Praise for Mortada Gzar

"Mortada Gzar's memoir, *I'm in Seattle, Where Are You?*, is a dazzling account of love, loss, and the complications of exile. This Iraqi novelist, filmmaker, and artist—a Whitman-like figure who contains multitudes in his embrace of the cosmos—understands 'that stories, like meteors, obey the laws of physics.' And what emerges in the stories he tells to an array of characters, including the statue of a vagrant, is proof that while 'their energy does not fade or increase' they will shape the lives and thinking of those who have the good luck to hear them. This is exactly the book to read in this fraught time."

—Christopher Merrill, author of *Self-Portrait with Dogwood*

"Gzar uses sharp criticism, irony and sarcasm to bring to the fore the devastating influence of the long war between Iraq and Iran that affected even minute details of life in Iraq. His characters and setting present the side-effects of the destructive war with Iran and the 2003 occupation."

—Dr. Waleed Al-Bazoon in his review of *My Beautiful Sect*, ArabLit.org

"The greatest success of *Al-Sayyid Asghar Akbar* (*Mr. Little Big*) is in building a space that links past with present and wonder tales with bleak contemporary realities like the American occupation of Iraq."

—Mohammed Khudayyir, author of *Basrayatha: Portrait of a City*

"*Al-Sayyid Asghar Akbar* is one of the few Iraqi novels that draws successfully on other arts, especially poetry. It can stand confidently beside the best Iraqi novels with its rich content and magical technique."

—Abd al-Khaliq al-Rikabi

"*Al-Sayyid Asghar Akbar* by the brilliant writer Mortada Gzar offers a unique, magical approach to prose narration. It is an entertaining novel with a surreal atmosphere that offers us a panoramic portrayal of the life of the city of Najaf and its ordinary citizens. Contemporary scenes blend with age-old symbols in it."

—Lotfiya al-Daylami

"This novel excavates the past, its characters' lives, and what they have deliberately concealed."

—Ali Abbas Khafif

"*Al-Sayyid Asghar Akbar* is a distinctive Iraqi tragedy saturated with comedy that Mortada Gzar has written with a unique lexicon. Its characters are drawn from the bottom of Iraqi society, from its margins. In this novel we hear the voices of people who otherwise are never allowed to express an opinion openly."

—Saad Mohammed Raheem

"*Al-'Ilmawi* (*The Scientismist*) was written by the skillful dreamer Mortada Gzar, who is an engineer, an artist, and a filmmaker. Its events are described by an imagination that is open full throttle. Twin brothers, Abbas and Fadhil, live through the period from the 1990s to 2003. One brother invents a manikin that answers questions but self-destructs when interrogated by a British commander."

—Maysalun Hadi, author of *Prophecy of Pharaoh*

I'M IN SEATTLE, WHERE ARE YOU?

I'M IN SEATTLE, WHERE ARE YOU?

A Memoir

MORTADA GZAR

Translated by William Hutchins
Illustrations by the author

Translated from Arabic by William Hutchins. First published in English by Amazon Crossing in 2021.

Published by Amazon Crossing, Seattle

www.apub.com
Amazon, the Amazon logo, and Amazon Crossing are trademarks of Amazon.com, Inc., or its affiliates.

ISBN-13: 9781542016575 (hardcover)
ISBN-10: 1542016576 (hardcover)
ISBN-13: 9781542016582 (paperback)
ISBN-10: 1542016584 (paperback)

Cover design by David Drummond
Interior illustrated by the author, Mortada Gzar

Printed in the United States of America
First edition

For Morise

Author's Note and Acknowledgments

Except for my name and the names of public figures, places, and actual events, most names in this book are my invention. For people represented as characters in my book, especially those who live in dangerous regions, I have chosen names quite unlike their given names, and obscured or altered identifying details.

I mention Dr. Michael Failla, though, because I want to thank him for the helping hand and advice he provided me on my journey to Seattle. I wish also to thank my six friends who are referred to in this book as sage monkeys and monks. In fact, I thank their entire circle of friends and acquaintances. I thank, too, Dr. Donald McCullough, Susan Moss, Mr. J. L., and also the people whose names I have avoided mentioning—especially my brothers, family, and friends in Basra, Baghdad, Iowa, and Lebanon.

Mr. Morise, this is what I have been able to recount. If this narrative does not suffice, you will understand that stories, like meteors, obey the laws of physics and that their energy does not fade or increase. The tales I have avoided telling today won't disappear. They will vibrate and simmer in heads and hearts until they find their place in a story or tale that we shall write.

And this, dear reader, is the book I have managed to write.

One

"I'm in Seattle! Where are you?" This is more than a question; it's a game that started ten years ago.

I once told him, "I'll come to Seattle. Then I'll call you and say, 'I'm in Seattle! Where are you now?' You'll recognize me by the white scarf hanging over my shoulder. It's not pure white—more like milk white verging on yellow. It's the turban I wore the first time you saw me." Its thin cloth, which resembles the gauze used for bandaging wounds, has aged and lost its whiteness. I've devised many uses for my turban's cloth since I stopped wearing it. It used to be five meters long when I unfolded it. Now, all that's left is this round shawl a meter and a quarter long. I've mended it, folded it twice, and placed it around my neck. Unfortunately, it is squeaky clean, because I have washed it repeatedly and rubbed it with dirt and soot to remove his sweat. One day, I unrolled my turban for him and made a carpet on which we slept among the bean plants on the banks of the Tigris. My turban became soiled with his sweat and semen. He polluted it that day, and I could no longer pray with it. I told him that anything of mine he touched, my

clothes, my turban, I would need to wash in running water to purify. He claimed he didn't understand, pretending he didn't comprehend my language. I haven't even mentioned the emotional impurity he caused me by this physical pollution, and for me, physical impurity was a prelude to spiritual impurity. Hearts cannot be cleansed with water or purified with dirt. The procedure to cleanse my turban of his pollution took only a few minutes. The fifteen years that have passed since that day have failed to cleanse my heart of his pollution, which seems to be a permanent stain on the heart for which human beings haven't yet invented an effective cleanser.

I am in Seattle, Washington, his city, where he emerged headfirst like a black piece of ice into a world overcome by fog, as he told me.

At Sea-Tac Airport in Seattle, I held my breath as I removed my shoes and belt before entering a security capsule. After the device scanned me, the huge, light-brown customs agent passed his wand over my body several times and smiled. He said, "You can collect your items now. Thanks for your cooperation." I smiled back at him and leaned over to tie my shoelaces. Then he asked, "Are you Iraqi?"

I replied, "How did you know?"

He spread his palm and waved it in front of his face as if washing it with air. Then he laughed and said, "The veil."

I leave my face bare now. I don't think veils could ever stay on it because I turn my head constantly and feel I need to keep looking, deftly and easily, in all directions. But I grasped what the man meant later, after I plunged into life in Seattle. He was referring to the invisible veil of exile and of the disorientations that spirits endure in transit, especially the reactions you see in airports and other public places. Iraqis aren't the only ones who wear invisible veils; perhaps everyone does. Even spinsters' cats do when they stare out the window on rainy days, waiting for their mistresses to return home from work. Each mask has its own purpose and occasion. Only a person wearing a similar veil will recognize its brand. I noticed on the security officer's chest a small badge with his name, which was very Iraqi. Then I felt sure he was an Iraqi too. You might feel something similar when you see a person wearing shoes exactly like yours. That person may relate to you, and conversation may come easily. What was different then at the airport was that the security officer had succeeded in scrubbing the veil off his face. I really wished I could ask him, "How many years did it take you to remove that veil?"

I'm in the Arrivals Hall. Where is he now?

I heard his voice shout my name but deliberately ignored him for a minute till I could hear it clearly nearby, until he approached me, or I drew nearer to him, pretending I hadn't heard. But his voice was drowned out by the sound of a child scratching his fingernails on the glass. As the other passengers and I dragged our suitcases from the hall, the bags reminded me of suppressed memories knocking their heads against the bars of a cell. I heard him call me a second time and twisted my neck to search for him. I felt a toxin spread through the tissues of my shoulders. My neck muscles had apparently become exhausted as I turned my head constantly—more frequently even than I blinked—for the past two hours, searching for him.

I had to stop and quit looking around. I addressed him silently. "If you want to show yourself, then do it the way normal people do. Appear quite simply in the waiting room. My neck can't keep turning around. Besides, I've grown tired of rubbernecking back. 'He who looks back never achieves his purpose': that's an Arab maxim I translated for you one day when we ran away from the farmers after we slept on legume seedlings and pink flowers and ruined a small garden plot near the Tigris."

I asked directions from a man puffing cigarette smoke out of his round red ladybug of a car parked by the curb on the way to the commuter train. Without looking at me, he pointed up. Before I could follow his suggestion and head for the stairway, I glimpsed your body, disappearing among arriving passengers. I left my luggage and raced toward you, slipping between people's shoulders and interrupting conversations as I shoved and dashed between them. I didn't catch you. I told myself, We're too old for these games. If he is really waiting for me in Seattle, he'll appear the way normal people do, not like an apparition.

I returned to my bags and found them leaning against each other, dozing. As I righted my suitcases, a young woman noticed that my body was shaking from fatigue. She came over to help and offered, "I'll carry the heavy one. May I?" I smiled, thinking I had thanked her, but my throat hadn't been able to utter the words. We made our way down the long concourse to catch the light-rail heading downtown. I heard the young woman talking on the phone with her mother. She stopped occasionally to listen, because the squeak of my suitcase made it hard to hear. Halfway down the corridor, she paused to answer her mother's question about the noise she heard.

"Mama, this isn't my bag. I'm helping someone at the airport.

"It isn't very heavy, Mama.

"I don't know what's in it," the girl admitted with embarrassment.

So I came to her aid and volunteered, "Characters. Tell her: characters." When I said that, the girl looked at me hesitantly. I repeated the words so she wouldn't think I had packed my bag full of carrots or Middle Eastern spices. I don't know what she heard when I said "characters," because we don't hear our words the way other people do, and my English wasn't fluent then.

I don't know why I told her that, and I don't think she repeated it to her mother. When we reached the station, she gave me the bag's handle, and I thanked her. She helped me buy a ticket. The train was completely empty when it arrived. She smiled and said, "Thank God! You'll find lots of seats for your characters!"

As I was about to board the train, we embraced, and she departed in the other direction. Before the doors closed, a wave of people rushed in and filled the car. I was covered in sweat from rising repeatedly to make room for women and the elderly. This ethical enzyme was secreted by residual teachings and maxims clotted in an ancient cranny of my "veil."

As the train started to move, when I was scrutinizing the placards and posters on the walls, I noticed that the young woman who had helped me was staring at the train, now packed with people, as it passed her. She had left me on an empty train, and it was suddenly packed to the gills. There was a shocked look on her face as she scanned the windows and saw how people were jammed together. I raised my head and smiled at her. When she saw me, her eyes widened.

Pointing to the swarm of people around me in the carriage, I moved my lips to say, "Characters, characters." That girl I met in passing was even crazier than me; she shouted at me through the train's windows, "Close your bags! You've filled the train!"

I clung to the strap with one hand and grasped my suitcases with the other. From the rectangular screens of the train's windows, I surfed the city's night and trees seen by lights from buildings. Then, as my eyes rested on a posted advertisement, one expression popped out at me: "I'm here." I felt he really was here—here, somewhere—or perhaps waiting for me at the station.

It took me three-quarters of an hour to reach my destination. Near me, three young men read and swayed with the train. A silent, white bitch with a turquoise collar studded with bells alternatively dozed and woke, seated calmly on her mistress's lap. She gazed, like me, at some unknown entity in the space created by a passenger's legs. It was invisible, but our eyes could fix on it and divert our vision till the minutes ticked away and the thickly veiled man glancing every which way reached his destination.

Erick's house stood on a hill. I carried my bags up the sloping sidewalk. We had agreed that his house would be my first residence in Seattle. When I neared the door, I sat down on the sidewalk to catch my breath. One of its windows shone with red and blue lights that were interrupted at times by the shadows of people moving inside with slow monotony. Some of the shadows fell on my shoes and spread across the pavement and across the acorn caps on the grass. Three round heads, which appeared to be bald, nodded sluggishly and moved from one place to another, one step at a time. One person was clearly using a wheelchair.

I took heart and used my shirtsleeves to wipe the oily sweat from my face. Standing on the stoop, I pressed the buzzer. The heads' shadows stopped nodding, and I heard them mutter, "He's here."

The doorknob turned, but the door didn't open. I heard a rat-a-tat-tat of footsteps, a commotion, and a mild struggle inside. I pressed the buzzer again and then heard someone repeat, "He's here." Something hit the floor and then rose. The crack of the door widened, and a face framed by white looked out as the beard covering the man's chest fluttered and gleamed in the relative darkness. He wore a green cap like a Sufi's, but his hat was decorated with beer mugs. As the door opened wider, the man's mouth did too. I had never seen anyone smile like this. It was Erick, who beamed like a superannuated god. I stammered without uttering a greeting or introducing myself and left that task to my face, with its conjoined eyebrows, and my lips, which were pursed from embarrassment. Even so, it wasn't hard for Erick to recognize me.

"Mortaada, Moorteeda, or Moortaada? Do you mind if I call you Morty?"

"Should I take off my shoes?" I asked, pausing in the entry. My response presupposed that I had greeted him. I still had difficulty stringing words together, because I had to select them from my Arabic dictionary and then extract and polish them before reformulating them in English. I translated for myself, for that twisting fellow inside me who felt that every language, except his own, was sign language.

"Don't violate our pact. We agreed to call him Mo," said the Black man behind Erick as he scooted his wheelchair back a little.

While Erick leaned over to untie my shoelaces, the man in the chair started moving my baggage. I felt their next step would be to place me in a cage with a glass of water and a dish of sunflower seeds.

"By the way, my name is Josie," said the Black man in the chair. He wore a lavender wig and had polish on his fingernails. He had drawn my suitcase to his chair and placed it in front of him to roll it inside with his chair.

I estimated his age to be between sixty and seventy. In fact, the three men were approximately the same age. Yes, there was a third man watching TV in a room with the door ajar. I heard Erick—as he leaned against the door panel and stroked his beard—call him: "Liao!" I hadn't seen him yet, but the melodious sound of his cough, which was loaded with phlegm, told me more about him than anything else.

"Liao! He's here!" Erick shouted in a louder voice, but Liao didn't respond. Then Erick asked me to have a seat on the couch. He entered Liao's room and closed the door behind him. I sat there, scanning the walls with my eyes and running my fingers over nicks in the couch's leather upholstery until Josie's voice roused me.

"Come here, boy. Let me introduce you to the features of the house where you're going to live." After saying that, he moved his hands like a maestro, and I realized he wore an earring composed of letters. I had trouble reading them, because Josie turned his head frequently, and the hair of his wig fell over his ears and hid the dangling word, making it barely visible. I followed him and stood by while he stopped at the furnace to show me the knob that turned it on. Then he pressed the controls on his wheelchair and moved toward the refrigerator. Spreading his palm and turning it over like a carnival barker, he pointed to colored slips of paper on the door of the fridge.

"This is the schedule for Heraclitus to walk and shit," Josie explained. Then he paused, presumably for me to ask who Heraclitus was. When I didn't, he added, "Heraclitus is our dog."

I succeeded then in making out the first three letters of the word that dangled from his ear and grazed his shoulder as he spoke. I examined that word intently.

Josie wore a padded bra and had sprinkled glitter on the deep wrinkles of his chest. He had on a sleeveless, olive-colored shift and had wrapped a rose-colored silk band around the remnants of his neck tattoos. His nails were painted different colors and made a sound when he scratched his short beard.

Josie led me next to the kitchen to show me the cooking pots, plates, spices, cereals, and cleansers and how the lighting worked. He explained to me the rest of the details about the kitchen. Even then, I hadn't been able to decipher all the letters of the dangling word.

Suddenly, he began to speak more slowly and to enunciate each word as though he were inventing it. Then I realized that he was listening to the voices from Liao's room. I couldn't make them out or understand what Liao and Erick were saying, because I wasn't proficient enough yet in English. Josie kept moving his chair around while explaining in his mellifluous voice what Heraclitus ate and cautioning me against feeding this "melancholy vegetarian dog," as he put it, any meat.

When the sound of the quarrel in Liao's room grew louder, Josie lurched forward and almost ran over my toes as he shot toward Liao's room. Spewing curses, he pounded on the door and entered. Then all three men were in there, and I didn't understand the bits and pieces of words that reached my ears through the cracks.

The gap below the door provided me an exhilarating inkling of what was playing on the large screen in Liao's room. I tried to busy myself with looking around and acquainting myself with the house in a simple meet-and-greet ceremony. The loud voices, though, really began to upset me and awaken some fears. I hadn't met any of these men before, although I had communicated at length with Erick through a mutual friend. I had informed him of my pressing need to spend time in Seattle. Naturally, I hadn't told him that I wanted to search Seattle for a former army officer I'd met in Iraq. That was my version of a priest's or saint's ultimate secret. I had promised myself not to mention you, Morise, until I felt totally at home, until my feet were on firm ground. I had spoken with Erick through this friend for many weeks, at intervals, before traveling to Seattle, but this was the first time we had met face-to-face.

I searched my mind for something to do to alleviate this awkward situation as their voices merged with the sound of the TV, and I struggled with the tumultuous thoughts in my head. Eventually, the men were all hissing, their bodies rubbing against one another. I thought at first that these three old men had left me alone in the living room while they played with each other and coupled. Once I could hear their voices more clearly, I felt reassured that they had dissolved into a shared sexual exchange. I heard them moan, spit, and gasp. All my assumptions fell apart, however, when I learned that the sounds I had heard faintly through the door weren't from a lovefest but from something else entirely. That happened when the door opened, and I saw Liao for the first time.

He saw me but didn't seem very interested in meeting me or making my acquaintance; he was probably preoccupied by what had happened to him inside that room. He took his long, black overcoat from a hook on the wall and left the house with an ashen face and an apparently troubled mind.

Josie and Erick trailed him outside to the steps but didn't follow. They sat there, smoking and hurling curses into the void.

I decided this was a good opportunity for me to enter the room and see for myself what the men had been doing. I took five steps inside and found that the room contained a small sofa, a tall bookcase, a china cabinet that displayed porcelain figurines and family photos, and a large flat-screen TV in the center. Red and blue fluctuated on the screen, and it wasn't hard to grasp that I had arrived in this house on the night election results were announced.

I watched Josie and Erick through the window and finally deciphered the words dangling from Josie's ears: "I'm a work of art."

Two

During the second week I lived in that house, I found the courage to leave its walls. It was almost three o'clock in the morning when I set off to stroll the streets, looking around.

Notions, ghosts, bits and pieces of stories invaded my head and occupied my mind while his name pursued me like the evening shadows no one sees.

The Space Needle peeked at me from behind buildings and through windows. It looked sympathetic and proud as it stood haughtily between skyscrapers. Lenin's statue greeted me, but with a woman's voice. I stopped and found a homeless woman below the statue. She asked if I had a lighter. I apologized and crossed to the other side of the street. Then I sensed that a shadow was following me. My heart rejoiced, and I told myself, Here he is, acting just the way I expected.

I let him trail behind me and didn't accost him. Although my back was toward him and he was following, I felt my eyes move to the back of my head like one of those weird fish the fishermen would spear in the region of the Arab Gulf shore where I was born.

I kept walking and offered him a whole hour to make a move without turning to look. I crossed a bridge and peed in the bushes. I sat on a bench and listened to the screaming silence a bird makes plunging through the currents of the air. I wanted to show him that the city had started to adjust to me and adopt me. I hoped to meet a passerby and strike up a conversation with him so he could hear my improved command of English, but that all ended when I noticed a wild beast with a long beard beneath the bridge. I hesitated, even though I love monsters. I waited for a vehicle to pass and light the beast clearly enough for me to see. And that's what happened. I walked to the beast and sat on its paw. I stroked its concrete beard. The beast's lower half was hidden in the ground. His nose covered half of his face, and hair grew from his cheeks, mouth, and the crown of his head, covering his right eye completely. I was reassured by his tender, speechless appearance, which belied his bestiality. I sat between his fingers. Then your steps stopped, and I sensed that you were quietly watching me play with the beast. What shattered the illusion was hearing Liao's voice instead of your sigh or breathing.

"Moortaada!" Liao pronounced my name as if imbibing it. "We need to leave here immediately. This Scandinavian monster is dangerous at night. You didn't tell us you wanted to visit the Fremont Troll. If you had, we would have organized an excursion for you during the day. I would caution anyone against visiting the troll at this hour. Do you know?" Liao asked, pointing to the monument. "I stood right here when they installed this statue beneath the bridge to revive this area, which was known for drug use.

"The legend recounted by Norwegian immigrants says that the gods sent the troll to guard vehicles on the bridge. But he delayed his arrival and retreated beneath the bridge when development in the city shoved him aside. I was here when he held a time-capsule bust of Elvis Presley. After that was stolen, the artists replaced it with a real Volkswagen Beetle." As he spoke, he moved closer. Placing a hand on my shoulder, he gently nudged me to leave. This conversation seemed to be Liao's way of making my acquaintance and introducing himself. He had repeatedly shunned the chance to be the third member of a trio, preferring to appear in his own special way and following me through Seattle's alleys.

Just as residents here made up this special legend, Liao devised a scary tale to urge me to return home with him. My eyes remained fixed on the features of this statue, exaggerated terror plastered futilely across its face, because the statue had retained its innocence and imbecility. It had become a shrine, attracting people who wanted to feel afraid or pretend to. As I walked along behind Liao, I experienced an overwhelming sense of leaving a theatrical production, feeling disappointment, fatigue, and ennui, because imagining you behind me had pumped my blood and kept my feet moving. Liao had toppled my dreamworld when he appeared and announced that he had been the person following me. That night, you were merely a specter and not actually present, but this means you are very present somewhere else.

Although a mature man, Liao moved faster than I did and cut through the air like a knife through a fish. He seemed keen to keep me talking. Taking my hand, he encouraged me to return to the house. I felt it was too early to desert the Fremont Troll, so I stood my ground and pulled my hand from his. He fell backward and extended a foot behind him to balance. But his foot struck something that rolled beneath it. Liao screamed in panic, saying something I didn't understand. It may have been something in Chinese. Perhaps he resembles me in this respect and returned to his mother tongue in circumstances of intense fear and fervent love. My father once told me that he was present when a soldier friend died on the front—the man started speaking Persian just before his death, his tongue suddenly erupting in the language of a people he himself did not know he belonged to.

Liao fell to the pavement. I kept my balance and held out my hand to him, but his limbs were dancing like a cartoon character's.

The object had rolled a few feet away, and Liao seemed to have fallen on some other object. When I hugged him and pulled him toward the statue, he shouted, "Careful! Don't step on my glasses!"

I found his blood-spattered glasses on the ground and picked them up. Before I could hand them to him, he screamed again and fell on the statue's hand. When he regained his balance and stood up, he started to race to the far side of the street.

I didn't succumb to the contagious fear Liao spread through the area. Instead, I turned back and grasped the rolling object by its ears. I picked it up and waved it at Liao. "It's a pig's head," I shouted.

I dropped the pig's head and picked up a cat's head, skin still hanging from the neck. I waved it toward Liao, who had leaned forward, not knowing what to say.

I noticed the heads of several different animals around the Fremont Troll. Someone must have been practicing weird rituals there. I ran to tell Liao these were animal heads, but he had disappeared down the alley, deciding to leave me in a protest against my interest in the heads distributed around the concrete beast.

We crossed a bridge that reared above several large buildings. Liao ran ahead and then stopped on a traffic island, where he waited to cross the street with five other people. A dog behind one of the men was wagging its tail to curry favor with its owner. I was amazed to see so many people out at such an early hour. When I approached slowly, intending to stand behind Liao, he laughed boisterously. My eyes had deceived me. These people and the dog were statues erected and installed here to represent people waiting for the bus, and folks had decorated them with ribbons and clothes.

"But I saw the dog's tail wag," I protested.

Liao replied, "Every city has its marvels," and then hurried to the far side.

I remained there to admire the statues. I noticed a hole the size of a small orange in the back of a man wearing a broad-brimmed hat and allowed my fingers to explore it. Liao returned to hurry me along but relented when he saw my fingers touching the statue delightedly. Perhaps he realized then that these statues upset me and made me lose my balance—that I'd spaced out from the world while I stroked them, my mouth hanging open like an idiot's.

He sat down and pretended to stroke the back of the inanimate dog, still trying to restrain his ringing laughter. Behind him, the sun yawned and attempted to shake off the blanket of clouds covering it.

"Liao, stories return to recite themselves like songs you've forgotten till you start to sing them." When I said that, I saw his face relax and open like a glass preparing to receive a liquid.

"Spill it. We've been keen to hear your story. I want to hear it from you. Drinking a story from the faucet is better than sipping it from a glass. Spill it."

"You seem to be talking about gas in the belly."

"I'm talking about a smart beneath the skin. We all sit on a story like a hen on her egg. Erick told me you wrote your first book when you were twelve. This means writing was the first thing you did in life. It also implies that you wrote before you spoke, and that writing for you is something like sex or eating."

"I'm not one hundred percent certain of this. But I know I was late speaking. My mother fed me a dove's tongue and once felt obliged to honor a local diviner's command to melt five bullets in a cauldron, cool them with ice and flour, and then cauterize my tongue with them."

"Your mother was resourceful. My mother spat in my mouth to make me speak."

"Liao!" I protested sternly, and then pinched his flank. We both laughed.

"Come on. You don't seem to have talked for some time. Mouths grow rusty too. Since you were a kid, you seem to have thought your strong suit was writing. Your brain grew accustomed to considering writing as a source of happiness. There's a disconnected socket now that is out of service. You need to reconnect your senses to that power source. Writing is your personal therapist, and your body will only respond to this therapy that you have relied on since childhood. Write down your story with that soldier."

"Soldier? What soldier, Liao?" I asked fearfully.

"Soldier! What soldier? I didn't say anything about a soldier. You must be tired," he replied without looking at me. I placed my palm on his back as I gazed at the hole in the statue.

I didn't grasp the point of this hole. There were five adults and a child that a woman carried in her arms, all of them waiting for the bus. I didn't understand then why we were squatting there, as if sheltering behind them. Liao seemed to think I was ignoring his words and discouraging communication. I avoided his eyes, which were staring at me, and instead peered deep into the dark hole in the statue, as if searching for an alternative world I could enter through it. I seemed to have grasped the point of the cavity, which must have been waiting for me. I imagined the artist had placed it there on purpose to make me narrate the beginning of my story to Liao.

"Liao, I was returning from school."

When I said that, Liao paid attention and moved closer to demonstrate his interest.

"I was returning from secondary school, glancing out of the corner of my eye at slogans painted on the walls. For example, President Saddam's saying cribbed from *The Stranger* by Camus: 'Keep your enemy before your eyes and outstrip him! Don't let him out of sight!' My companion was laughing under his breath, because the president's slogan presupposed an enemy outside the limits of time and space. A student's father had been arrested recently for kidding at home about this motto. He had learned it from his father and repeated it at school. His father had said in jest that this saying meant you should ride together on a bus with facing seats. We had laughed ourselves hoarse. But slanderous students reported the incident, and law enforcement pounced on him. The incident ended with the arrest of the student and his father. That's why I bowed my head when I passed walls adorned with drawings and Saddam's sayings. I would almost retract my head into my neck, like a tortoise, but those sayings would reach my heart somehow. The sayings and parodies of them sprouted everywhere like thick underbrush in the forest. The saying that lingered most stubbornly in my mind back then was *Akhshushano!* Live rough! This one-word Arabic slogan may have been taken from a longer sentence. The timbre of this word in Arabic is truly rough. You feel you are rubbing a hedgehog's back when you say it: *'Akhshushano!'* This word used to appear in tandem with the regional party leadership's emphasis on manliness, virility, and bushy mustaches on clean-shaven faces. This was the sole face that all men should present.

"People were advised to return to manliness, to the epochs of Nebuchadnezzar, Naram-Sin, and Sargon the Akkadian. There were diatribes against the effeminacy that was spreading everywhere. We were even punished in school for having a limp wrist!

"I didn't realize that my daily walk from our house to the school was meant to toughen me. The smells of human and feline urine and the branches of eucalyptus trees blended to create a putrid stink that my nose still recalls. Back then, I kept a large notebook that I carried as top secret wherever I paused or ventured. There was a place where I would hand it off to Qahtan, who was a plump youth with a lisp and curly hair. Two years my senior, he was my first boyfriend. Because I wrote so much, it wasn't practical for me to use a pen. The American trade embargo was at its height, and virtually all families lived below the poverty line. Pens cost so much, it took days for a secondary school student like me to save enough to buy one. I used pens for my school homework but made entries in my secret notebook with a reed pen and food dyes. On Fridays and school holidays, my mother would place on my back a cork box containing a dozen colored Popsicles with a wooden stick in each. My job was to tour the alleyways, shouting, even though I usually didn't speak much, and touting my treats on blazing hot summer days.

"My share of all this was the Popsicles that melted before anyone bought them. Since their primary ingredient was dye, I used that liquid as ink. My notebook became sticky, and it was hard to separate its pages. All the same, it was crammed full of entries without rhyme or reason. I just kept writing, feeling a need to record events and the conversations of the real people around me. It provided me with a great sense of relief. I would sit in our house's lofty attic and watch the world breathe and people move around like ants in the distance, looking for a bite to eat. I became a little demon, so eager to record everything, spill the beans on people, and report on them. My demon self communicated with an unknown power. Having served as one of this power's spies and having reported on the world's cruelty, my demon self would be a major proponent for it when this power landed on Earth.

"That notebook wasn't well hidden in my bag. Its secrecy was a mental concept I constructed to afford myself peace of mind and comfort. Normally, I tore up anything that people peeped at, feeling that people's eyes ruined food-dye words. All the same, as I hiked to school, I would feel elated by the dangerous, sacerdotal secret I carried tucked among my schoolbooks!

"Every day I saw an elderly man dressed in a white dishdasha with his arms held behind his back. Whenever I glanced at him, he would look away. I repeatedly saw him with another man. When I approached them, proceeding on my way, they would separate. Then, they would immediately clasp their arms across their chests like clever pupils.

"One day during my walk, at the place where I normally met Qahtan, I heard the statue of the president bark. Those two men were sitting beneath the statue, and the shadow of the president's hand, which was raised to greet the masses, fell on one man's shoulder as he sat embracing his friend. I stopped to listen carefully to the statue bark. As I approached, the two men started to leave, and I saw them lengthen their steps to flee, because the presidential statue shouldn't bark. These two men shouldn't even remember an incident like this, because talking about it could destroy them. Heads can't always be trusted to lock up stories and not betray their intellects.

"I felt the small hole in the statue's heel. It seemed a little wider than this hole and provided a peek into the statue's dark interior. I noticed the eye of a small puppy whose bad luck had drawn it into the statue. I seized a sturdy stick and tried to excavate beneath the president's base till the puppy could push out half its body. It had trouble freeing a leg twisted inside something in the president's interior. Hearing the voices of students approaching in the distance, I remembered where I was and that my schoolbag was lying on the ground. Then I panicked and pulled the small black dog farther out of the statue, but it continued yelping and whining in pain. It succeeded with difficulty in getting its third leg out, but the fourth was still inside.

"Drops of sweat from my temples fell on the base of the statue, and the dog licked them. I shoved it back inside so I could find some water before getting it out entirely. I grabbed my bag, turned tail, and raced to find water. A distant water faucet glittered beneath a palm tree. It was connected to a rubber hose from which a line of saline water trickled to irrigate the plants and shrubs around the president. The water was, truth be told, much sweeter than the water we drank in our house. I cupped my fingers and held them in the water; but when I hurried back toward the statue, I spotted a khaki vehicle from which a group of masked men had gotten out. From their all-black uniforms, I immediately recognized them as members of a group called Fedayeen Saddam, or Saddam's Men of Sacrifice. They spread around the area with swords drawn, searching, as usual, for something to dump into the back of their vehicle. I noticed from the far side of the tree behind which the two men squatted, fettered and sheltered, that the statue was barking sweetly; this was what had upset and rattled the Fedayeen.

"A pair of men appeared from the other direction. They were man-handling and dragging three teenagers, one of whom was buck naked. They grasped them by their collars, ears, or hair and sat them down beside the two men. I heard the naked boy shout to me, 'Mortada! Tell my mother! Tell my uncle!' When everyone turned toward me, and I realized that the naked youth was Qahtan, I raced away with my hands still cupped, even though my fingers held no water.

"It took the short Feda'i only a few steps to catch me and drag me back by the belt of my trousers. He pulled me by my sideburns and sat me down among the others.

"They rained punches and blows on us with hard rubber hoses, and I felt hot blood run down my face. I sensed its salty taste in my mouth as it slid down my throat. When I came to, I was in the back of the vehicle together with the two old men and the three teenagers. The unexpected presence there in the vehicle was the president's statue.

"But it was given a warm welcome. The Fedayeen, frightened when they heard it bark, feared the consequences, so they had decided to remove the sculpture to another location where the defect could be corrected. In any event, the statue was already wobbly, and my small excavation had left it near collapse.

"'Where are they taking us?' I asked the old man who seemed compassionate and sympathetic to my situation because I was the youngest of the group.

"'The president is going to a veterinarian, and we're heading beyond the sun,' the elderly man replied. In those days, everyone understood the phrase 'beyond the sun' to mean lengthy imprisonment or permanent disappearance.

"Qahtan was speechless and seemed oblivious to everything. His features were rigid, but his eyes glittered with disgust and bitterness. I had met Qahtan five years earlier when I was at the door of our home, admiring a rainbow that arched over the houses. He informed me that the rainbow belonged to him and that he would sell it to me for a fistful

of change. I handed him the money with the understanding that he would hand me the rainbow the following day when he was done with it. Qahtan, though, later denied the deal, and whenever I complained about him to a member of his family, the fellow would burst into laughter and mock my gullibility. I harbored a grudge against him till one day he held his arms out to me to steal a kiss while I sat watching him play goalie for the school soccer team. That was the first time he kissed me, stirring the little animal between my thighs.

"I must have dozed off from fatigue. The Fedayeen's boots woke me, pressing against my head. The dog had escaped somehow from inside the statue and kept jumping around on my belly, which held nothing but fear.

"The president's statue was no longer near me. Instead, I found myself with the old men and the boys on a basketball court, in what looked to be a school or sporting club."

Recounting all this, I hadn't noticed rays of sunshine reach my ear as Liao listened to me. He was still patting the back of the concrete dog, which for its part was sticking its head between the feet of the people waiting for the bus that hadn't arrived for decades. This monument had been erected in response to a commission from the Fremont Arts Council in 1978. Then some years later, it was moved a hundred yards to another street, where the figures still wait.

"A Feda'i called al-Sayyaf—the swordsman or executioner—appeared, wearing a mask that hid everything but his pointy nose and green eyes. After he brandished his sword by waving it in the air, he drew a paper from his pocket and read its manifesto, which was filled with the same sayings, the ones extolling virility and punishment for effeminate men. It concluded with expressions about the leadership's determination to promulgate virtue and to hold accountable individuals—male and female—who were promiscuous and deviant. We were in the middle of a 'Belief Offensive,' which was the Salafi Muslim fundamentalist phase the entire state entered after Saddam was defeated in Kuwait. State TV became religious and blasted out religious anthems and hymns. Turbaned men, whom the state employed to glorify the president and to link religion with the authorities and to embrace the state, appeared front and center. These men also devised a family tree for the president, tracing Saddam's lineage back to the Prophet Muhammad. The state suddenly donned a white turban and the fake kind of beard used by actors.

"Al-Sayyaf read the manifesto aloud as lamely as a primary school pupil. Because I was sick of all the linguistic rules and corrections of pronunciation at school, I privately corrected his errors and may have murmured these criticisms under my breath at times.

"He grabbed the elderly man's neck and kicked his chest. Then the man fell to the floor. The executioner struck a blow to the man's neck with the sword, and the old man's head rolled away, spewing a mass of thick blood that spattered my eyes and made it hard for me to see."

I noticed Liao take off his glasses and wipe away the blood that had spattered them when he fell on the animal heads.

"His lover, the other elderly man, thrust his head under my arm and rolled up like a cabbage worm, becoming much smaller. I sensed that he wanted to plunge inside me. When al-Sayyaf grabbed him, the old man clung as tightly to me as if he were part of me and immediately began wailing. When he was dragged off me, he continued to plead with al-Sayyaf, swearing by the spirit of his mother and then by the spirit of his father that he would never do 'it' again. After al-Sayyaf laughed, the man offered to swear by the name of His Honor the President, which was posted on the facing wall beneath the saying 'Sweat more in drills and spill less blood on the battlefield.' But the executioner tightened his grip and brought the sword down on the man's neck as he told him, 'I will slay you not for your sex crimes but because you defiled the president's name by uttering it.' Then he dropped the sword on him with a blow that sent a piece of his scalp flying away. So he struck a second blow. Eventually, he finished him off with a third blow, after the second failed to sever the man's neck completely.

"Al-Sayyaf temporarily excused the sexual behavior of us young guys, and we began to weep bitterly and loudly enough to be deafening. In less than a minute, I expressed all the prayers my heart had stockpiled. One of us lost the ability to speak, but his farts blanketed the place and served as his orisons. I literally placed my cheek on a pool of urine and shit. Then I saw al-Sayyaf tie an electric cord around the puppy's neck, toss the dog in the air, and twirl it around as if he were a shot-putter at a track-and-field meet. I heard the puppy's yapping fade, dwindle, and totally disappear as it was thrown far away. But the puppy recovered and fled, nursing its hurt leg."

Liao stood up and took my hand to help me rise, since my leg had fallen asleep. I noticed that he walked behind me now and let me stride ahead with the agility of a person freed from some heavy weight.

"Don't you want to hear the rest?" I asked.

"Al-Sayyaf came toward you, holding your secret book. He had seized your diary entries written in food dyes: the maxims, descriptive passages, poems, and sexual fantasies about men you saw in your daily life. You copulated with them on paper. You exchanged love letters with them and asked if they were like you. You queried God why he had burdened you with this major sin. You demanded to know why he had afflicted a child like you with this disgusting habit that causes the throne of the compassionate God to shake. You had recorded everything in your notebook and incriminated yourself. All the Fedayeen needed to do was deliver you to the party Brigade's headquarters. Then this man led you to your house, after kicking your ass and cursing your mother and father for raising you so poorly. When he reached the door of your house, dragging you behind him, he opened it without knocking. Actually, he kicked the door open, entered, and threw you down in the middle of the room. Everyone in your family was terrified to see you tossed on the floor while the Saddamite comrade kicked your flank, your mother pleaded with him, and your father cajoled him. Then the Baath Party comrade explained to them that their son was a sodomite but that the party Brigade had generously pardoned him."

"How did you know?" I stopped walking and turned back toward him, softening my tone.

"You repeated the story three times in less than an hour, Mortada. Don't tell me you weren't conscious of that! Never mind. That didn't upset me. I'll take you to breakfast. I'll watch you eat. I'm not hungry. I don't think I can eat right now."

Three

Between three and four o'clock in the morning, I opened my eyes to find Josie, Liao, and Erick standing stiffly beside my bed and staring at my face. They drew back quickly when they sensed that I was surprised to find them watching me sleep. Each one found something to do. Liao pretended to be cutting his fingernails; Erick went quickly to look out the window; and Josie asked if I needed anything. Then he quickly looked down at his lap, where he had a pile of letters. Apparently, he wanted to make an earring with a different phrase. After I rose and soaked my body in the bathtub, a song spilled from his lips and dominated the large house, which was composed of wood, nails, and all the short sentences uttered by its inhabitants.

When I was looking for tea in the kitchen cupboards, I found a book tucked among some jars. It seemed to have been thrust in there quickly. I pulled the book out, but before I could flip it over to read the title, Erick's hand quickly seized it from me.

At noon that same day, when Erick was providing me more information about the house and the rooms downstairs, he told me about the three plastic boxes inside a small cabinet at the center of the house. Each container had one of their names written on it and was filled with white and colored pills. He explained they were all required to take one pill a day, but that Liao's pill differed from Josie's, and his pill was different too. All these pills strengthened the immune system and blocked the AIDS virus they had been exposed to as young adults, although Josie had been exposed when he was a teenager. All three men were HIV positive. During his explanation, he watched my face to see my reaction, but I merely nodded. When he returned a box to its place, he dropped the book to the floor, where it fell on its cover. I lunged and grasped it. Then I found it was Thesiger's account of living with the Marsh Arabs of Iraq.

Erick's face looked troubled, and he seemed embarrassed. I returned the book to him, and he quickly put it back in its place and closed the wardrobe, saying, "Apparently some naughty girl in this house has been looking for a guide to your interests!"

Josie's song resounded again and climbed the house's walls like a plant. He kept singing the same phrase, which suggested that he was amusing himself by making an earring from it. The steam rising from Liao's coffee also rose into the air as he sat, legs crossed, by the window. He was resting his bald head on his palm while three-quarters of his body was hidden in his overcoat.

Since Erick's preoccupation during this period was introducing his housemates to me, he chose to acquaint me with Liao's essence through short sentences he delivered while showing me cleansers or trash bags. He would say for example, "Liao speaks English, Chinese, and Portuguese. He is a famous choreographer. His mother is still alive and owns a bakery on the far side of the city. A person should stay at least five yards away from him when he's angry, because words drop from him like cigarette butts. In a previous life, Liao was a dictionary. He resembles a ninja, vanishing and reappearing. If you open his closet, you'll find yourself in a utopia of black overcoats. I met him about thirty years ago, but he always insists on using English words I don't know. He appears suddenly, and you're rarely conscious of his arrival or departure. It's hard to tell whether he's here or not, because he will disappear for days and then suddenly turn up. He loves the rain, walking in the rain, and shaking off the water's spray with high-heeled shoes, which he likes. He will give you his kidney and spleen if you tell him he's between forty and fifty. He likes to swim and dive, and swims laps for an hour almost every day. We fear he'll turn into a seal. He doesn't speak to Josie, although he might occasionally touch him, without being conscious of that. He doesn't drink alcohol but is generous in buying drinks for others. He wants you to make him feel that he is discreet and cryptic. Liao's stomach was a heart in a previous life. There is another version of Liao preserved in the refrigerator, in case you need more Liaos. He is an extraordinary rice cook. His real name is also Liao. His body is devoid of tattoos, and his heart is devoid of grudges. He is tooth blind, and this isn't a rare condition. All three of us are tooth blind. You could even call us that. Frequently, one of us will pop in someone else's dentures."

Erick would expand on these sentences from time to time. He might add something in Liao's presence, even personally intrusive comments, but I never heard him speak ill of Liao.

In fact, Liao was far vaster than Erick's characterization of him in three terse sentences. That was the message of his eyes, which gladdened anyone who saw them. They could also turn into deep craters into which a person conversing with him might tumble. That happened to me when Liao finished his coffee and began staring through my face instead of through the window.

"What does your name mean?"

"A person who is desired and sought or who provides satisfaction."

"Seven," said Erick, who was observing our conversation from a distance.

"Eight," countered Josie, who had arrived to claim the space between me and Liao.

I was confused by these numbers. I didn't know what they referred to or how they related to the meaning of my name. All the same, I was loath to express my surprise. So I let them toss numbers at each other as if they were at an auction. When I added the phrase "a man whom God favored" to my reply, I realized that they were counting the number of sentences I uttered that day. That was their way of encouraging me to speak freely.

"Nine," shouted Liao decisively. Then he shifted his posture to avoid losing his balance in his enthusiasm.

The way they looked then reminded me of the three Confucian monkeys that respectively hear, see, and speak no evil. But this wasn't the Japanese version that condemns the transmission of evils and negative feelings. These monkeys also never lowered their eyes, held their ears, or shielded their heart to avoid seeing, hearing, and feeling forbidden things as in the Arab version. Nor were they the Socratic version that clarifies reports and cautiously examines concepts like justice. They were, quite simply, Seattle's monkeys, and what they had in common with the monkeys in the other versions was that they were sages. In my opinion, this parable's meaning wouldn't have been altered by the addition of "lascivious" to the Confucian version, since Seattle's three monkeys were gods of wisdom and impudence.

I excused myself from the scene and sat on the toilet, thinking, like Americans in films. My disappearance put an end to the counting but not to their chatter. Five or six minutes passed. Everything seemed normal until a ruckus suddenly broke out. I heard papers being crumpled in their hands, making a sound even louder than their elderly voices. They were near the bathroom door, browsing through the papers and making themselves squawk by grabbing them from one another. Josie led the assembly that confronted me from outside the door. He must have learned something. I could hear Erick muttering. I heard Liao, but

he wasn't speaking. I heard his overcoat flopping around as he played with it. That's what he usually did when he was silent, listening but not speaking—confronting an important issue with silence.

To harass me, Josie began, "Come out."

Someone else said, "If you come out, we'll go easy on you."

I opened the bathroom door and slipped but didn't fall to the floor. I twisted my torso away and headed to the kitchen, which I entered, closing the door. Seattle's three monkeys didn't succeed in catching me. So they broached the same topic from outside the door.

"Open the door. We want to talk with you," Josie said as he tapped the papers with his fingers or a pen. "There's no cause for alarm. The gist of the story is that I didn't know you had a true love," Josie added.

"Morta, Morty, Mortada," Liao sang, turning three versions of my name into a song.

"Listen: I have an idea," Josie suggested.

"Yes, Josie has an idea, and everyone needs to listen to Josie when he has an idea," Erick said in a dismissive way, which reminded me of a verse of ancient Arabic poetry: "If Hadham said that, believe it *because* Hadham said it." Hadham was a woman who lived hundreds of years ago and had keen eyesight. Her tribal members didn't believe her when she told them she saw trees moving, but they regretted their skepticism when they were attacked by an army of ruffians that used branches and dirt to disguise themselves as trees.

"We engage in almost the same discipline, since writing means choreographing words. I picture your writing as belly dancing. We've been reading your correspondence with Erick," Liao added, trying to convince me to come out. "Your story is like the scenario for a film."

"The scenario for a film! Don't believe him. I, for example, if I wrote my autobiography, I would need a director who wouldn't diminish its gravity to make it seem credible. What happens in films is much lighter than banal reality," Josie said. Then he added, "I have an idea that will make you talk like a parrot and tell us the story."

34

A long time passed—perhaps an hour or three-quarters, while I listened to their breathing on the far side of the door and their slow steps when they checked on me from time to time.

They may have grown tired of waiting and decided to push Josie to share his idea.

"What it boils down to is that we want to be nice to you. We are happy that a lovestruck novelist is living in our house," Josie began, before presenting his idea.

"Open the door just partway or a crack, I beg you, Mo," Josie said plaintively.

I opened the door, and he quickly poked his foot through.

"Take this," he said as he held his foot out and waved it. I saw a foot wearing a sock with green and sky-blue stripes and bears with white wings. "Put this sock on your hand. Hold it outside the door, where we can see it, and move its jaws as if it were talking to us."

He tried to remove the sock using his other foot, so I helped him with my hand. He drew back when I removed the sock from his foot and closed the door. He may have returned to the living room with the two other monkeys.

"Tell us your story. Tell it." Then he clapped his hands as if welcoming actors behind the curtain where they were waiting to come onstage and perform.

Liao began to whistle, and Erick chortled.

I made them wait, but not as a ploy to allure the audience to the presentation and make it seem precious. I did that to collect my thoughts. I placed the sock on my right hand, removed it, and put it on my left hand. Then I noticed that the sock puppet's jaws wouldn't work properly because of my defective left hand; my middle finger stopped growing when I was in my twenties. Placing the sock on my right hand, however, would mean I had to show part of my body, because of the way the door opened.

One of them: "I'm growing drowsy."

Another: "We'll give him another fifteen minutes."

The third said, "I'm going to feed Heraclitus."

"My favorite show has begun. Good night," said one.

Then I heard a drumroll of footsteps on the stairs and realized that everyone had left the living room to tend to their affairs. I slipped slowly to my room, closed the door, curled up, and fell asleep with the sock still on my hand.

The next morning, when I stretched, I felt the sock, not my mouth, was yawning. I had grown accustomed to the calm of this house in the morning, but the light that shone through its windows, which were thoroughly scrubbed with disinfectants, wasn't strong enough to prompt me to go out and discover the city, where I didn't even understand the cries and squawks of the seagulls yet. When I was a child, I used to hear collared doves call out, "Hey, sister!" They didn't literally say that, but that's how I learned to hear it. The tongues in our heads make the dove say, "Hey, sister!" The dove asks everyone mournfully about its missing sister, and its lament has become a child's chant. Legend says that the eagle ate the dove's sister, and people should tell the dove so it can reconcile itself. People seem to want birds to say what they think, and the story of the missing sister is our way of anthropomorphizing animals and attributing to them concerns and desires like ours. I soon grew convinced that the seagulls and crows of Seattle were saying, "Morise, Morise!" I started to hear them utter his name and squawk it.

That day, I started hunting for my pens, which I normally hid in my shoes. I removed some pieces of colored paper from a museum guide I had taken from a communal book-sharing box and made three cards. Each of these Seattle monkeys would receive a hand-decorated card with an official stamp. These adornments were refined and vulgar at the same time and featured vegetative and foliate arabesques, Andalusian forms, interlocking rectangles, monkeys, unicorns, and bears—because these men loved bears; they were everywhere in their

house. There was a large space for owls, frogs, crows, scribbles, curli-
cues, stars and bars, and random, meaningless shapes. All these detailed
designs surrounded the card's text, which read:

> Dear So-and-So,
> I, Mo, Morta, Morty, Moortaada, value highly your
> noble desire to forge a name for me. I will outline for
> you below the best way to pronounce the Arabic letter
> *ḍad*, which is found in the final syllable of my name,
> which is and will remain Mortaḍa! My father was
> in the army when he learned of my birth. Then he
> requested leave and hopped on a bus heading to Basra,
> my city, which is located at the north end of the Arab
> Gulf. When he stared at the forest of sleeping army
> boots on the bus, his attention was attracted by the
> arm of a soldier sleeping among the feet. This soldier
> wore a white scarf over his nose to protect it from the
> smell of the feet. The tattoo on this soldier's arm read
> "Nothing has harmed me save the people I've met."
> For the duration of the trip, which lasted five hours,
> my father kept searching his memory for the name of
> the poet whose poem that verse came from. Before he
> left the bus, he had found another soldier who was
> tattooed with the second line of that couplet: "May
> God reward the person I haven't met." They told him
> the poet who recited the couplet that he loved was
> al-Mortaḍa, a medieval Arab poet from Baghdad.
> So he decided to name me Mortaḍa. My birth certifi-
> cate and name had been officially registered before he
> discovered that the author of the verse was actually
> not al-Mortaḍa but al-Ma'arri, who took a long time
> to discover that man is the greatest source of harm to

himself. You are not obliged to call me by my name, but I will answer only to my name. I know the Arabic letter *ḍad* is hard to pronounce and that Arabic has been called the language of the letter *ḍad*, as it is the only language that uses this sound. Even though few Arabs pronounce it properly, because it's difficult even for them, I feel my name isn't my true name without it. If you become exhausted trying to pronounce it, just listen to the seagulls and imagine they are saying my name.

In conclusion, I wish you the best of luck in following the steps below to the proper and appropriate pronunciation of my name. Once I find that you can utter it, I can complete the story. Remember always that since you can say "Tchaikovsky," "karaoke," and "algorithm," you will be able to pronounce my name.

First: raise your tongue till the tip touches your upper gums.

Second: coordinate this touch with the expulsion of air from your lungs to your mouth.

Third: increase the amount of air behind the tongue to create pressure on its front so that the sound of the letter *ḍad* emerges.

Fourth: after pronouncing the letter *ḍad* in the middle of my name, you need to open your mouth a little and push out a small puff of air so that the letter *alif* will emerge: ah, half of aah. This isn't the "aah!" people say when they are hurt. It is half of that "aah."

Fifth: you can call me Mo, but my name isn't Mohamed, and people here say Mo to refer to people named Mohamed. The *o* in my name is more like the sound *u* in "too" and "boo."

Sixth: I've changed my mind. If you clap once, I'll come. You really don't need to learn how to pronounce my name.

After this, I chose to hide. When I found the courage, I began to look out the window and spy on the world. I felt that I was a single matchstick staring out of an open matchbox and that it wouldn't have anything to write in its diary if it left the box. I saw Josie coming toward the house but didn't see Heraclitus. An entire week had passed without my encountering this dog or hearing him bark. His name was repeated everywhere, and he was mentioned in brief conversations, without even his shadow showing. I found I couldn't remove the sock puppet and continued wearing it. This sock helped me remember and arrange the story that was forming in my head. There was something else I kept doing: I wore large red earphones so I could pretend to be listening to music or telephoning someone. That way, I could laugh or speak Arabic aloud without my housemates thinking I was crazy. I hadn't yet cured myself of the habit of speaking to Morise.

Four

I met Josie at the door and stepped forward to open it for him. We wished each other a good morning, and he shot off in his wheelchair as if he had lost control of it, like a passenger on a runaway boat.

Liao was checking the mailbox and soon returned with a pile of parcels and packages, which he placed on the large counter beside the kitchen sink. He began to cut them open, one by one. I left him doing that and went to look for my sock puppet. I put it on my hand and busied myself with cleaning the back door to the garden. Although I hadn't slept well, I was flooded with vitality and lofty ambition. A rectangular mirror taller than me was attached securely to the garden door. This mirror held me in its embrace as I stood gazing at my reflection. I had grown a lot. I remembered my father once remarking, when I was a child, that America turns your hair white. Back then, I had imagined that it would turn your hair white if you went there. You wouldn't be old, but your hair would turn white the moment you set foot in the country.

"Mortada, do you plan on keeping your beard?" I heard Erick, who was also looking in the mirror, ask.

"If you shave it off, or at least trim it, you'll have less trouble finding a job," Erick suggested as he twisted his thick, white beard and looked back at his computer screen. Erick worked from home most days.

That afternoon, I set out to buy a razor and shaving cream but met Josie heading back to the house. He said he had been out taking Heraclitus for a walk, as usual. But I didn't see Heraclitus. He asked me to accompany him downtown; I agreed as my errand was taking me in that direction but suggested he wait while I fetched an umbrella. He laughed then and shook his head no.

"Don't carry an umbrella. You'll look more like a resident of Seattle without one. Everyone will know you're a newcomer if you take it."

"It's not for me or you. I'll get it for Heraclitus."

"You're a really fine person, Mortada. You go, and I'll wait for you here."

Heraclitus wasn't there, but I tried to play along and give him the impression that I would fetch it for the imaginary creature I didn't see.

I drew an umbrella from the gray container by the door and returned, but Josie wasn't where I had left him. I stood there as the breeze and misty rain began to annoy me. I may have waited fifteen minutes without him appearing. Then I noticed an enclosed park behind me and saw Josie sitting there with his hands together and head leaning against his shoulder. This small park was devoid of other human beings but chock-full of small shrubs and sidewalk drawings. I slipped inside and approached Josie. I touched him, but he didn't react. When I asked why he hadn't told me he would be here, I realized that he was sound asleep, snoring loudly, saliva dribbling from his mouth.

I left Josie peacefully asleep in the park and went to make my purchases. I departed the store, carrying a bag that contained everything I needed to shave. Josie was still asleep, even though the windows of passing buses were crowded with the frowning faces of young people returning from work, and the sun was retiring behind the clouds, somewhere on the horizon. When I pushed Josie's wheelchair up the arched bridge, I started huffing as though I were Sisyphus shoving the boulder toward the top of the slope. But Josie wasn't a boulder, and I wasn't being forced by the gods of Olympus. All the same, I felt a kinship with Sisyphus at some level when I pushed Josie. My effort, sweat, and muscle fatigue all reminded me of Sisyphus, although I still found it hard to consider Sisyphus a true hero. All the same, he posed an essential question for me: Did what was happening now compensate for everything that had happened previously? Would Seattle prove a safe spot for someone like me? Would it protect us from being killed and terrorized? Would it safeguard us against attacks by the demons of memory?

Josie's wheelchair would occasionally veer right or left. He had begun to wake up and yawn but didn't know that my left hand was merely for looks and lacked any force. It couldn't push even ten pounds. I noticed that he had started to fool with the buttons controlling his chair and was attempting to seize control of it. He seemed unwilling to cut the Iraqi Sisyphus any slack, because he used the controls on his motorized chair to back it directly into me. I threw myself out of the way and rolled down the slope after him. Josie didn't go far, because the chair turned over. Then I landed. Before I checked on him, a huge load of outrageous sorrow clouded my heart, and I began to weep out loud. I bawled, determined to release the tears of the last thirty years.

I wasn't sure whether I had released everything in this tearfest, but I felt lighter. What I sensed then was that this bevy of sweet tears wasn't demeaning.

Stretching, Josie asked, as he pretended to smile, "Are you okay?"

"I'm fine. Sorry! I blanked out for a moment, and the chair got away from me."

"Don't worry about it. I enjoyed the game. Come on: we'll try it again."

I walked back to look for Josie's wig. I turned left and right but didn't find it. I stretched to look beneath the bridge but couldn't see whether the winds had carried it there. Josie came toward me and tried—like me—to peer between the bridge's railings but failed. Attempting to grasp the bars of the railing, he said, "It's not your fault. Let it go. It's a good time for me to get some air on my head. Have you ever worn a wig?"

"Almost."

"What do you mean, 'almost'?"

"Listen, Josie. You don't need me to push your wheelchair. Let me walk beside you, and we'll go home."

"I want to see what you look like in a wig."

At that time, I used Josie's brain as an ashtray for my memories and surprised him with the second installment of my story. Without any introduction, I continued with Josie what I had begun with Liao.

"Yes, I wore something larger than a wig on my head. The Fedayeen Saddam threw my body into the center of my house and humiliated me in front of my family, telling them that their son was a pansy—that he was 'pierced,' meaning that his anus had been used for sex. They threw me down carelessly, and I felt I was a useless tool returned to its owner, who was told, 'Your tool has been pierced, and its manhood doesn't work.' My father did nothing for the next three days. Eventually, he bowed to our tribe's pressure that I must be punished. He was obliged to inform them that he had formally disciplined me. He limited himself to fastening my leg with a chain to the window bars. I heard men whispering outside the door. I heard bits and pieces of their suggestions because their words reached me truncated and incomplete, whispered beyond walls coated with plaster and lime. I felt that my father's head was becoming a landfill for worn-out ideas and other men's advice. As I was only fifteen, my father rejected the idea of marrying me off. They decided to feed me dates and milk, which was a relatively decent diet; I would have eaten the same things if I were free. The catch was that this meal arrived once every nine hours. One of my cousins—on my mother's side—was charged with opening the door and shoving the food inside, without looking at me or touching me. I was a moral leper. My father wasn't strong enough to look at me and waited two whole weeks before he peeked through that window at three o'clock in the morning, when he thought I wouldn't see him. He was mistaken, because I was wide awake and pretended to recite ritual and personal prayers. I cried out, 'Zahra, Zahra, Zahra,' repeating the name of the Prophet's revered daughter Fatima al-Zahra to curry favor with my father—or, better put, to punish him and transfer to him a share of the tortures I was enduring. When he poked his head up partway in the darkness, I wailed louder and began fervently to sob the name of the Prophet's daughter repeatedly. This proved successful, because I heard him weep and repeat, 'Zahra, shield us, O Zahra. We are good people, and this child is affectionate and radiant. I'm sure he will dedicate his life to your service, to promulgating news of your deeds, and to lamenting for your auspicious, young, shackled, martyred offspring, O Sovereign over the world's women.'"

I watched Josie's face as I recounted this. Even though I was no longer a Muslim believer, the name Zahra still provoked a fiery sensation in my heart. When beliefs perish together with their formulae, they leave behind perforations like nail holes in the heart, and these are hard to patch or paint over. They are like the shadow left by a painting that once hung on a wall.

"I still wonder what you meant by 'almost' wearing a wig," Josie said, drawing an imaginary wig with his hands over his head. We were nearly at the top of the hill.

But we rushed downhill again, even though this time we didn't topple over and weren't hurt. We returned to where we had started silently and shot off again.

"According to the beliefs of Shi'i Muslims, Zahra was an incarnation of Our Lady the Virgin Mary, whom you revere, of Our Lady Hagar, the wife of Abraham, and even of Our Lady Eve. Between you and me, I wasn't a total hypocrite when I repeated her name. I was buttering up my father, to be sure, but in some portion of my mind, I truly was confiding in her. I hated everything that had happened and felt impure. When I heard my belly growl with hunger, I sensed that I was purifying myself and that the flesh of my body needed to waste away and be replaced with new flesh that wasn't on my bones when I was a sodomite and polluted with sin.

"My cousins entered the room and unfastened the chain. I wasn't overjoyed, because their faces didn't look happy. They began to sweep the room and to shake off the sheet of cardboard I had been sleeping on. They handed me a metal brush and Dettol. With one word, they ordered me to scrape from the floor the mounds of filth my body had left. They watched me while I did. I expected them to wait outside, but they chose to train their eyes on me. There were three of them, and the third had a bandage over an eye, because he was a cock fighter, and his cock took out his eye one day. They stared at me in a mean way, and I sensed that this was to satisfy their lust for punishment. Their strategy soon changed when I finished cleaning the place. They fastened me to the chain again, but by my wrist, and stuffed me into the trunk of a Toyota Crown sedan. It wasn't pitch black in there, because the cover wasn't latched. Fastened by an electric cord, the open cover exposed me to the exhaust fumes. I caught sight of the broadcast tower, seesaws in a barren park, and gray walls covered with presidential sayings. There was plenty I couldn't see because the gap was only a few centimeters high, and the opening changed size as the Crown bobbed up and down. Words written on fences leaped about with each pothole we drove over. The letters forming the president's sayings surged and collided with each other. I noticed that many periods, commas, and parentheses were missing, effaced.

"My view broadened to include all of their faces when they opened the trunk and pulled me out. I saw that one of them held a shovel, which he used immediately to begin digging. I was sure they wouldn't kill me and bury me here. The goal of this exercise was to frighten me and make me conscious of the gravity of what I had done.

"This party ended when it began to hail: small hard hailstones that the sky spat down on this scene. Basra, my city, which is almost tropical, does occasionally have hailstorms. Then its fetching slopes and hills are covered with white. This hailstorm caused my cousins to hasten to complete their assignment. They quickly kicked me in the mouth, and one of them broke his toenail as he shoved his big toe against my teeth. I remained passive and merely uttered a sound like a dove: '*Yakhti*: Sister!'

"I was wrong. They did quickly bury me in a hole, planting my body in it like a dwarf palm. Then they hid behind the car, laughing together and occasionally arguing. I could smell the whiskey to which my cousins were becoming addicted and realized they would start fighting each other if they consumed enough alcohol. I was waiting for that moment, which might alleviate my own feeling of shame, because one of them would get beaten the way I had been. That might diminish my humiliation. It seemed that this time they were more amicable, but before two of them departed, leaving me with the cock fighter, one cousin urinated on my face. Then he bruised my neck with a kick from his shoe. He left in the sedan with his brother. The cock fighter kept glaring at my face as he squatted on the ground. His cheeks were flushed, and his eye had lost its luster. After pulling me out long enough to pee on my butt, he told me, 'I'm going to put you back in the hole till the smell dissipates. Dirt is good for purification. That's why we use it for ablutions before prayer if there's no water. Do you know that? Do you ever pray? I want to hear you pray.'

"I don't know where the other two brothers disappeared to. I don't know whether this was a deliberate fraternal ploy. When they returned, they were more relaxed and less hostile. They took me back to my house, to that same room, where one of them appeared to have sprinkled water and perfume and lit incense. I would learn later, though, that my mother had done that.

"Another week passed without their deciding what to do with me. I learned from visits by my cousins that what had happened with the cock fighter had not been part of their plan; it was something sneaky that needed to remain our secret. Early the next morning, my mother came and placed my head on her thigh. She sat in the center of the room with a small brazier and a pot in front of her. Her fragrance perfumed the whole space, because she was always careful to scent her clothing with incense from the tombs of the saints. She wore her habitual long silk scarf. Her favorite color was black, which was the typical choice of Iraqi women after the war—a major fashion influence. I never saw my mother wear any color but black except in family photos. My father, the teacher who had married her and brought her to this city, wanted her to adjust to Basra, at least in family pictures. Thus, in them, I would find my mother clad in a short, colorful skirt with her hair carefully twisted on the crown of her head: oiled, neatly combed, and coal black. These photos reveal that her brown complexion wasn't a result of Basra's sunshine but of a Black lineage that mixed with that of her ancestors who lived in Iraq's marshes. There was no family tree, because the preferred system was to refer to lineage by *fakhidh*, or clan. Since the word also meant 'thigh,' I would think of the thigh of a chicken or the haunch of a sheep. Tribes were composed of clans, and my mother's clan resulted from the intermarriage of the daughters of the shaykhs with other tribal chiefs' slaves, who came from Mozambique, Zanzibar, or other East African communities. The gist of the traditional story was that these women were captured in violent battles on land and on water between the shaykhs of the marshlands.

"My mother didn't recite a favorite verse of the Qur'an above my head and didn't repeat Zahra's name or variants of it. My mother did

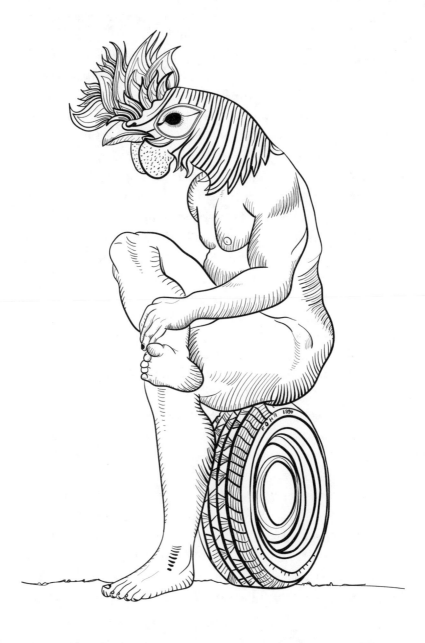

not know much about Islamic creeds, but her head was filled with stories of the marshes' saints and female diviners to whom people made vows and presented sacrificial offerings to request assistance with satisfying their needs and achieving difficult tasks.

"My mother appealed frequently to Fouada Umm Hashim, an ancient saint of the marshes. She was a blind woman who wandered with her livestock every day through the thickets and cane. Everyone mocked her and referred to her as 'the ignorant blind woman whose smell would stun your senses and blind you.' They made fun of her and composed songs and doggerels insulting her. Fouada had a weak, broken mind but a sound, unsullied heart. One day when Fouada returned from the pasture, no one blocked her way. In fact, everyone fled from her and avoided her, even though they had humiliated her almost daily when she returned each afternoon with her livestock trailing after her, quite meekly. That day, however, was terrifying for every member of the tribe. The moment she entered the alleys, everyone ran from her, screaming and wailing, instead of laughing and mocking her as usual, because Fouada arrived with calm dignity, followed closely by her animals. What was new that day was the pair of lions that trailed behind her as obediently as the water buffalos. Fouada had tamed the lions and the other wild beasts, which walked demurely behind her. The Shi'i imams had granted her this amazing, compensatory, charismatic gift of conquering lions and their ferocity, and this spread terror through the tribe members' hearts. It also sufficed to turn Fouada into a saint with disciples and students who believed in her charismatic gifts and her power, which was undeniable.

"For my mother, Fouada was a person who could accomplish everything and who did all types of good deeds. Even so, my mother saved Fouada for grand tasks and major problems. She wouldn't invoke her name if it wasn't important. Summoning saints for trivial matters demonstrated disrespect for them and for the power of the prophet Adam. Her mouth uttered the name Fouada in tandem with prayers while her hand stroked my temple and pressed on it. On the small brazier, she melted lead figures in a pot. I watched them change shape as she stirred and agitated the forms with her spoon.

"The idea was that this lead, which was extracted from shrapnel and bullets, would tell us a lot, because the heat would cause it to assume random shapes that would alert us to what should be done. This approach doesn't differ much from the language of signs and the communication between a viewer and a complicated, postmodernist painting. In fact, it also resembles the mistaken, juvenile way of interpreting the secrets of complex paintings. Some people love abstract art for the puzzles and enigmas it contains. I don't remember what shape appeared in the pot, but my mother apparently thought it resembled me. It showed her things that made her smile, and she exhaled a gallon or more of air. She seemed to be ridding herself of toxic fantasies and thoughts by puffing out all this air. Then she reheated the lead but placed a metal cup on my forehead; I was so curious, I froze motionless. Then she poured molten lead into the cup as I gazed fearfully at its bottom, anticipating that a hole would open in it and that lead would pour down on my retina.

"She kissed me and hugged me to her chest, blew her nose, wiped away her tears, pressed on my skull, pulled her abaya around her body, and left.

"I gathered from the hullaballoo the next morning that a tribal trial would be held between members of my tribe and that of Qahtan, who had sold me the rainbow. For this reason, they took me out, bathed me, and shaved my head.

"There would have been no need for anything to happen and no reason for a trial, had the scandal not spread far and wide. The tribal elders feared what people would say—that they didn't respect manly exploits. In short, they would not be appeased until they had blathered about these matters and reconciled the adversaries. To be sure, there hadn't been any quarrel. What had occurred was that people had spread the story after the Fedayeen set out to create a scandal about Qahtan and me. Then these tribal elders had felt they had to placate the government by punishing both of us.

"During the hours I waited for the trial, I was buoyed by my mother's smile and her laughter, which followed her weeping and subdued sobbing. I asked myself what Fouada had told her and what the molten lead had revealed about me.

"I don't know who neglected to lock the door to our yard and allowed boys and women to sneak up on my prison. I turned my back on them when they peered at me through the window and whispered to one another. Then they began to laugh, and some of the boys felt they could chat and recount incidents that bore no relationship to me at all. Eventually, matters evolved to the point that a large crowd entered our yard and claimed their right to disparage me and provide their version of the story. None of these people troubled themselves to ask me what had happened, and I heard them whispering whatever stories they wanted, no matter how contradictory or fabricated. They eventually grew tired of talking but not of staring at me. I heard one man ask his wife as he looked at me if she would iron his white shirt because he needed it for a relative's wedding."

Josie rolled down the hill again, but he seemed to have done it on purpose because he wanted time out to play. I let him slide to the bottom of the arched bridge while I stayed at the top. He raised his glitter-covered eyebrows and tinted eyelids and signaled with his head that he wanted me to continue my story. I went to him and pushed him back up the hill again.

"The guesthouse where the trial was held consisted of a large chamber constructed from cane and papyrus. These reeds were braided together in a geometrical fashion that was fascinating to observe. I was preoccupied—as they shoved me into the center of the crowd at the middle of the chamber—with observing the skillful way reeds had been bundled together to form cylindrical columns that were joined at the top to make the arches that held the building up. That *mudeef* was in a working-class neighborhood where most houses were built of red brick and concrete. These tribes, which had immigrated to the city from the marshes during the first half of the previous century, had committed themselves, though, to continue making houses from cane and erecting halls for the shaykhs and thus to preserve this folk architecture, which had originated in the coastal wetlands.

"Custom required the family that had committed the offense to offer its apology, express remorse, and castigate its son in the presence of the family of the adversary or victim in order to smooth the way for the judicial proceedings and to soften hearts. But, to tell the truth, I didn't know who the guilty party was. No one had asked me, and my testimony had not been sought. I saw Qahtan, kneeling behind his huge father, who wore a thick, camel-hair cloak embroidered with gold thread. I then found myself lowering my gaze to the floor and contemplating the arabesques woven into the carpet.

"This was more of a theatrical performance than a judicial proceeding designed to determine the truth. The gist of what the adult men said in the session was that two sons of these two tribes had committed an act that causes the heavens to shake and frightens the angels. For a male to mount another male is a matter that angers the compassionate God and makes his throne quiver indignantly. Such a stain of dishonor cannot be erased, and this bad behavior is inappropriate for anyone. Therefore, it was decided to chastise both boys. The Baath Party leadership would be satisfied with this when it was made cognizant of the judgment."

I succeeded in escaping from Sisyphus and crossed the bow of the bridge safely, pushing Josie. I certainly wasn't Sisyphus, because he was punished forever in an endless labyrinth. In fact, Josie was done with his game and began driving his chair himself. So I walked along beside him and continued talking.

"They threw a wig at me. It wasn't a real wig. Instead, it was a mound of black wool that was arranged and enclosed by a thread net. Then they tossed at me a voluminous, one-piece, scented woman's dress that glittered with beads and silvery bangles, which rang like a bell. They shouted in my face, demanding that I put it on for everyone to see. I thought that wearing the wig would suffice and spare me from having to put on the dress. But they scolded me after I placed the wig on my head and demanded that I don the complete outfit. Once I had put everything on my body, they summoned someone from the opposing tribe. They didn't give him any directions, because he knew what to do. He flipped me over, laid me on my belly, lifted my dress, and continued to bear down on my back with his midriff. He was attempting to seek vengeance by making a public display, in accordance with the tribal judgment. He merely displayed his virility to everyone and demonstrated my submission and my temporary feminization. Yes, I have worn a wig."

Josie began to mumble some words I didn't understand. Then he started to sing as he gazed at my face, which was wet from the rain. We reached the house when the night and quiet were competing to take control of the whole neighborhood. I disappeared into the bathroom and immersed my whole body in the tub. A long black hair like the wool of a ewe floated to the surface.

I heard Erick inquire about me and Josie reply that I was in the bathroom, bathing and shaving off my beard.

Everyone was waiting for me at the dinner table. Liao was slowly stirring his soup, taking care not to make a sound. Josie had intertwined his fingers as he spoke with Erick. I appeared, sat down, and started eating. I noticed that they were stealing glances at my face and whispering. Once dinner concluded, Erick couldn't bear to hold his question any longer. "I thought you were going to shave off your beard."

"No, I shaved something else."

They may have understood what I had shaved. They merely changed the subject to talk about the suit Josie would wear to some party. He spoke enthusiastically about his investment in its many details, explaining that the matter had required much thought, deliberation, and expertise. As he rotated his rapt face slowly, I was able to make out the words that dangled from his ears: "Hard to forget."

Five

When I returned from work that night, the monkeys' door was locked.

Liao had found a job for me at a marijuana farm on the outskirts of Seattle. My supervisor there placed five blooming cannabis stems in my pocket as my weekly wage. I discreetly handed these to Erick and Josie, because I hadn't tried pot yet, although this claim isn't 100 percent true, because the pot scent filled my nostrils during every hour I worked at the greenhouse. My clothes and fingers were sticky from various types of cannabis flowers that kept me gliding and wandering in the realms of the imagination. I would walk the three miles home and watch my shadow divide into three shadows resembling soccer players on pickup teams. When dim streetlights split these players' shadows, I didn't hear the colors breathe—unlike hashish users such as Arthur Rimbaud. Instead, what I heard were the breaths of stories falling naked onto the pavement only to rise, race away, and enter houses through their windows. I was rehearsing my conversations with Morise and reworking my responses to him. I amended our conversation from the day he told me about his love for hashish and that the word "cannabis" was derived from the Arabic word *qanab*, which does mean "cannabis." I pushed back then, because I'm not a person who thinks that all words are derived from *his* language. Like me, Morise loves words, plays with them as he utters them, dismembers them with his tongue, and then traces them back to their ancient roots. So, when I heard him say, "I love you," I heard an extremely condensed expression that harbored traces of mariners' shanties, soldiers' groans, mothers' letters, and horses' hoofbeats.

I didn't have my own house key yet. They had told me they would provide me with one soon. I tucked my legs beneath me at the door and waited for relief. I may have nodded off and begun to snore gently. Perhaps I stretched out with my legs apart. I don't remember precisely. In any case, I suddenly woke to find a snowflake on my shoulder. Snow penetrated my clothing, and its chill stung me. Once the snow roused me, drowsiness abandoned me, and I decided to walk toward the center of the city. I was very embarrassed because I reeked of marijuana but had no alternative to smelling like that. I took the bus and got off two stops later. I found a coffee shop with umbrellas to catch the snow, selected a chair, and sat down. I tossed my bag down, brought out a large sketchpad and my pens, and started drawing. A dog with a large head approached me and kept nudging me and rubbing my foot. I was submitting contributions to a magazine in Lebanon. I would send them a five-hundred-word essay that included a caricature. That was the type of submission they welcomed, and they paid me regularly. That newspaper and the marijuana farm were my only sources of income since the oil company in Dubai and Basra had fired me. "If you're thrown on your head, you'll land on your feet," my mother used to tell me when she wished to list my strong points.

I rose to go inside to use the restroom and noticed from my reflection in the coffee shop window that my fly was open. For weeks I had kept buying used trousers because they were cheap and still looked new. But I had discovered time and again that their zippers were defective.

I had taken to referring to this condition as the open-zipper syndrome and subversively defined it as typical of Arab homosexuals, who are always twisting one way and the other.

After I returned to the table, I was startled by the large dog that had seemed friendly before it unexpectedly attacked me. Apparently, the zipper hadn't remained closed long, opening again seconds after I zipped it in the restroom. The dog, which was a huge Japanese Akita, had noticed that something wasn't right with my trousers and bit me in the groin. I managed to restrain my scream and muffle my yell, but my face flushed red, and I started jumping and hopping on one foot to relieve my pain.

At that point, the dog's owner, a lady, stood up, yanked it away, and held its jaws closed with her hand. She sat back down in her chair; then she seized the dog by the ears and settled its head on her lap. She apologized effusively with affectionate charm. She left her table and returned moments later with a large cup of coffee and a slice of lemon cake on a plate. I had both my hands between my legs and bowed to thank her. A light breeze flipped the pages of my sketchbook and attracted her attention. She expressed her admiration for the pages she glimpsed, even though she was still embarrassed by what her dog had done. I was yawning and feeling drowsy, but the smell of coffee helped me pay attention to what she was saying and to her tender way of communicating with me. Her voice, which rose from a cup of warm rose water, could have stopped rain and tamed dogs and lions—like Fouada's. She was blonde and short like me, and her curiosity could open windows in boulders. She offered others a hint of her brilliance and surprised them with her knowledge.

After I returned to my sketchbook and took out my pens to continue drawing, I noticed that she was watching my hand and peeking at the sketch of the caricature I was making. It was a drawing inspired by *The Thousand and One Nights*: a statue of Shahriyar climbing on Shahrazad's shoulders. It was a commentary on the continuing dialogue in Arab culture on "honor" killings of women. Shahrazad, the heroine of *The Thousand and One Nights*, was forced to tell Shahriyar an exciting story to keep from having her head chopped off the next morning. The cartoon was a riff on the statue of Shahrazad and Shahriyar in the heart of Baghdad near the Tigris River. Instead of depicting him seated in his typical fashion with flowing garments with which the breeze toys while he holds a glass of wine and Shahrazad curls up before him, telling her stories, I drew the man climbing on her shoulders, even though she could scarcely support his weight.

We discussed the drawing, and the woman learned that I was a newcomer to Seattle and that I was still looking for a real job in programming and digital simulation, which I had done professionally for the last five years as an engineer for oil companies.

"Why did you choose Seattle?"

"It's a long story. I'm looking for someone."

The woman seemed very interested and paused every time I said something. I could feel her curiosity bounce from her eyes and become a throng of people encouraging me to tell them more. She asked whether I was searching for a family member or an old friend, a girlfriend or a wife, a kinsman or a relative.

"All of those and none of them," I said, using a traditional phrase with vapid conceit, because I was proud of it.

"Are you married?"

"No, I've come here to search for my boyfriend, from whom I was separated by circumstances beyond our control, several years ago. He lives here, somewhere on the Hill."

I love the way Seattle makes it easy to express proclivities and abridges a dozen sentences as people converse.

The woman sensed she had learned enough and chose not to pry into details. Before she rose and said goodbye, she wrote her telephone number on a piece of paper and asked me to give her my number. So I did, thanked her, and rose to give her a hug. I opened my arms, interested to see that I still reacted spontaneously to warm human emotions. My response didn't disappoint me.

Night fell, and its arrival was accompanied by rain. The streets glittered with drizzle, reflecting the cars' lights. The rain intensified as I walked quickly, my bag on my back, trying to catch the bus so I would reach home in time to read before going to bed at a reasonable hour. That way I could rise at dawn the following day without feeling groggy.

My eyes caught sight of a homeless man sleeping on a bench. He was all wrapped up in an overcoat, and all I could see of him were his feet, which were heavily scarred. I laughed quietly despite myself when I approached him; I had meant to offer him my leather jacket but discovered that this homeless man dozing in the rain was a statue of a sleeping vagrant.

I leaned against the wall near him and allowed myself to scrutinize his body, facial features, and the folds of cloth covering his form. The sidewalk was deserted, and the street was silent except for the scraping sound of the windshield wipers of passing cars. I searched for the vagrant's face but found none, because it was hidden in the marble.

These circumstances didn't keep me from continuing my story with him.

"Listen, my dear dozing vagrant, after implementation of the tribal judgment, the tribe was keen to reform me. Everyone felt personally responsible for guiding me and fashioning me anew. In those days, my father was trying diligently to leave Iraq to work abroad and had quit his job as a history teacher, because the Iraqi currency had fallen in value incredibly, and his monthly salary, which amounted to only a few dollars, wasn't enough to buy dinner for his family. The government had forbidden teachers, engineers, and physicians from traveling out of the country. So he, like thousands of other government employees, was forced to buy a counterfeit passport in order to flee to Amman to work there and send money back to my mother. But they caught him at the border and put him in prison, where he spent two years, which he devoted to memorizing the Qur'an. He came out a pious man. His chin was adorned with a short beard, and his forehead bore a black spot that attested to many prostrations in prayer. A black forehead became fashionable with middle-class men suffering from the economic embargo imposed by the United Nations in the 1990s. A joke circulated then that men grilled eggplants and branded their foreheads with them so that they would look like righteous, good-hearted people. The eggplant was referred to as 'the monster of the skillet' in those days, because they were abundant and cheap and supported people's tendencies to disguise themselves, hide, and adapt to difficulties. 'Monster of the skillet' was an expression derived from a phrase used for famous movie stars, who were called 'monsters of the screen.' Now the skillet was the screen, because it was the magic window of hunger, and poor people stared at it.

"Also popular then were supererogatory nighttime prayers and visits to supposititious tombs of ancient saints and those of saints who had never existed but whom people sought out, hoping for the chance to die more than once—since poets who celebrated the president and the war deafened people with the slogan 'Brave men die just once; cowards die again and again.' Meanwhile, the government was rolling out a program to turn the populace into pious Sunni Muslims, even though most people betrayed the government by secretly persisting in their embrace of Shi'i Islam. This practice of saying one thing and believing the opposite was compatible with the Shi'i principle that in dangerous situations, it is permissible for a believer to conceal his denomination. My father didn't use an eggplant to stamp his forehead. Instead, he had devoted every night he spent in prison to a complete spiritual retreat during which he communicated with God in his own fashion. He had never mastered the set, statutory prayers and merely made some gestures and mumbled phrases along with the imam leading the prayer service. He did recite the Qur'an, performed supplementary prayers, and was interested in the enchanting spiritual tales of fallen angels and penitents. When he first caught sight of me after he was released from prison, he asked me whether I prayed. As I answered him, I took from my pocket a booklet entitled *How to Teach Your Son to Pray*. This booklet, written by the greatest Shiʻi Muslim authority in the world, instructed fathers how to teach their sons to pray. So I started reading to my father from the prayer book and demonstrating the gestures for him, while he imitated me. Then he commented that the title ought to be changed to *How to Teach Your Father to Pray*. This may have helped me change my image gradually in the family and erase their perception of me as a sodomite who shook the foot of the Lord's throne each time he had sex.

"My mother found me another profession, which was more precisely—from her point of view—a suitable punishment for me, because what I had done could not be allowed to go unpunished by some form of exile and banishment far from the city. Three-quarters of the youth in our alley worked collecting used copper and selling it to factories that smelted it to make weapons. At noon on the streets, you heard the cries of men selling old stuff or searching for old copper containers; these formed a counterpoint to the voices of muezzins calling people to prayer. I set to work and traveled to the city's outskirts, making the rounds and calling out to people that I would buy their outdated and used wares and old containers. We frequently did find used items that could be resold—even though we were ill-treated by people we didn't know and insulted by guards and soldiers. This trade caused me to miss many days of school, and the principal reprimanded me. Then my father took pity on me and intervened with my mother, convincing her that I would work only on school holidays and feast days. She consented on the proviso that I would begin working in the desert near the city, scavenging war materiel.

"That desert was al-Faw, which was the name of an ancient ship that became the name of a city on the Gulf. It was once known as the city with the most date palms on this planet, and it fed thousands of men during the war; it lived off its date plantations. The Iran-Iraq War bombardment in 1986 transformed it into a barren wasteland with charred palm trunks that resembled matchsticks.

"At first, I went to the desert alone. Then I discovered a group older than I was: two men and a woman. I would follow them early in the morning. Once I felt comfortable at a site, I would deliberately leave them and meet them again at noon, when I stashed my possessions and took a truffle from my provisions. I would break my routine of eating truffles with a boiled egg and a chunk of grilled eggplant.

"In one hand, I carried a canvas bag with its mouth open and its edges folded. In the other, I held a spade the size of my hand. I raked the earth with it, turning the dirt over to search for scraps of metal and shell casings—for any metal debris left from the war. When I looked up, my eyes would fall on a swarm of people wandering through the wilderness to dig for al-Faw's gold, which was copper war waste. One kilo of it would bring enough to feed a family for three days. As for me, my goal was to provide my family with some cash and to save up enough to buy Muhammad Mahdi Naraqi's book entitled *The Collector of Felicities*. I had frequently heard about this book on broadcasts from opposition forces. The shaykh, who presented programs on philosophy, had chosen this book as his text for Aristotelian ethics. He was trying to show connections between Greek philosophy, philosophy of religion, and Shi'i ethics. The happiness the book discussed was, therefore, virtue. Each chapter of the book discussed the essence of happiness. As I walked across the sand dunes, I grew convinced that there was a parallel between gathering metal fragments and gathering types of happiness.

"Scrap metal was graded by how suitable a piece was for smelting. As I attempted to find bits and pieces of metal in the dirt and pull them from whatever stuck to them, they would frequently deceive me. People paid more for clean metal free of blemishes.

"A flock of sheep passing by on the horizon suddenly became a ball of white dust. I raced to find myself in the middle of that dusty dirt-devil. I was covered with wool and realized that the sounds from the explosions had become magnetic fields when the dust exploded into the air. People shouted to each other, and men scattered through the area, fleeing from the dormant land mine these lively animals had tripped.

"Terror penetrated us, and hearts struggled out of their cages but quickly returned as people recovered their zeal to search for the desert's gold. I caught sight of a gleam on a small hill. I stretched out my fingers to pick it up and discovered it was a large fragment the length of a pen. Before I could grasp it and blow on it, a hand in a black glove snatched it from me. This hand belonged to a large woman enveloped in black cloth that resembled her, except for the sparkle of her eyes, which were outlined with kohl.

"'This is ours!'

"'I found it, but you can keep it. There is a lot of shrapnel.'

"The woman ignored me. Instead, she strode toward the hill and returned the fragment to its place. I watched her move with difficulty. Her body leaned forward as she walked with a bent back, looking almost lame. I decided to leave her alone, preferring to observe her from a distance. I saw her move between the small hills and open her bag. She took out metal fragments that she returned to their places, as if replanting them.

"A group of people passed, crying out and clapping their hands to show they had finished work for the day. When their route took them near the woman clad in black, they shouted at her, while clapping and laughing together. 'Hey, Three Legs. Hello, Mother Three Legs.' She just ignored them and continued planting shrapnel in the field. I realized at once that she had fought them for fragments and taken some from them. A few moments later, I saw her return to the places where she had planted metal fragments to pluck them out again and put them in her sack. When she approached the metal that she had taken from me, though, she pulled the bits out of the ground and placed them on her palm. Then she approached me and pointed. The moment she gave me that shrapnel, she turned her back and limped down the hill.

"'Auntie, I don't want it. Take it.'

"'It's ours, but you take it. It's ours.'

"I noticed she said 'ours,' not 'mine.' Before I could turn the matter over in my mind, I found her repeating the same thing louder while spreading her arms to gesture toward the entire space surrounding her. Her voice, which didn't sound like other women's voices and which was hoarse from smoking, was enjoyable to hear. So I ran after her and watched her do the same thing with the metal fragments she found. If she kept doing that, she would lose all her take for the day. Then I decided to leave her and to penetrate farther into the sands, anticipating a plentiful harvest before nightfall.

"I continued to watch her from a distance as I gathered scrap metal and filled my bag. The ground was free of scrap metal collectors, although they had been distributed throughout it, far and wide. The two of us were there alone. I wasn't comfortable staying there as the sun set. People told unpleasant stories about what happened when the sand dunes swallowed the sun."

Six

"Keeping my distance from the other scrap metal vendors, I retreated alone behind the garage to wait for the bus that would take me home, my sack of scrap metal beside me and a large notebook on my lap. I had made enough of a fortune to buy a Parker pen with the lion emblem. I no longer needed the Popsicle dyes that made my words sticky and attracted flies. I usually waited for everyone else to board the other buses and stayed behind till the red air-conditioned buses arrived after sunset, because I didn't like to mingle with other war materiel scavengers. The red buses carried people from the scrap metal peninsula to the heart of my city on the Shatt al-Arab. I wrote random observations very rapidly, without dotting letters or using punctuation. I considered writing without diacritical marks a skill characteristic of eloquent people, because I had heard a shaykh in the mosque say that the Prophet's caliph had been an eloquent man who wrote in such a magical fashion that he composed a sermon without any jots or tittles, even though the custom in writing Arabic script is to mark letters with various arrangements of dashes and dots. For this reason, I thought I had to avoid using letters that needed dots, and this reduced my alphabet by almost a third. This notion held sway over me for days, even though I didn't keep what I wrote. After the incident with the Fedayeen and the tribe, I was fearful and panic-stricken about anyone seeing what I recorded in my notebook. For this reason, my compositions had the life span of tiny insects, and I tore them up within hours of writing them. They would die before the next day dawned. I would shred them and cast them into the wind, only to gather them up again to check whether they still said anything. I didn't abandon them till I was certain that no one gathering the bits of paper could decipher their lines.

"I hadn't seen Mahiya for weeks. What made her name unique was that in the language of Arab philosophy, *mahiya* means essence—as opposed to existence. But instead of meaning 'nonexistence,' it referred to what truly is. On the other hand, in the vernacular language, it does mean 'nonexistent.' Mahiya now actually seemed nonexistent, since no one had glimpsed as much as her shadow.

"When I inhaled the exhaust of the big bus through my nose, I put aside my notebook, after tearing up the pages I had written and tossing them into the wind. Then I grabbed my stuff and raced to the bus, which wasn't at all crowded. No soldiers stood in the center aisle, and many seats were empty. I boarded the bus and headed to the 'monkey corral,' the customary name for the rear seats. Before I could reach them, Mahiya seized my hand and patted the seat next to her. I realized that she wanted me to sit beside her. You could smell her from far away, and many passengers seemed to have avoided seats near her, to steer clear of her stink. After fifteen minutes, my nose had adjusted to the smell, and I began to regain my equilibrium and sit there without turning my neck away from her. Halfway through our commute, she took some dried dates from her bag and began nibbling on them.

"I pulled out my large new notebook, spread it on my lap, and stared at a blank page. From every direction, I heard the snores of shrapnel collectors. These were noisy wheezes skillfully orchestrated by heads exhausted by the sun and the sands, and racing to flee from land mines. Mahiya and I were possibly the only ones who weren't asleep. She was gazing at the window's void, and I was staring at the emptiness of my notebook, which I was scared to write in, feeling that words resembled a trail of gunpowder and that rows of them might lead to an all-encompassing explosion that would destroy my whole life.

"I was focusing on the crack between the pages of my notebook when the bus stopped suddenly, and my head banged into the seat in front of me. I heard a drumbeat of footsteps and agitated tongues complaining with annoyance and astonishment. The snoring stopped as the sound of the brakes assaulted ears, and the vehicle gushed with the passengers' pandemonium and questions. I watched Mahiya open the window, lift her leg to the sill, pull her things together, jump from the window, and disappear. Before I could stick my neck out to keep track of her, a wave of people started to disembark. I followed the others, left the bus, and witnessed a horrendous sight. The bus had collided with a truck that had run into another vehicle, which was apparently filled with cages of cocks bred for cockfighting. It had been overloaded with these crates. I don't know how the driver had managed to cram dozens of crates into his vehicle, shoving them in haphazardly. Feathers fouled with the blood and flesh of the chickens flew everywhere, and the people gathered around were shouting. The driver, who kept hitting his head with his hands, was forced to remove crates of chickens from the back of the truck that his had slammed into, mounting it. That truck had been filled with props for a national celebration: balloons, glossy streamers, and colored flyers that seemed to have been prepared to commemorate Saddam's birthday. What caught my attention were aluminum letters crafted by calligraphers to form the president's sayings. These would have been displayed in a well-lit exhibit in the square where the ceremony was staged. I noticed that the Arabic letter *seen* س had crushed a large rooster and left him breathing his last.

"The arteries of roosters heading to cockfighting venues had been cut and their necks broken by these letters that formed things the president had said, even before their razor-sharp beaks could be tested in the cockfighting arena. The driver, who had thrust up his head the better to beat his chest, sat wailing on the sidewalk. He would presumably pay mightily that evening for the demise of these roosters.

"Mahiya, her abaya knotted behind her back, appeared, pushing aside people who stood rigidly around the accident, uncertain what should be done. The long truck with the aluminum letters also contained stacks of books. Mahiya didn't wait for the dust to settle. Instead, she stepped forward and grasped one from the stack, which appeared to contain many copies of the same book. No one stopped her or criticized her conduct. She seized the book, opened it, and shoved her nose in it.

"The sight of her reading left me incredulous, because I wouldn't have thought a person who looked like her could read. I reached out my hand and lifted the cover. The book's title was *The Fortified Castle*. In place of the author's name, the cover said, 'A novel by its author,' even though everyone in the country knew who had written it. This novel, which was distributed with all the government newspapers each morning and sold in kiosks, had become a mandatory purchase for citizens when they bought the document stamps. Many citizens were reprimanded for criticizing and disparaging this book or were reported for using its pages for cleaning, to wrap sweets, or as bags, because President Saddam was the author. It was forbidden to disclose this—perhaps to prevent anyone from saying that the head of state was neglecting the state, his stressful duties, or the hard work necessary for the state's welfare and that of its citizens, by busying himself with writing stories. This naturally added to the importance of the several novels attributed to Saddam. They were treated as almost sacred works of Baath Party literature. Replacing the author's name on the cover with the expression 'A novel by its author' was meant to glorify it and to lend the topic an exciting secrecy. Meanwhile, everyone knew that Saddam wished to establish himself as a very humble author, not to feed his ego. All the same, critics in government newspapers were allowed to attribute the novels to Saddam or to refer to him as 'the mighty soul.'

"When she noticed my curiosity, Mahiya slapped the sides of the book together and shut it. She did so angrily. Then I felt the characters of the novel jump about and flee through the window. Meanwhile the drivers had begun to wrap up the crisis and settle accounts, since no one had died, and the president's metal letters had only killed roosters. As they put it, 'No big deal—we can handle it.'

"I decided to walk the rest of the way home. After I collected my haul of scrap metal from the bus, I followed the sidewalk by the water. Mahiya caught up with me there and poked a finger in my flank. That appeared to be one of her ways of communicating. My body wasn't expecting that, so I jumped, tripped, and scattered the salvaged scraps on the ground. We both bent over to pick them up and put them back in the sack.

"'I'll show you where war materiel is hidden, if you teach me to read, just to read. I don't want to write. Would that be easy?' she asked as she poked me, pressing her finger deep into my belly.

"'Reading? I think you're asking the right person.'

"During the five subsequent weeks, I wouldn't return home till after the sun's disc had fully set beyond the charred palm trunks, because I was following Mahiya, who led me to places where excellent shell casings were hidden. Although I wasn't a particularly compatible

companion for her, given her fondness for belittling other people, she loved the way I taught her to read.

"The gush of enthusiasm that swept over her showed clearly on her face, which blushed red with excitement, and learning made her an eloquent speaker. She told me how rebels in the marshlands had shelled the little house where she'd been learning to read as part of the state's program to wipe out illiteracy. But the state shelled it because the rebels were sheltering inside and using it as barracks for combatants. She also became extremely generous in leading me to scrap metal left from the war. She got so involved that she would seize my hand and pull me toward a little hill or damp hole and point to it as if leading me to a honeycomb.

"I asked her, 'Why did you scold me that day and take the metal scrap from me?'

"She replied, 'I thought it was ours.'

"'Ours?'

"'When we were fasting during Ramadan, a shell dropped on my family and blew them up, here, where you found me. This was our house. You were collecting shards of metal from my brother's bones. But you're a good boy, and that's why I returned them to you. The members of my family were very good people. If they were alive, they would have let you have those remnants of shells and bullets. These things don't come free, as you know. When Saddam executed my maternal uncle, they demanded that his family pay for the bullets used to kill him, and we did. These items cost us a lot, and the people who traverse this land harvest them free of charge!'

"I would take her to the bus station and have her look at the placards on the buses. She would read their numbers, the names of their destinations, and the witty sayings drivers placed in the rear windows. Her voice, as she sounded out the letters and then assembled them at once, seduced me into tempting her to continue the lesson, even though I realized she was exhausted. I knew she was truly a reader once she began to walk with a straight back. Knowing her letters seemed to have strengthened her spine. She walked with her head held high, and that left her prone to stumbling at times. All the same, she would quickly straighten up. She went even further at times. When she saw people's shadows on the walls, she wanted me to teach her how to read them. She did the same thing if she caught sight of arabesques, squares, and triangles, the tracks of tanks, lines on the highway, and clouds undulating high overhead. Was I a lousy teacher?

"Mahiya felt she wasn't fully formed yet and wasn't ready to say she was a reader. She repeated the same question every time I met her: 'Do you think I'm good at reading now?' Even when I replied, 'Yes, you can read now,' she would pucker her lips, turn her neck, and say, 'No.' Then she would leave me. After an exhausting episode of searching for me among piles of rubble and the remains of military vehicles, when she finally found me bending over to pick up something, she would repeat the same question. She would show me a page from a newspaper or from the president's novel and ask me to listen to her read it. When I applauded her, admiringly and appreciatively, for how well she read it, she would look sad and dissatisfied. In denial, she would complain that she didn't feel she was a good reader. Then she would disappear, only to return, torturing me with the same question, 'Boy, do you think I can read?'

"Once, as if overwhelmed by this complaint, she began to drag me by my shirttails and carry my full bags for me. Then she took me to a pile of rubble.

"'Will you swear to me that I actually am a reader?'

"'Yes, I swear to you, by any prophet or imam you choose, and attest and certify that you have become a reader.'

"'Then, why can't I read this?'

"As she said that, she raised her shift to reveal her belly, which was very white, because sunlight never touched it. The tattoo above her belly button read quite clearly '*Uhibbuki*: I love you.' I expressed my amazement to her that she couldn't read this word above her navel and asked why she needed me rather than any other person to read it to her. How was it possible that she didn't know the meaning of this very old tattoo, which had been etched on her skin so long ago that it was losing its dark green color?

"'Everyone I bring here pronounces this same word. They all read it the same way. The one who wrote it on me said it differently. I have never heard anyone pronounce it that same way. I learned to read so I could read it the very same way the person who wrote it said it. When I showed my tattoo to people, I didn't believe it was the word *uhibbuki*, because the way he pronounced the word was totally different. I don't think it's the same word. I want you to teach me more letters, all the other Arabic letters, so I can discover what this word *really* says. It isn't *uhibbuki*. Yes, it's like *uhibbuki* and has almost the same pronunciation, but I'm searching for that original pronunciation. I just feel people aren't saying it the way the one who wrote it on my belly did.'

"When we heard the voices of shrapnel collectors approaching us, she quickly covered herself and stretched out on the ground, pretending to be digging up something. When the sounds of the other people moved farther away, Mahiya remained lying on the ground glumly as she turned something over in her mind. After she learned to read, she became more introverted—retreating into herself and disappearing into her thoughts for a long time.

"I didn't see her in the following days. But whenever I rode the bus and passed the village where she lived on the banks of the Shatt al-Arab, I heard other passengers and the shrapnel collectors repeat Mahiya's name. I assumed that, as usual, they were mocking her or padding her life story with untrue and inappropriate comments. My suspicions evaporated, though, when I saw them point to the throng of people congregating at the entrance to the village, which seemed to have acquired the new name of 'Diviner's Village.' When I decided to get out there one day and learn about that female diviner for myself, I found—as I expected—Mahiya seated by the head of the road, inside a glass-fronted case with a circular opening. She still wore the same type of traditional garments, but these looked clean and modestly elegant. They emitted no foul odor, and she uttered no profane words. She was characterized by a dash of dignity and a trace of grace. She asked her clients to hold their hands through the opening so she could disclose their fortune to them. She had prophesied some elements of their true destinies.

"'Give me your hand. Hold it out. I won't eat you.'

"'I doubt that will help me, and I think you're exposing yourself to problems. The Fedayeen won't leave you alone.'

"'Give me your hand, boy. The Fedayeen have been here before you, and I told their fortunes. They left happy. In fact, they blessed me and took pictures of me.'

"'The right or left one?'

"'The hand you use to clean your butt.'

"I put my hand through the hole, and she pulled it toward her. She took out a book and asked me to close my eyes and then open the book at random. I did as she demanded, opened the book, and allowed her to return it to her lap as she pushed my hand out of the glass box.

"She hid her face and was silent for a long time. Then she said she was sorry. She struck her head lightly several times with her hand and sat up straight.

"'Look: you face many problems and potholes. I don't know what to say, but you must not go back to the shrapnel fields again.' She said that out loud while reading under her breath from the book, so I couldn't hear. Then she raised her voice to explain the words and to decipher the lines.

"Her words didn't frighten me, and I accepted them with a smile. That caused her to give me a hard time and to confirm what she had said, as though she had truly read a sliver of the future, which shimmered before her between the words.

"Before I said goodbye, I allowed myself to look into her case and to pull out the book. She exploded with anger and shoved away my hand, which was injured by the edge of the glass. Even so, I caught sight of the first page of the book from which she had removed the dust jacket, replacing it with a white cover. It was obvious that she was reading and revealing fates and the future from *The Fortified Castle*."

Seven

I don't know whether the stone vagrant listened carefully to my story in the rain, but another, animate homeless man had arrived and now sat on the statue's head, with his hands over his ears so he wouldn't have to listen to me. They seemed to have each other's back in times of need. At times, it's appropriate for us to protect our innocence and refrain from hearing other people's memories, since our own memory is quite capable of destroying us.

That night, I decided I would make an important confession to the three monkeys. More precisely, I wanted to tell them about Morise, why I had chosen Seattle, and my reason for coming here.

Liao was my first stop. I knocked on his door, which he opened and closed with the grace of a professional dancer. I asked him to assemble the monkeys in the living room, because I wished to tell them a few things. I sauntered to my room, intending to change clothes quickly before heading to the living room. But the next thing I knew, I was waking up from a long sleep, and it was between six and seven o'clock in the morning. Apparently, the monkeys had waited a long time, till, like me, their eyelids were assaulted by drowsiness. I had been exhausted, and my head was dazed from handling cannabis.

The opportunity came a few days later when I returned from work, not wanting to affront anyone with my unbecoming smell. Erick sat by the space heater, wearing his glasses with red frames, dressed in red, with the Christmas sweater he was knitting spread over his legs, while he struggled with forming the reindeer's antlers. He would plunge in his needle and pull it out as the reindeer's horns grew and intertwined with other designs on the sweater. I drew up a stool and sat right in front of him, aiming my face straight at his.

Without any introductory remarks, I began. "Listen. I want you to help me search for someone. This person naturally has a name, but I would prefer to describe him to you, because I don't know his full name and don't have a picture of him. All the same, I have memorized every blemish and cut on his forehead. I'm an expert on everything about him and can draw a picture of him or make a sculpture if you want. Don't tell me to search for him on social media, because I've already tried that." I concluded by sketching Morise in the air.

"Don't look for problems, Mortada. You need to focus on Seattle. It's your new life, so reap all you can from it at every moment. Allow the person you're looking for to search for you. That's been my policy for decades."

I kissed Erick's head and nose, pretending to demonstrate respect for his wisdom. He may have sensed my sarcasm, because he mumbled something I didn't understand.

That evening I had promised to accompany Liao to a small theater attached to a restaurant, which was rather dark and had wooden carvings of monsters on its walls, as if it were a Gothic church. Except for the two of us, everyone in the audience wore a woman's dress, and their faces were hidden beneath thick layers of makeup. I sat in the back row and engaged in my hobby of looking every which way and surfing the sea of faces. I waited for the audience to laugh and then allowed my face to smile at the jokes the actors delivered from the stage, being careful not to laugh too soon or too long. I synchronized the opening and closing of my mouth with all the other mouths, without anyone realizing that I literally didn't understand a word that was said. When members of the audience started giving dollars to performers on the stage, Liao handed me two dollars and gestured to me; then I understood he wanted me to do the same thing. I walked forward without any hesitation and motioned to the performer that I wanted to put a dollar in his bra. He immediately leaned toward me as he gazed into my eyes and bared his chest. His eyes protruded, and his teeth were gleaming white. Strands of his lavender wig swayed forward with him but did not hide his focused gaze. My eyes, for their part, stared steadily into his. My hand relaxed as it pressed a dollar against his firm chest. Before the dollar fell, the dancer did, twisting his ankle. As he fell, he said, *"Akh"*; that was a word I had taught Morise. No one else said it just that way; only Morise did. *Akh* is an Arabic expression that means "my brother" and "my darling." It is also said by someone in pain. It's a way of asking for help from the person physically closest to you when you're hurt. Before the dancer regained his balance, a colleague hurried out from the wings to support him. The music didn't stop; what stopped momentarily was the breathing of the audience. I felt a pool of light encircling me. It was a sad moment that would make Liao treat me with sullen suspicion.

"Do you know each other?" Liao asked, even before I sat on the chair.

"I'm not sure. How can I be certain? Could you take me into the wings so I could find out who he really is?"

Liao drew me by the hand and took me out of the theater as the heads of people seated in the restaurant tracked me to the back door. I found myself in a smoking area in a narrow alley outside the rear door. The cloud of smoke there had trace scents of lipstick and hashish. Below this cloud swayed some audience members, and performers on break leaned and stood. Liao asked me to look carefully at the faces and see if I could find that dancer. I felt dizzy, and my body became numb. I leaned against the wooden wall. I dozed off momentarily and then found I was alone, without Liao. The number of smokers had dwindled, and I found a chair to plop my body onto. I spotted the dancer, surrounded by three friends. They were rubbing his back while he squinted and cleaned away eyeliner and powder. He had removed his dress and wore a green T-shirt with the logo of a homosexual dodgeball team. While he was hidden by his friends' shoulders, his image formed in my memory. I recognized him. I recalled all his gestures, pauses, laughter, and the way he enunciated words like a waiter arranging knives and spoons on a white tablecloth. I also sensed the smell of an electrical short circuit from his presence whenever he arrived or left. A tremor raced through my limbs when I considered approaching him. From a distance, I watched him drain a full glass of beer into his tiny belly. His pointy Adam's apple, which moved like a cogwheel, helped me recall every detail about him and his daily routines, which my memory seemed to have preserved through the crush of events of the last ten years. He had quickly matured before rehearsing to forget. I would have liked to reach him in a single bound and open all the passages of his memory with my lips, a door at a time. I would take him back to Baghdad, or bring Baghdad to him, displaying it before his eyes. There was still an Arabic tattoo hidden beneath the sleeve of the T-shirt: "Love is a characteristic of generous men." That was a translation of the tattoo, which was written in a poor-quality computer script. Morise must have gotten that after we parted.

Once his body was freed from the costume and his face came more clearly into sight as he wiped it clean, Morise's features were slowly liberated like a butterfly emerging from its chrysalis. When he saw me approach, his eyes adopted that same mysterious look. He told his friends to leave him and make space for me. Before I reached him, he succeeded in sporting a fitting smile.

That lessened my hesitation. So I smiled and sat down in front of him.

"Hello. I'm sorry my appearance startled you. I didn't introduce myself then, because, just moments ago, you reminded me of someone I know. When I approached you now, it became clear you're someone else. Will you permit me to touch your forehead?"

"What? This is a super way to begin. But I don't think you need all that. I like your beard. I can suck your cock in that alley. Come on. Come!" His tone was affectionate and calm at first but reached a crescendo when he said, "Come!"

Then he turned his head right and left before bringing his face near mine as if to share a secret and whispered, *"Yalaa."* That sufficed for him to identify himself—as if he were a spy identifying himself to a fellow spy with a secret password. *Yalaa* is a colloquial Arabic word American soldiers used, even in Hollywood films about the Iraq War, when racing off to a mission, breaking down a home's door, or liberating a hostage. It was a cinematic stereotype of a word and may not really have been colloquial Arabic. The dancer wished to suggest he had been a soldier in Iraq. Perhaps he had been—as the tattoo on his skin suggested. But he had seen Iraq on a Hollywood screen, not through the window of a Humvee. His *yalaa*, which means "Let's do it; hurry up," rang false and failed to convince me.

He placed his glass on the table and turned it around, making a wet circle. He set it down in another spot and made another circle. It seemed to be my turn to speak, so I said, "Thanks, but my friend Liao is waiting for me somewhere. Do you know him?"

He jumped out of his chair. "Okay, it seems you want to suck my dick. I have one too. So come on. Come on!"

I gazed at his face, searching for some last resemblance to Morise before it evaporated.

"Seattle! Damn Seattle. No one wants me here," he screamed into my ear. Then he left.

I knew the way home by public transport but preferred to walk along the shoulder beside the swift line of cars. I don't know how far I went before I realized I was still a long way from the house. I didn't bother to look at my watch, because I felt that the moment a man lives riding on the hand of a watch is one devoid of minutes. It's a sure way to pass bitter moments. Perhaps you won't feel time's sting when it passes if you ride the hand of a clock.

What would happen if I slipped into the bay, beyond the restaurants overlooking the waterfront, paddled a little till I reached the Seattle Great Wheel, and sank in the waves there? My greatest concern would be that cameras might photograph me. I didn't want to be watched shrugging off this life, which rode me like a she-jinni while walls butted against my head, punishing me, hour after hour. I wasn't concerned about my body surfacing the next day like a dead fish driven by billows toward the bluff, where my hairy body would stop tourists running on the shore: the body of an Indian, a Latin guy, Arab, North African, Turk, or Persian, covered with hair, cast up among the beach grass, brush, and beer bottles. "Suspected suicide," I imagined Seattle's local newspapers would write the next day. I was neither reluctant to kill myself nor obsessed with terminating these nightmare days. When I stood on the shore, I felt that I had committed suicide a hundred times and grown weary of killing myself and reading the headline in the newspapers.

I stood like a small nose on a boulder that held out two hands, shielding me from view. I didn't resist; I didn't question who I was. I wasn't concerned about who would close my eyelids, because I didn't want to imagine it would be anyone but Morise. I decided to fill his palms till they became buckets overflowing with bubbling tears. But I couldn't. I wasn't able to weep. At such moments, I find I'm closer to laughter than to tears. Laughter is infectious in Seattle, but weeping is hard to communicate to anyone. The dancer hadn't shocked me, as one might think. He had not struck the lethal blow. What the dancer had done was to pull back the curtain to reveal something—just as he had on the stage.

The boulder's two hands hid me entirely from view.

I don't know how long those misty fingers lingered before my eyes, but I was very silent and still. I didn't move a muscle and didn't ask the master in the haze to leave me and my affairs alone. Instead, I told him a story. I didn't ask the unidentified person, didn't request his permission to recite more of the story. I began it this way, as usual, without any introductory remarks.

"I looked for Mahiya that evening, because she no longer came to the desert and no longer chased people away from her family's shrapnel. I had benefited from her tips about finding caches rich with steel casings and copper bits of weapons and munitions. The longest battle in modern history had been waged on this land. Men's brains had exploded in the air, and their ribs had commingled. We were here, on the stage, after the show had ended, but the earth itself had failed to swallow all those bodies and still needed more time to crush and pulverize them. I saw a man grasp someone's rib cage and remove shrapnel from it. With his hands, he dusted off those scraps of metal, cleaned them, and placed them in his sack. Then he put the rib cage back where he had found it, beneath a damp, leaning wall. I noticed a boy my age using a screwdriver to scrape plaster out of cracks and crevices. I went to him and helped him clean off the layer of dust that had covered his face. I handed him a piece of cloth to wipe his thick glasses. When he felt tired, he retreated, gasping for breath, and sat on a hill. At that time, I allowed myself to approach the wall and found he had been prying human teeth from it.

"The boy may have felt afraid, because he brought his limbs close to his body and hugged his small sack. He drew a pouch from his sock, opened it, and quickly rolled a cigarette from his tobacco and paper. When he lit it, he blew the smoke over his shoulder, as though he feared his smoke would affect me. I approached him, planning to ask him about those teeth, but he jumped up and retreated about three meters. Then I heard a group of people shouting at me, 'Don't go near him! Get away! Get away! Get away! We told you: get away!'

"I don't know what spurred me to ignore their warning. I moved closer and closer. Each time I drew near him, he would retreat farther away, as if we were two wheels racing each other. Then I noticed that he was ignoring me and stretching his neck to watch a large ant emerge from a hole. I didn't understand why his entire body quivered as he leaned over the ant and put it back in its hole. He seemed to be telling it, 'Get back in there! Don't even think about coming up here.' All the same, he forbade me and himself from watching an ant as he preached to it to stay away from this world, which he seemed to consider ill-suited to life.

"'Get away from Little Hand,' I heard a voice yell at me again. Then I immediately asked the boy, 'Why do they call you Little Hand?'

"'That's an odd question!' he responded quickly, protesting its pettiness and absurdity so vehemently that I almost believed my query was pointless.

"I was reassured minutes later when the boy moved, leaving his hillock, and took a few steps toward a nearby barhi date palm. Barhi date palms are known for their sympathy, tenderness, and fellowship with people, and for the sweetness of their fruit.

"Beneath that barhi palm rested people who looked a lot like this boy. Their eyebrows met in the middle, their faces were yellowish, and their heads clean-shaven. They lay around the palm like numbers on the face of a clock. A girl who lay north of the palm was at twelve. There was a girl at three, and another girl was beneath the palm at six o'clock. A small boy represented nine. The father was the big hand, because he slept leaning his feet against the palm's trunk.

"The boy, who took his place and slept like his father, represented the clock's little hand. They moved together with the motion of the palm tree's shade fueled by the fiery sun.

"They formed a real-life sundial that sheltered itself from the heat and the hot, dry desert wind. Steeling myself, I approached them, but Big Hand threatened me and threw toward me a large pebble he had stashed beneath him. He seemed to keep stones there to ward off intruders, mischief makers, and curious folk like me.

"The stone struck my thigh, causing me to limp and scratch the bruise, amazed by the accuracy of his aim and the strength of his right hand. I gathered my possessions and turned on them, heading back to the bus garage. But I heard them pursue me and noticed that people were shouting to caution me that the clock family was after me. I didn't heed those warnings and instead turned to greet the family. Contrary to the expectations of the small crowd of onlookers that had formed around us, the man leaned forward, bowed, and held out to me—without approaching closer—a sack full of metal scrap. I bowed and thanked him. When I wanted to embrace and kiss him, he fled and ordered his family to return to the palm tree.

"I left, delighted with this scrap metal, even though my load had become heavy. The fatigue and troubles of that day faded when I emptied my sacks on the scales. The scrap metal dealer—who wore a headcloth carefully coifed around his forehead—was amazed. He laughed, congratulated me, and said it was the largest load of shrapnel he had bought at one time.

"He paid me enough to keep my mother happy for two weeks. It was also enough for me to stay home from work the next day, a government holiday honoring the president's birthday. School attendance then was a formality and almost not mandatory. So I took the bus to the Venerable Mahiya's post.

"Yes, this was what she was called now. It is a sacred title, and I don't know how she was able to convince people of her descent from the lineage of the Prophet Muhammad. This spiritual elevation caused me to hesitate and feel uncomfortable about visiting her, because I wasn't sure how she would receive me. I thought she might pretend she didn't know me, take on airs, and deny she recognized me, even though I was the one who had opened the doors to prosperity for her. My reservations were totally misplaced, for she welcomed me hospitably and spread a mat for me on the banks of the polluted stream near her glass booth. She asked how I was doing and patiently listened to my terse replies. She seemed more fluent and thoughtful, and her pronunciation of consonants was more polished. Perhaps what helped her with all this was her conviction that I was a shy boy.

"When I told her about Little Hand's family, she hugged me and put her mouth to my ear to ask, 'Boy, my child, did any of them touch you?'"

Eight

"Once when it was almost time for me to stop scavenging for the day, I encountered the shell of a tank that was shaking and wheezing. People had already removed its heavy, valuable parts to sell. Since the wind wasn't strong enough to cause such shaking, my oversexed imagination suggested that people were having sex inside it. I slipped closer, taking care that my toes didn't bump against anything solid. Walking as softly as an ant, I circled round the tank. After I heard human panting inside it, I felt terrified, cowered, and lay down on my belly. Listening intently, I edged closer and peered through a small opening. I saw an adult man pull out his plump penis and masturbate as he moaned from the sweetness and pleasure of the feeling.

"He was sweating profusely, and frothy saliva drooled from his jaws. The way he rubbed his thing, which was oozing with fluid, made enough noise that he didn't hear my movement or realize I was watching him. When he sat up and turned in the other direction, I recognized him as Big Hand.

"Mahiya had told me that the members of this family had been exposed to radiation and fled from the government's quarantine to this desert. No one would touch them; no human being would come near them. Mahiya, like many others, was convinced that this radioactive family would die in a week or less. Even so, some of the shrapnel gatherers followed them to try to learn where they stashed their loot, because they were the richest people she had ever met. Their bags were packed with thousands of dinars, and their pockets overflowed with pure gold coins. This was because they were the best scouts for fragments of metal war detritus, which they sold for staggering amounts to top merchants and major scrap metal dealers. They would precede the 'People's Teams' of excavators and work as human land-mine detectors. Since they were light in weight and their complexion was the same color as the sand, soldiers didn't see them, and squads of Fedayeen didn't notice them creeping over dangerous hills planted with mines and traversing forbidden territory like turtles and lizards. At night, their glowing eyes resembled red lamps, and their voices were so raucous that people who heard them were scared away.

"I forgot all this while I leaned against the rear of the hollowed-out tank. Once the man ejaculated and his breathing calmed, he napped for about fifteen minutes. Then I heard a rattling sound from inside and hid. The same man had begun to masturbate again, and the tank was shaking, because he was excited and was moaning loudly.

"His tank didn't stop shaking till I heard yelling coming toward us. His family was running and dragging behind them thick electric cables they had apparently stolen from a nearby power plant. I concealed myself behind the hill and watched them enter the tank. All of them, including the father, left it together and proceeded to wrap cables around the decrepit tank so they could pull it as they headed toward the bands of shrapnel collectors, who were scattered through the area like ants. All the other waste metal pickers dispersed and made way for them.

"I sketched a plan in my mind to meet them without anyone noticing. I ran around them as if tracing half the circumference of a great circle till I was ahead of them. It seemed they would expend a lot of effort and time crossing to this other section of the desert. So I got out my notebook and began to write. I don't know what I penned, but I'm sure it was about them. I wrote them up, recording what I knew about them and chronicling their every action and sound. Then I climbed a small hill nearby and began to cast my eyes back and forth between them and the paper, giving concrete expression to the idea that writing is drawing with words.

"I felt I was the angel who stands on people's shoulders and records all their sins and good deeds. A velvet picture that hung in our kitchen had woven into it the image of a man kneeling between a recording angel on his right and an observing angel on his left. That was imprinted in my mind, where it served as my special text about the act of a writer writing. A writer is the person who records people's deeds and preserves them in an archive that will be presented on Judgment Day and read aloud!

"The man noticed me and was able to prevent his daughters from attacking me, because he was confident that I was just writing. For my part, I did not stop first observing them and then busying myself with my paper, the way a draftsman does when drawing from life.

"The radioactive boy, who, as I learned from his family, was called Samir or Little Hand, watched over his sisters in compliance with the conventions of brotherhood. Iraqis love their sisters and celebrate them at times.

"Little Hand temporarily abandoned his task of dragging the tank and headed toward me. I cracked my fingers and pressed my toes into the ground to welcome his arrival. He was handsome, and 'his nose almost dropped into his mouth,' as people used to say in those days to praise beautiful women and handsome men. He wore baggy pants and walked with a slight limp that was synchronized with the movement

95

of his head. I think he assumed that a long forelock still hung over his brow. So he kept turning his head to keep the hair out of his eyes, forgetting that he no longer had any hair or bangs. His baggy pants rode up over his belly, because Samir had lost several kilos during the past days on account of their strained relationship with other people and difficulty obtaining food. His father was unfazed when Little Hand stopped pulling the tank and came toward me. One of his sisters, though, gestured obscenely to him from a distance and thumped her chest three times, as if to send him some message.

"'My father says you're writing us. We've watched you write for weeks. My sister says her eyebrows have grown back, thanks to your writing. My other sister, number nine on the clock, the little girl, asks you to write a braid for her and breasts like a dome. She says if you do, you may sleep with her in the tank, for free.'

"I grew furious and stood up. I seized my notebook and yanked it in two. Then I tore it into four pieces. I was trying to show him that I rejected what he had said. I had been writing about them—not creating them. My words weren't responsible for his sister growing eyebrows again.

"Samir simply fled from me and walked away with his radioactive family. I didn't see Samir or meet his family again and didn't write about them for a long time. Approximately six months later, though, when I was selling my scrap metal on the shore of the al-Faw Peninsula, I saw a dozen fishermen standing around the tank, which was actively rocking. When I approached, one of the men told me to join the queue. I heard Samir inside the tank. He was moaning loudly and beating his feet against the wall. I realized that these fishermen had lined up to have sex with him. It became clear to me how this tank had been repurposed. I didn't see his father or sisters there, and—based on the hoarse sound coming from the tank—his voice seemed to have become raspier, as if his words emerged only after wounding his throat with their sharp edges.

"I planned to wait till they finished with him and I could signal my presence to him, but the fishermen treated me rudely, and I was afraid they would harm me. So I hid behind some large sea creatures fishermen had dumped on the shore. These beasts had landed in their nets, but no one would buy them. They now filled the air with a foul, putrid stink. In the waves behind me, water mixed with petroleum, and all the colors of the rainbow struggled for predominance till blue finally won out at the shore. Some retreating waves reclaimed dead turtles and rotting fish for the waters, which swallowed them again. I heard one fisherman explain to another how he used a special kind of fish for sex: he would poke his tool into the fish, which would act like a woman's vagina. They argued about which kinds of fish were best for that. They each tried to have the last word and ended up laughing together.

"'Scoundrel, why did you tear up the notebook?' I heard Samir shout at me from behind. I turned to protect myself but saw that he was exhausted and that a line of blood trickled from his baggy pants down to his ankle. He was wet all over, as sweat oozed from every pore. I found that he held me responsible for everything that had happened to him and his family. I had torn up their happy life, as it had existed in the notebook. That's what I grasped from him.

"I drew him away from the boat slip, the fish and octopus carcasses, and the fishermen's lewd conversation. I learned from him that he had lost his family when his sister tried to dismantle a grenade, which had burned part of his body. A mobile clinic of the Red Cross had doctored him. After his smell proved even more putrid than that of the rotting fish, I kept my distance from him. When he sensed I was pulling back, he told me he absolutely did not want to return to the tank and felt it was a gross rotten egg that he must quit. He needed to leave the womb of the tank for some other place, some other egg or nest of scrap metal. It didn't matter.

"'I forgot to tell you something. Swear you won't tell anyone. Swear! On your honor.'

"'I swear by that tank I won't tell anyone.' I don't know why this strategy fooled him and why he believed I considered the tank sacred and suitable to use when swearing an oath.

"We were standing, and he drew closer and kneeled before me. Afraid he might offer to do something lewd, I sat down opposite him. He took my hand, held it behind his neck, and began explaining. 'Fine. I wish to confide that we weren't a radioactive family. We were never contaminated by uranium. But people said my sisters were prostitutes and that I would offer my arse for next to nothing. That's what they said. Our reputation was beyond scurrilous. We were polluted, because they thought we practiced prostitution. People boycotted us and abstained from sitting with us or conversing with us. They didn't deign to associate with us. So my father contrived the radiation ruse to negate our bad reputation. We were originally shunned as a family of prostitutes. After that, we were shunned as folks irradiated with cancer-causing agents. We were just poor sick people, nothing more! Isn't that brilliant?'

"'That was great, Little . . . Hand.'

"He took me with him to the city, where they were showing Indian films in the Karnak Theater. These weren't new films of Amitabh Bachchan or Mithun Chakraborty—they were ten years old. But the halls were packed, because they also showed lewd scenes from the 1980s with actors who spoke various European languages. But we referred to all of them as French, because all the sexual positions were French in that cinema, and the phrase 'French position' meant having sex in general. All positions were French there, even sexual trysts between the rows of seats and sexual acts for which a cinema employee would arrange a suitable location in exchange for a tip, behind the screen, in a screening room, or somewhere even more restricted. They did that in the restroom, too, but guys who did it there hailed from other cities. Regular customers knew the ushers took people there for sex so they could threaten to call the police and the Fedayeen. Their goal was to extort exorbitant sums of money from them.

"I found that Samir was a habitué of this world and had many acquaintances and customers in it. When alarm bells of fear and panic went off inside me, I grabbed Samir's collar and told him I was leaving that cesspit.

"I was walking through the market's narrow alleys, which resembled corridors with stairways, on my way home, when I found that Samir was pursuing me to ask me to spend the night with him and join him the next day as a member of a small team to gather war materiel. I noticed he was wearing splendid new clothes and gleaming shoes of the type called snakeskin, which had an attractive shine and sparkle.

"Morning dawned to find us sleeping beneath the bridge. Samir had packed his new bag, filling it with bread and ripe dates. It took us only three hours to reach the shrapnel peninsula.

"I had forgotten to buy a new notebook that day and felt I was missing something, because the pen I stuck in my notebook was also me; it was like part of my digestive system or a bone in my joints. I felt on edge, especially after Samir introduced me to members of the team. He made the rounds of clusters of people, addressing them like a commander whose kingdom had been attacked—as if he were trying to assemble his army by conscripting everyone he saw. I saw him ascend the hills and climb on guys' shoulders to rally people, trying to convince them to join his foray. From each cluster he enlisted youngsters with spindly frames or ones with weird names that were either calculated to make them seem more threatening—like Jiju or Hihu—or names that kids had heard on the radio and distorted, like Hilter for Hitler and Bushi for George Bush. Then he ordered them all to stand behind him. These recruits treated me like his lieutenant, and I embraced that designation completely, feeling that it cloaked me effortlessly.

"Before the sun disappeared, he had assembled a team of six boys, and I was their median age and height. Walking together, we crossed a field of cucumbers and tomatoes. We dug into the ground with our feet, making a trail of indentations in the ground like the narrow line of perforations between two postage stamps. We ate till our bellies were full and drank water from salty wells. A strange plan occurred to Samir. The gist of it was to fill the wells with soldiers' boots that were strewn across the desert in the debris of wheels and war materiel. In this way, we would make the wells overflow with sweet water. We quickly agreed and down a well threw a dozen shoes from soldiers who died in a war that had ended a decade earlier. Then we waited for fifteen minutes to test his claims, but when we dropped the bucket down the well, the water we drew out was fouled with rubbish and mud.

"This misadventure didn't lead to any disenchantment with our leader or cause us to lose confidence in him as someone who would steer us to a dazzling flow of water. Beyond the farmland, he told us we would find a cache of gleaming scraps of copper at a crossroads. He told us a battle between the Iranian Revolutionary Guard, which had held that position, had flared up there with the Iraqi Republican Guard. Confirmation of his claim was provided by concrete structures that still bore Persian inscriptions, even though pockmarks from shrapnel had turned their walls into lattices.

"The boys, who were singing sea shanties, dispersed through the roofless, ruined structures and over gentle rises covered with prickly pears and desert grass. Truth be told, Samir was out in front of the group as we cut our way through the area, searching for pieces of copper. I led the rear, perhaps luckily for me.

"I heard a violent roar and saw a cloud of gray smoke rise from the building, accompanied by the boys' screams, which quickly became grievous moans. Some lads rushed back as fast as their feet could carry them. They plowed into me and toppled me to the ground. I was so terrified by the situation and its chaos that I couldn't rise. Even their moaning, which could have guided me, totally faded away, and nothing remained but the dust, which grew increasingly thick and murky.

"When I regained control of my body, I turned and fled toward the fields. One of the boys followed me, holding on to my shirttails. I grabbed his hand, and we advanced, jumping back and forth between the hills, trying to find the shortest route to safety. The boy suddenly escaped from my hand, and I saw him fly into the air, fall first on his heels and then his head, and finally lie there motionless. I gazed at his corpse, which had sunk into a profound sleep, without considering my own condition. I was covered in blood and was losing sensation throughout my body. I remember that I could control only my eyes, which I turned right and left, without seeing anything. The last image in my brain was the sight of the boy who had hit the earth lifeless. My hearing was totally blocked, and I wasn't aware of what I assume was the screaming of the other boys or the drumbeats of their feet fleeing toward safety.

"'I'm blind.'

"That was my first conclusion. The second was that a thick mixture of liquids was flowing over my left hand, the one I wrote with. These hot liquids, which were contaminated with pebbles, caused me atrocious pain. I wasn't nearly as concerned about blindness as I was about losing my left hand and my ability to record my daily doings in my secret notebook as well as my long-term dream of becoming a writer. The image of Cervantes popped into my mind, because he had wounded his left hand fighting Turks. I saw him writing about his Don Quixote while laughing with rosy cheeks and going easy on his paralyzed hand. Then Ibn Muqlah entered through the door of my imagination. When the caliph amputated the right hand of this famous ancient Baghdad calligrapher, he wrote with his left. Then the caliph cut off his left hand, and he wrote holding the pen in his mouth. I saw an army of writers, each fluttering one arm blissfully. Why had all of existence suddenly become vapid, quiet, and melancholy? Where had Samir and his mates gone? In fact, where had my fingers gone? I felt a sting. Then I sensed that someone was standing on my hand, not merely resting all his heavy weight on it but also rubbing it and mashing it. I screamed at the top of my lungs, as loudly as I possibly could to counteract that pain, but that creature didn't quit me. Then another feeling overwhelmed me: that my hand was nailed to the ground, that someone was hammering on it and pulverizing the bones of my wrist and plunging it deep into the cucumber patch.

"I realized that I hadn't taken the route through the cucumbers. Instead, panic had led me in the opposite direction, behind the building tattooed with green Persian words.

"I regained consciousness in the hospital, and the ward resounded with the screams of boys awaking from sedation. I hadn't encountered Samir yet or any of his other boys. My mother was stroking my head and squeezing it, reciting Fouada's name in a string of incantations and prayers that carried her scent, which was reminiscent of the perfumes and shrines of the saints.

"Together with the moisture of her hand, I felt pain slip from my eyes and condense on my forehead, but I still wasn't able to see. My father was pressing my feet, and I realized he was signaling to me that I still had both feet—because while I was sedated, I had wept, bewailing my lost limbs. When I felt certain my parents were with me, I quickly recited a few sacred names, to make them cry, pardon me, and not blame me, or perhaps feel that the saints were surrounding me and I would be fine. Besides, a boy who survived being injured by a leftover land mine was assumed to possess a charismatic power. A miracle might happen and return sight to his eyes. Approximately a week later, the dark screen my brain had imposed on my eyes lifted, and I slowly and gradually regained my sight. The first thing I saw was a child in the ward. I watched him steal oranges from the plastic sack under my bed. The theft wasn't what infuriated me. It was his ability to draw on them with a marker. At that time, I felt my left arm, which was encased in a cast from the elbow to the tips of my fingers, only one of which was visible. My father later shared with me the physicians' diagnosis. Even though I hadn't lost my fingers, the nerves controlling their motion had been severed. That made it necessary for my fingers to remain bandaged until some miracle occurred, or my hand responded to ultraviolet therapy after I left the hospital."

Nine

Seattle is waking up. I'm conscious that light is hitting my eyes and darkness is dissipating.

Before someone lifted his hands from my face, dawn had slipped between his fingers, and seabirds had tempted Arab tourists to come outside and snap pictures and feed them. Liao had retreated and found himself a stone bench. He sat there and watched me liberate myself from the surprise, rubbing my eyes. I knew he was the one who had covered my eyes, blocking my vision, and he knew that I knew. But an hour of delicious fantasy is sweeter than an hour of reality. I prolonged it and trapped it in a moment of restless lethargy. It had been Morise, even if it hadn't been Morise. I had to work hard to free myself from my feeling that he was the lord of the city and its shaykh, on whose crown falcons dozed, because everything in Seattle pointed to him and led toward him—each detail and sign. He did not merely dwell in this city; he was its creator, who had woven it from warp and woof. He had re-created it and then shaken the dust off it as if it were a carpet from Tabriz. Everything in the city carried his signature and his fingerprint:

the joyful queues on weekends at pot stores, the empty seats in outdoor cafés sprinkled by drops of rain, girls' colorful wool caps, tech workers' badges dangling to their laps, the panting of elderly Asians climbing its heights, the spoons of busy restaurants clicking against the teeth of children of wealthy Indians, the turquoise fingernails of young women writers at the Elliott Bay Book Company's coffee shop, the dripping coffee stains on the rims of the cups, the smiles of homeless people beneath Native American totem poles, the chagrin of umbrellas failing to shield a Chihuahua that straggles behind its owner, the helmets of cyclists who pause to look at the tranquility of the Japanese Garden, the sigh of buses as they lower a lift for an elderly white woman in a wheelchair, the roars of laughter of Saudi teens in the swimming pools of the University of Washington, the pride of victory of the algorithms of artificial intelligence when they decipher the taps of my fingers and show me the prices for tickets for the debate between Slavoj Žižek and Jordan Peterson, the fragrances of perfumes in Pacific Place Shopping Center, my shoelaces as they come untied while I cross a street painted with the rainbow gay pride flag, the moans of a gray whale dying outside the city's Western Yacht Harbor—all these tell his story. Everything glorifies his name. I still think of him as the city's lord, whose guardian angels bring him news and delights. The entire city is hidden in his pocket or hangs from his throat like a necklace, which bumps against his chest and becomes saturated with his scent while its citizens are condensed like grains of sand in an hourglass.

I don't know what brought Josie here, but Liao is the one who placed his hands over my eyes. I didn't say anything to them. I sat on the bench, staring at the seagulls' faces. They did not abandon me in this condition. Liao kneeled in front of me, and Josie stopped right before my face. They encircled me with their arms as we experienced a long moment of silence.

"Listen, you two. I want to find Morise. You don't know Morise. But I'm here because of Morise." That was the first time I mentioned

his name to any of the three monkeys. Unlike Erick, they didn't push back against my wish. Instead, they promised that this was a problem that could be solved. During our conversation, I felt they made these pledges as though they were prepared to act on them. Their words implied that. I had my doubts but shook them off and returned the rest of the way to the monkeys' house, while repeating to them that they should help me. Even after they swore to me three times at different points along the way, it should have seemed odd to me that they never asked me who exactly Morise was. Or why I wanted to contact him. I had merely indicated that he had been in Iraq and that such a clue couldn't help me find someone, not even if we knew his name and skin color. But they did not press me further and did not ask for additional information.

Two weeks later, during a break on my first day of work as a T-shirt designer for an apparel company, Liao texted to say he and Josie had something significant to tell me. It was easy to discern they had information about Morise. My fingers were still covered with glue and scraps of colored paper. I had been determined to demonstrate my initiative on my first day with this firm and keep this job so I could liberate myself from the smell of marijuana. In one day, I designed about ten logos, a few penguins, foxes, simple graphic designs, signs, and a camel they used twice—once alongside charming words and again with rude ones. Those camels were printed on T-shirts!

In a single day, a wide spectrum of human beings had passed before me. A Baha'i wanted me to print a gold rose on his shirt. One individual wanted me to print the word "Allah" over his heart on his jacket. When he ascertained from my accent that I might be a Muslim, he almost prostrated himself on the floor to thank God, considering it a miracle that a Muslim worked in the shop where he had chosen to have the glorious word "Allah" printed—without any infidel designer touching it—or that's what he said. While he stood there, a transgender person passed by, and this customer pointed at them and said, "Look at those unclean people who don't seem to know whether they're women or men. May God assist you, young Iraqi man, with what you suffer here. In any case, they're all created by God!" That same day, before I received the text from Liao, I finished work by printing "Make America Great Again," for a child of six. Because I am unfiltered around children and begin conversing with them like someone their own age, I helped the boy try on the red T-shirt. I cajoled him and congratulated his father on buying him a new shirt, which his father said would be his favorite. Seeing me—a brown-complexioned, bearded person who made mistakes speaking English—hold that red T-shirt apparently seemed odd, because the other designers stopped working and started staring at each other. I didn't realize what was happening and perhaps still haven't. I may have grasped what occurred but pretended I didn't understand or care, because nonchalance at times is more lethal for cats than curiosity, and whatever cats think doesn't matter anyway.

Downtown, Liao, who was accompanied by Josie, pulled me to a wooden table in a nearby restaurant. He opened his briefcase and brought out a small notebook that had "Mortada and Morise" written on the cover. Josie, for his part, brought out a large blue folder, which he spread open on his lap. He put his glasses on and cracked his fingers to indicate that they had something important in store for me. I needed to salute the step they had taken and the time they had devoted to all this, but I had a headache and didn't absorb all the details that evening. What roused me, though, was the way they leafed through their notes, which seemed to be packed with entries, scribbling, marked-out lines, and crooked arrows, as if the entries were the draft of a novel by an author who had just discovered that his heroine's name was almost the same as his own aunt's.

I rose and ordered lentil soup and glasses of water without ice for us. Before my butt landed back in the chair, Liao began quickly profiling three Morises who had lived in Seattle or its suburbs during the last five years: Morise I, Morise II, and Morise III, whom he presented like members of a royal lineage. He continued by recounting their titles, professions, complexions, and appearances by heart.

Morise I, who was thirty, worked as an airline steward. Morise II, younger than Morise I, was a cartoonist. Morise III was a choral singer who had an amputated nose. He also worked in a coffin-making shop. But none of them had been a soldier. Josie had turned up two Morises. He took his time as he approached Morise IV, but his eyes weren't on his papers. He sighed, rubbed his glasses, scratched his forehead with his fingernails, and then said, "Morise IV moved a few days ago to Canada. All I know about him is that he was in a relationship with a waiter at a bar, and they separated amicably. We could meet that waiter; I know where he works."

"Morise hasn't left Seattle."

"Let me finish, Morta. The last Morise is a well-known Seattle journalist, who writes a weekly column. They are all Black Americans, but I can't confirm that they were in Iran."

"Iran?"

"Sorry. Iraq. 'I' like 'eye' and then 'rak.'"

"You know I don't care about the word and am happy to joke about it. You can contract your eyebrows when you say it in response to the violent freight the name carries now. Pronounce it however you want. What's important is to inform me you are referring to the land where my mother's belly discharged me."

"Your mother's belly discharged handsome things, it seems," Liao interrupted.

"I'm pleased you feel that way, Liao," I said cheekily.

"Will you give up on this idea, or will you travel to Ottawa to meet Morise IV?" Josie said, trying to emphasize the importance of his abbreviated search.

"I told you: my Morise is in Seattle."

"Fine, fine. Don't get upset. We seem to have made a mistake. You've caused us to waste our time," Josie complained. Then he slapped his folder shut and left the table. Liao followed him and closed his own notebook without missing a beat. Meanwhile the waitress spread her smile over a white cloth and set the soup on it.

"Liao! I'm truly sorry." But he ignored my words and headed for the restaurant door. The crowded Morise network he had mapped via his multifaceted relationships with the creatures of Seattle had fallen apart.

I stood, leaning my arm on the railing of the fence along the waterfront. I had received a voice mail from a woman who identified herself as the owner of the large Akita that bit me in the café. Her enthusiastic tone of voice didn't awaken my joy but did harden my resolve, which had been sapped by the reports from Liao and Josie. She wanted me to do a drawing of her dog. I agreed immediately and sent her my email address. When I reached home, a photo of the dog was waiting for me. I immediately started the drawing while Erick sat before me, knitting the reindeer's leg on the garment, which he was embellishing with bells, snowflakes, and musical notes. In the picture, the Akita's front legs were spread, and its head was on the ground, jaws parted in a smile, or at least what people perceive to be a smile and demand from dogs.

After that email with the dog's photo, I received another from a newspaper in Beirut, telling me it would cease distribution in paper form but continue online. The editors offered me a choice between continuing to contribute without pay or quitting, with their thanks for my past efforts. I quickly decided to support the newspaper by writing a few articles and then to quit. The Akita's smile, which I didn't really think was a smile, had achieved its desired effect—it had spread across my face, helping me bear the sad news of the paper's demise. I learned later that the paper's final print edition appeared with all its pages white, without any words and with only its masthead, to protest the cessation of financial support by its former patron.

I completed the drawing of the dog but thought I would work on it some more. So I drew another one, a second, and a third. I didn't find the Akita's face convincing until I set the drawings down and went outside to run. I jogged for twenty minutes and then found I was satisfied with my latest drawing of the Akita, even though I hadn't changed anything. Late that night, I decided to send off the drawing after adding a frame and some other final touches. Two days later, during my lunch break at the design company, I saw a missed call from the Akita's owner and received an email that shared her lavish admiration for the drawing's attention to detail, although she objected to the coffee-colored spot over the dog's eye. She said her dog's face was all the same color and had no spots. There *were* spots on its neck and other very small ones to the left of its nose. She asked me graciously to correct this. I didn't understand what could have inspired the dark circle on the dog's face. Once I returned home, I scrutinized the picture and saw I had really misrepresented the photo. My hunch was that I had been too tired to draw straight the previous night.

I re-created the drawing and sent it off quickly. The dog's "mother," who was delighted with the new illustration, thanked me and then asked me to draw another dog, which she said belonged to a friend. While I was drawing the new dog, she sent me a respectable sum, which was five times more than I expected! I thought she had made a mistake and declined to accept it, but she insisted. So we reached a simple settlement; I would draw the new dog for free. What was remarkable about this situation was that I couldn't keep my fingers from drawing a circle on the dark, unmottled face of this dog, above its eye. I noticed this problem early, before I afflicted the dog with my liver spots.

In less than a week, she sent me another dog and then two plump cats sitting on a basket of orchids. By accident or design, I drew a circle above the eye of each animal. I repeated the same thing with an Iraqi shepherd dog that belonged to a breed of shepherd dogs from troubled cities in the north of the Land of Two Rivers. I branded it with a spot over its eye, yielding to the accidental design that lurked in my fingers. I nourished many suspicions about the source of that spot. Then all my fantasies evaporated when I saw a dog sleeping on the couch in the three monkeys' living room.

It was broad shouldered and lay prone as its body sagged—like a hot-air balloon losing its gas. It was also an Akita and was snoring—sound asleep. Over one eye was a coffee-colored spot. I had never seen that dog here before and soon deduced that this reclining animal was Mr. Heraclitus, who had finally returned!

Before I could ask myself how his dark spot had burrowed into my senses without my ever seeing him, I was flooded with a hopeful feeling as I examined this dog's face, which was calm, sociable, and friendly, despite his lethargy, and his dejected, glum expression. He was still, and the thin ray of sunshine that fell on his damp nose only made him look more distinguished and majestic. Heraclitus was a dog whose name required no explanation once you saw him, because his mysterious, weary, unique appearance served as a living placard for, or an incarnation of, a critical metaphysical philosopher who prophesied the world's decline.

Naturally, I would need more time to ascertain the extent of the correspondence between this dog and the characteristics of his Greek philosopher namesake. I had to wait for the dog to wake up. After he slept for a long time, I found myself eager to criticize the person who named this magnanimous creature after an angry man who devoted a large portion of his life to cursing others. I doubted whether a canine incarnation of Heraclitus would agree to live in a household of homosexuals. I didn't think that the human Heraclitus was comfortable with homosexuality. I found myself criticizing Erick, as he was most likely responsible for branding this dog with the name of the philosopher of fire and brimstone. I don't know why I felt that. Perhaps it was because he sat in front of us, his legs crossed, knitting a Christmas sweater, as if he were the Lord God who had just finished naming everything.

"Hera sleeps like philosophers, doesn't he?" Erick asked when he saw me stroke the dog's head.

"Yes, I'm waiting to see whether he wakes up like them too."

"Oh, Hera doesn't wake up. When he does, occasionally, he dozes off again seconds later. Josie holds him on his lap when they go out. Hera hasn't walked on his own for years. He only has one hind leg. The other one was amputated by the vet two months before you arrived."

As he said this, I looked around the room. I don't know why I hadn't noticed the three cartoon portraits of Hera's face—with a dark spot above his eye. Unbeknownst to me, his image had penetrated my imagination, and I had introduced his spot into every dog drawing I did. The next morning, I noticed, sandwiched between the towels in the guest bathroom, a small picture of Hera, closing the eye below the spot. So I had repeatedly seen these portraits, which had drilled themselves into my imagination before they emerged from my fingers onto the dogs of rich women.

"'You can't cross the same river twice,' the human Heraclitus says," I muttered to myself.

The dog Heraclitus says, "You can't walk in Seattle twice." It's not possible. Seattle runs faster than a river and inevitably changes. Morise's Seattle might no longer exist; there are millions of Seattles that take turns here. I feel this while I walk the amazing streets in the heart of the city or its outskirts. I sense its skin corroding and another skin growing, only to be shed and replaced again.

Ten

Erick taught me how to lift Hera, carry his massive body while keeping my balance, and place him on his large pillow in Josie's room. "Careful," Erick whispered to me. "Don't twist his legs."

We closed the door behind us, and then Erick decided to tell me the rest of the story of Heraclitus while we sat on the steps.

"This is Heraclitus III. My previous dogs had their own names. I started referring to them as Heraclitus I and II years after they died, when Heraclitus III fell ill. He was a birthday present from my sister. This dog is now fourteen years old. I've never encountered a dog as clever and smart. Believe me. When I was a kid, I worked as a dog walker. I consider myself a superb friend of dogs and someone who understands their lives, concerns, languages, motions, and interests. Liao and Josie had never lived with a dog before or owned one, but Hera became their dog, a dog belonging to all of us. He's like a relative or an in-law. When he accompanies you, you feel you are stepping out with a judicious man. This has remained true even during his medical treatment. His intellectual acuity has gradually diminished, though, and his incandescent spirit has begun to waver."

I left Erick as he threatened to repeat his story, and headed to my room, intending to slip into Heraclitus's chamber. That night he seemed alert. My entry roused him, even though I was walking slowly and cautiously. He opened his eyes and directed them toward me. Then, turning his head away, he closed them. He seemed to be saying, "Oh, a gay, Muslim, Arab refugee—he is in the wrong place at the wrong time." That was what a well-intentioned taxi driver had told me during my first days here. He had allowed himself to say this for some reason—perhaps because, as he told me, he had been homeless for many years, even though he had earned several degrees. He seemed to have preserved the spirit of a homeless person just as I still preserved that of a scavenger of shrapnel and scrap metal. He had observed, "A homeless person can do what others can't." That comment removed the barrier of reserve and the thick skins that blanket people's natures here. He disclosed his spirit, thus shortening the time a person normally needs to cleanse our mirrors of the stains of flattery and the rust with which diplomatic notions of proclivities, colors, and conduct coat them.

"Why did you repeat the words of the amiable driver, Heraclitus?"

He replied with a snore, "Hummm, khukhukh."

"My dear Seattle philosopher, have you seen an individual descend from the sky with a parachute, someone named Morise? Did you hear from your father about a coffee-colored boy whom your grandfather said kneaded and rinsed words before uttering them?"

I spoke to the dog and conversed with him, man to man. I told him, "We share a handful of characteristics, but I think I lack your wisdom and discernment. Like you, I lay in bed, so blind I couldn't see light as sedatives and liquid medicines washed my throat. When I left the hospital, I had to prepare myself to sit my examinations with only one hand, because my original writing hand was damaged. I had to address the practice exams with my right hand, a hand I had used when I peed, not when I wrote. My father offered to help me write and to go with me to the examination hall at the school so I could dictate to him and he would record what I said. He was highly motivated to undertake the task. He was also eager to restore agility and strength to my fingers. In those days, Heraclitus, I could not move my left wrist or fingers, in fact any part of my writing hand. I looked weird in the hospital, because my middle finger was bent, as on the day of the accident when they took me to a nearby clinic, where they sewed up my wound quickly, without anesthetics. They completed the damage to my hand that the land mine hadn't finished. When they took me the next week to a specialist, the top surgeon in our city, he felt entitled to express himself rudely enough to dominate everyone present with his personality and extraordinary expertise. He shouted in my face: 'Why did you let assholes whose sisters you fucked destroy your hand? Are you happy now? These fingers have stopped growing forever, you son of a shoe!' When he said that, he glared at my father, whose head was bowed as his tears hit the floor.

"'We just need to return your bent finger to its place so the whores in that bed will stop laughing at you.' He was referring to three girls who were perched on the neighboring bed, studiously observing the people there, chewing seeds, and using lewd language while they visited their mother. Yes, I was in the women's ward, because the men's ward was overcrowded. Perhaps I was lucky, because women's wards are like women's public baths. Both are teeming with stories and inquisitive storytellers who stick their noses in the midst of events to create a ripe and well-considered version of some scandalous tale.

"Thus, Heraclitus, after they removed the bandage from my hand, I had to visit a physical therapist every day, in the heart of the city, at the convergence of little streams that branch out from the Shatt al-Arab, which, more than a thousand years ago, was described as having thousands of creeks descending from it.

"The physical therapist, with her sweaty, sympathetic hand, kept massaging the palm of my hand, which had lost any sense of feeling, and then shining warm violet light—which they called 'ultraviolet' even though it looked violet to me—on it. This is the opposite of us human beings who refer to each other by color, even though we are beyond colors. I was obliged to walk a whole hour every day, except for holidays, to submit to the therapist's care, and shelter beneath her words, which were full of calm compassion. That atmosphere was the exact opposite of my home session, which was supervised by my father, assisted by some of my maternal uncles and my brothers. They would lay me down on my stomach and spread out my hand, squeezing it and playing with the erect finger till they bent it or until its awkward angle opened up a little—while they said things like 'Be a man. We don't want to see you with a deformed hand when you grow up. Don't complain. Men bear pain. Do you want to be a sissy?'

"It was a therapeutic form of torture, dear Heraclitus. The blades of the ceiling fan assisted me valiantly by listening to my screams and allowing me to entertain myself by counting the threads dangling from them. Even the spiders, as they complained about the soot and black fumes emitted by the oil lamps, watched me as they amused themselves by gnawing on the bodies of dead flies in the corners. My father, who was terrified by the idea that my hand might remain stunted, suppressed his sorrow, addressing me with apologetic silence. The bullying word 'disabled' still follows me today, although scarcely anyone notices the deformity.

"For the Arabic language exam, on which I received a nearly perfect score—the highest mark in Arabic in the entire country—my father had suggested I dictate to him the essay I had to compose, while the proctor stood over us to monitor the legitimacy of the exam. He listened to my father ask me which topic I would choose. A student usually had a choice of two prompts. The first was to write about an essay attributed to His Excellency the President. The student needed

to write about what the essay brought to his mind: words of praise, discussion of characteristics of the essay, and philosophical observations gleaned from the sagacious essay. The other topic was deemed a poor choice, because it would be unbecoming for a secondary student to ignore the essay of the inspired president and 'the historic necessity' and risk everything by writing about the other topic.

"My father carefully considered the exam paper, looked me in the eye, and guided me by slightly lifting his upper lip to the first choice. When I grew calmer, he asked me out loud which title I chose. The proctor heard him, leaned over him, and told him to keep quiet. My father sat back in the chair and exhaled. Then, trying to humor the proctor, he apologized effusively.

"I snatched the pen from my father and, with help from my damaged hand, grasped it with my right hand. I wrote down the title, which amounted to 'The Ant and Abd Allah the Believer.' After a quick look to see if I was writing legibly with my right hand, the proctor lowered his mouth to my father's ear and asked him to leave the room immediately, as his handicapped son didn't need him. When my father was slow to rise, because he wasn't sure I would be able to complete the exam and scribble all the words, the proctor warned him that if he did not leave immediately, his lingering presence would be recorded as an attempt to cheat.

"Heraclitus, my exhausting drills paid off, although my handwriting was truly atrocious. It was legible, though the consonants had inappropriate dips and squiggles. My father, who continued to watch through the windows, wasn't so worried about the legibility of my words as about whether I would finish recording the words and scraping away my mistakes, slowly and deliberately, in the allotted time, because I hadn't written with my right hand before. He was also anxious about the sweat pouring from my temples onto the paper. In addition to all this, he was quaking about the troublesome title I had written down. No one would overlook the choice of the president's essay and choose instead the prompt that read 'Write what comes to your mind about a story that you have experienced, that happened to you, or that you played a part in, and supply it with all the diacritical marks.' This seemed at face value to be an easy choice, but you had to maintain the serious and official tenor of an examination.

"My father did not realize that I did choose the first prompt. He might have guessed that, if he had remembered Abd Allah the Believer is one of the president's ninety-nine names. Iraqi literati had adopted a list of names for the president, referencing his rare, superhuman attributes—just as the ninety-nine names of God are mentioned in the Hadith of the Prophet and recited by chanters in mosques and at religious festivities. Poets have even composed essays and odes about the names and marvelous attributes of the president.

"I seemed to have chosen the second prompt and ignored the president's essay, by using what I might call a 'double entendre.' In Iraq at that time, this rhetorical device was commonly used, and many authors created stories using codes and figurative or metaphorical references in literary texts, apparently to celebrate the president, only to turn in a different direction. This syndrome culminated with a generation of writers in the 1990s who wrote in codes the authorities did not break. My composition, though, consisted of a prose essay with a limited goal, and that was to pass the Arabic language examination while I trained my hand to embark on the scientific exams, like math and physics, where there would be no place for the president's essays.

"In the tale, Abd Allah the Believer is a dignified man and a brave leader, whose subjects love him passionately and adore how he is gentle and tender toward everyone. Poets celebrate his feats and rhapsodize about his generosity, nobility, and manly qualities. One day, just as the story in the Qur'an says about the prophet Solomon, when Abd Allah the Believer marched off to war with his victorious army, he caught sight of an ant, with which he began to converse in the ant's language, because, again like the prophet Solomon, he excelled in all languages. It so happened that this elderly ant was a mute. She gestured to him with her head to follow her. He walked behind her for three days while his army dragged his gear, weapons, and supplies behind him. The army left the sultanate and the affairs of its citizens to follow their leader, because they were prepared to march behind their leader and their godfather, even if he led them to their destined death.

"The ant stopped at an ancient library that dated back to the sixth century BCE. The Babylonian commander had built it to serve science and knowledge. I used here a boy's hypocritical hunch about a correspondence between the president's life story and that of Nebuchadnezzar. Saddam loved to compare his life story with those of the kings of Babylon, Ur, Akkad, and Sumer. He adored citing the record of that imaginary bridge between him and those ancient leaders as a sign of the continuity of civilizations and of our technological skill in engineering, construction, and national defense. A mural that showed Saddam receiving a concrete chalice from Nebuchadnezzar was famous in those days, and government media showed it frequently.

"When the ant enters the library, Abd Allah the Believer is delighted, and his army dances jubilantly, because they have discovered the historic library of Nebuchadnezzar! They follow her inside, and she stops at a book, which lies open. My decadent imagination suggested that a book of the Babylonian library was written in Arabic! I don't know how I allowed myself that childish error. The ant stopped at the Arabic letter *ya* and then dragged herself, as her energy flagged, to the Arabic letter represented by ʻ. Meanwhile, the president's scribe recorded all the letters the ant approached till she completed the Arabic word *yaʻish*, which means 'long live!' The ant stopped to rest, and then the commander Abd Allah al-Mu'min ordered his army to enjoy a brief period at ease while drinks and delicious foods were served and female dancers performed and musicians sang. The ant resumed spelling a phrase by stopping at the Arabic letter for ṣ, which was followed by *d* and *a*. Even before she reached the letter *a*, everyone burst out applauding and rejoicing. Then the ant felt she didn't need to finish spelling the name, which was 'Saddam.'

"The hardest questions came on the physics exam, and my physics grade was lower, but my overall average was solid thanks to my perfect scores for math and chemistry. My family was keen to have me enter the Department of Petroleum Engineering in the College of Engineering at the University of Baghdad. Its graduates were the only ones who lived comfortably and well, and petroleum engineers made the most money. My father was motivated to promote the idea of my future financial security, because with me as a petroleum engineer, he wouldn't need to worry about me. His son would be an employee of the national oil company, and as his father, he would be able to boast about him to everyone. This is what actually happened. The disabled guy who had trained himself to write with the hand he didn't naturally use for writing was accepted into the College of Engineering and traveled to the capital by himself. 'Perhaps he will work there and repay us for all the money we have spent on him and the exorbitant price of his books that are read only by history buffs and scholars.'"

As Heraclitus rolled onto his side, still sound asleep, he observed, "Would that she had given birth to a turtle instead of you, Son of the Provinces!"

I heard the same thing when I was at university and was forced to alter my accent a little and make it more central Iraqi and less southern. My father counseled me to do that to avoid paying more for taxis, as the southern accent cost a person a lot, because it suggested you weren't from Baghdad or some other central city. This meant you became an easy target—easy prey for drivers.

Eleven

Liao humored me by meeting me at the Seattle Art Museum. I found him waiting there, waving to me from behind a Native American totem pole. At the door leading to the special exhibition of Sumerian and ancient Iranian statues, the guard asked to see my ticket. I noticed that Liao had passed in front of me and started to head to the escalator. I showed my ticket to the guard, who smiled as he turned it over. He gestured for a woman to pass after she waved her ticket at him. I was standing alone before him when he asked me to check my bag. I had turned to head in the direction he indicated just as I saw the lady enter with her large bag, which he hadn't asked her to check. I started toward the cloakroom, plastering on my face the kind of phony smile we affect at the end of a hard day. When I was two steps away from him, I heard the guard tell me, "Yes, your bomb might explode inside!"

I stopped and swung around toward him. He wasn't even looking at me. He was gesturing for an Asian woman, who carried a black bag big enough to hold a small bear, to pass. Then he stared at my dazed face. His words descended on me like a Siemens refrigerator falling on a Bedouin in an empty desert. The Bedouin wouldn't expect that—manna may fall from the heavens but not a fridge! I never expected to hear such a comment in the Seattle Art Museum, which I love dearly.

Admittedly, my blood boiled, and there was nothing in my hand except the ticket, which I condemned to the punishment of being shredded. That wasn't all I did. I threw the bits of paper on the floor in plain sight of everyone, even though there were trash receptacles nearby. Then I shoved the door open and marched out with an invisible column of smoke rising from my ears.

A tear that spilled from my eye may have extinguished the fire. I recovered my composure and balance as I crossed the street before the "walk" light flashed on. A voice inside me screamed loudly, "Where's Morise? Shouldn't he appear now and take me to the water's edge so we can discuss different types of fish or seagulls and escape from the filth of this world? Can't we hide together in an invisible fissure and grant our exhausted senses a time-out?"

But I heard him whisper back to me, "What's this! Do you find this story painful? My dear Worm, it's just an outing. It's nothing. It's like a pinprick. A giant worm won't be harmed by a pinprick!"

So I headed to the Seattle Public Library instead. In a reading room there, after I stood up to get a cup of water, I tripped over the leg of a man who was reading. The man smiled and then looked up at me. We exchanged warm greetings. Minutes later, I returned to my place, carrying the water and avoiding readers' legs that were crossed in my way. Unintentionally, with a face as despairing as Chaplin's in his youth, I collided with the same man's leg, and some water spilled on his clothes, book, and shoes. He flashed another smile, which he seemed to have stored somewhere between his jaws for just such an emergency. This smile was broader and higher. He extended his legs and accepted my apology very politely. Then he rose and left his place. Embarrassed and blushing, I quickly stuck my head in a Moroccan book about the healing arts in Stoic philosophy. The man returned shortly with a cup of water and a handful of paper towels. He wiped off my table and offered me some towels. He proceeded to dry off the book's cover and pat down his clothing.

He asked me my name and where I lived, after he closed his book and set it aside. I told him about myself briefly, encouraged by his interested look and the repeated expressions of amazement he offered in response to my quick, abbreviated account. He didn't forget to introduce himself and then proceeded to tell me about his circumstances. He had recently arrived in Seattle and chosen to live here with his two friends. He continued in this vein till another young man, who resembled him, interrupted us and took a chair beside us.

"Steve, this is Mortada. Christ has brought him to us," he added, turning to his friend.

This man considered the times I had stumbled into him a sign from the Lord or a blessed nudge and one of the Messiah's glad tidings. Or, that's what he said. Glancing at his clothing, I realized he was a priest, and from his smile, which glowed with a fraternal spirit, I gleaned that he wished to continue our conversation and become friends.

The priest seemed about to extend his hand and squeeze my shoulder, sighing with compassion and succor. His hand advanced across the table and stopped at the edge. His friend's compassionate black fingers were intertwined and drawn up toward his lower lip, touching it, while the man focused his eyes on my features and my mouth, which was speaking softly, answering their questions with truncated sentences.

The priest rose and then returned with a large paper cup of coffee and another handful of paper towels. He placed his bounty on my table and presented it to me, as if *he* had poured coffee on my clothes. The two men sat before me, drawing my narrative from my lips and pushing the conversation to continue.

"Do you see at the corner of the street—the redbrick building with those lofty turquoise windows? Behind the building, immediately below it, is our church, where we go every day. You are welcome there as our guest. We are friends now. You must dine with us in our residence. Our house is half a mile from here. You are a breath from Christ's blessed Gospels. This has not been a chance occurrence. You mustn't think that. We also need to introduce you to our third friend. We live together," the man said, pointing to the library's glass wall and the view outside.

I was looking for a suitable opportunity to escape from the bubble into which they had thrust me, while trying to avoid seeming ignominious or ungrateful for their gracious treatment. I was preoccupied then by wondering what the point of my existence was. Figments of my imagination and various thoughts were attacking me, and my head was hemorrhaging disappointments. Even as I gazed at them and pretended to listen, I was busy weaving webs of self-loathing.

We were sitting in the quietest corner of all the floors of the building. To be more precise, it was the place where the library's architect, the designer of this edifice, got down on bended knee before his true love, and she said yes. That corner had become a favorite of mine, and I rejoiced in that romantic moment, which the architect mentioned in interviews. Even so, I treated it as a secret story that I alone—out of all the readers distributed throughout the building— knew. I excused myself from the priest and his friend, who was also a priest. I headed to the library's Book Spiral, where shelves have the rich bouquet—the smell of books—that keeps me alive. I need to inhale it from time to time to feel there is something to live for, even though most things aren't.

"I don't like the term, but you seem to be a bookworm like us," the second priest whispered from behind me. It struck me then that these two monks resembled the three monkeys, who would appear suddenly behind me and whisper. I was surprised by the thought that all these men belonged to the faction of sudden whisperers!

I replied, "There was an Iraqi joke popular in the 1990s about an alcoholic whom people blamed for drinking too much wine and then staggering through the markets while speaking incoherently. When they begged him to stop drinking alcohol, he retorted, 'My father died from alcohol abuse.' They were amazed by his statement and asked, 'If it killed your father, why don't you swear off alcohol?' He replied, 'You're stupid! How can you ask me to stop pursuing my father's killer?'"

Books didn't kill my father, but I consider them a prime suspect that mustn't escape, even if the quest is hurtful. Over the past years, wherever I have wandered, books have piled up on my bed, almost without my noticing, and created a small hill, spreading out, uninvited. The priest may have felt that he and I shared this same trait, because he had lost himself in the Spiral, where he was wandering like me, running his fingers over the spines of the books. He asked me then to accompany him to his church the next morning—as the other priest had done. I apologized, saying I had to work, even on weekends. Then he said we could postpone that visit to another day.

When we left the entry of the library, the two men introduced me to their third friend. Then I was walking along with three priests, clad in black, who spoke Guinean English and opened their umbrellas at the first sprinkle of rain, while we discussed a new book by Yuval Noah Harari. Then the six books I had checked out fell from my hands as I stumbled. They all bent over, before I could, to pick up the books. They told me about an ancient poet from their land who had perished when his books fell on him. So I told them about al-Jahiz, a man who had lived in my city of Basra hundreds of years ago, who discussed the theory of evolution in his book *al-Hayawan*, or *The Book of Animals*, and who had also died when his books tumbled on him. I did admit that his attitude toward homosexuality wasn't very humane. My mentioning that last point to them was something that homosexuals do when they wish to hint at their homosexuality in some way, without there being any special reason to and at what may even be an inappropriate time.

They may have grasped at this point that I am attracted to men, and I realized that I had more or less painted myself into a corner. I felt that even more acutely when they talked together in a language I didn't understand—some African language. They all laughed and shouted at each other, before regaining their composure.

"He's gay too," the first priest said, pointing to the second, who parroted that phrase and repeated it, gesturing toward the third priest. Without missing a beat, he pointed to the first priest and said it again.

I took a deep breath and began to laugh. I almost slipped on the sidewalk as I tried to recover from this new Seattle joke. How could people say the residents of Seattle are coldhearted, that people here are hard to meet, that it's difficult to socialize with them, and that they all live in isolation chambers?

We reached an intersection, where the three priests gathered around me for a group hug. I told them that we had been to a library, that we weren't emerging from a bar, and that the excessive displays of inebriated emotion were inappropriate. "You all need to postpone this till some other time. When we all go out together, next week, for example." They chortled and told me, "This is who we are! We pride ourselves on a spirituality intoxicated with love and try to extend it till it embraces the entire day. We consume our fill of it and pass it around with hugs. Hearts needed to be charged and plugged into the sockets of other people's hearts for them to ignite and for happiness to flood into them. Then scars, nicks, and pains vanish as minds catch fire and devote themselves to thinking about what is truly beneficial."

We took leave of each other.

My head was still steeped in the spirit of books. I tipsily crossed the street, imagining that it would become my magic carpet, the way streets lift up righteous people and saints, but it didn't. Everything was quiet on the sidewalks, which were wet from the drizzle and tinted by

the lights—until I came to the area containing shelters that attract masses of homeless people to the edge of the southern portion of old Seattle's downtown. I saw a young man penetrate the wall of calm, racing as fast as his body could. He shot past me like a bullet—I had never seen anyone run that fast.

I continued walking and eventually reached the Western Yacht Harbor. I realized at this hour that strangers' eyes shape cities. Each street, sidewalk, tower, and bench is an amalgam of all the strangers' eyes that have passed this way, but Seattle does not allow you to remain a stranger. The dragon suspended from light poles in Chinatown steals your eye and hangs it here, somewhere. Then you will be both from it and in it. In fact, the city will come to resemble you and become your twin brother, so people remark how much the city looks like you, even though you have never noticed that. When I stopped at the fence separating the sidewalk from the Sound's water, I heard pounding footsteps and heavy panting. Behind me, someone's pharynx was gasping, wounded by air, and braying forcefully as air rattled through it. It was the young bullet man. But how had this happened? I had reached the harbor before he did. I smiled privately. I told myself that perhaps the road had lifted me up and that I may have become a saint after my session with the gay priests.

The young man reached the edge and quickly climbed over the fence. He was near enough for me to watch his body strike the water when he tried to commit suicide.

He didn't seem to be thinking straight, because he bumped into the boulders, and the darkness deceived him. He rose again and climbed the fence. He was closer to me this time but seemed unaware of my presence. He stood erect at the edge of the fence and spread his arms open to the air. Before he leaped, he shouted at me, "Don't you recognize me? Has my appearance changed that much?"

"Who are you? I'm a newcomer in this city."

His response was a prolonged silence as he turned to face me. I know only one person who announces his silence in this resounding way.

"Morise! I don't want to believe you're Morise. I want to suffer a little more before I find you. I want to catch you off guard and appear to you as a nasty surprise. Don't be Morise, I beg you. That would spoil my story." I said this, backing away from him, afraid he was Morise. I averted my face but was still close enough to hear him.

His face was totally covered by a navy-blue wool balaclava, but wisps of steam emerged from the small slit. He was the same height as Morise. His shoulders were as massive. His calves filled his khaki jeans the way Morise's calves swelled *his* camo military trousers. His chest didn't seem broad beneath the bands of his expansive jacket, and there was no way to tell whether his nipples protruded like Morise's spearpoints.

I was also confused about his smell. I could not say decisively that it was Morise's smell, even though they were quite similar. It might have been Morise's smell, or it might not, because before this man appeared, the entire area had been saturated with Morise's smell. This was totally natural, since I was standing by the Yacht Harbor, where winds off the Sound collided with the boats' sails, galleys, engines, oils, and the laughter of children on board them as breezes toyed with portholes' latches and penetrated them. Morise's smell was certainly a composite of all this.

The man turned toward me angrily. "I don't know what Morise you're talking about. I'm here to kill myself." As he said this, he raised his balaclava, revealing a young man's tanned face covered with blemishes and cuts.

"Sorry. I thought you were him. Sorry, again. I'll let you jump."

"Cheers."

"Cheers to you too."

I turned away to look for some other spot where no one would intrude. Nearby was the statue of a man feeding seagulls. These metal seagulls were cloaked in a deep layer of the night's darkness. Before I touched the statue's protrusions and indentations, before I could enjoy the curves of the bodies, and before my fingers would savor the sharp corners of the birds, the bullet man appeared and climbed toward me again, leaving his previous place and crowding me here. He interrupted my beloved retreat with the statues and repeated the same queasy scene.

"You seem offended. Should I plead with you and grasp your feet? Should I weep and counsel you to embrace life's charms and keep you from killing yourself? Do you wish to live out that cinematic scene? Or, perhaps you aim slightly higher than that. Perhaps you want me to punch you, bloody your nose, and make you fall to the ground with a sound like a pillow stuffed with pains, despairs, disappointments, loneliness, sexual assaults, hunger, and homelessness. Then I'll kick your midriff as I scream at you, 'Why are you killing yourself? Huh? Are you in more pain than me? Have you experienced being burned, kidnapped, hung by your ankles from the ceiling, sodomized with a broken bottle, and had salt and pepper rubbed into your wounds? Have your friends and kinsfolk abandoned you because you're queer and one of Lot's sodomites, who are cursed in the Qur'an? Oh! Are you the sort of person who searches for tragic stories to make his own personal stories seem less valuable and more painful?' Oh! Sorry, asshole, wait a bit, and perhaps such a person will arrive and provide you just such a silly, edifying, sermonizing, dramatic scene. You're distracting me from the pleasure I find with statues and intruding on my personal space. You need to back off. Otherwise I'll call the police on you."

"Relax. I won't grant you the opportunity you seek. I don't want a failure like you to vomit his past in my face," he said, facing the water. He exhaled deeply and removed his jacket to reveal a man in his early thirties.

"I'm happy that you're a cultured and educated asshole. I'm happy, too, that you have recognized me for what I am, characterizing me as a failure. I envy your discernment. I'm usually trailed by people who are slow to realize what a loser I am. In any case, I ask you to leave. I will contact the police and tell them that an individual is disturbing me by committing suicide before my eyes."

I don't know if I was angry. Perhaps I was just pretending.

I don't know why both of us started laughing uproariously at the same time. He climbed down and stretched out on the ground as he continued to laugh. I felt he was extending and prolonging his laughter, squeezing every guffaw out of it and turning it every which way. When it started to die away, he would revive it and push it with his tongue a little, treating it the way a thirsty person does with the last drop of water in his mouth.

"You should have seen your face when you said that," the man remarked as he propped himself up on his hands and extended his legs in front of me.

"I'm here to help you, if you want, return to the suicidal mentality from which I jerked you unintentionally. I apologize for that. I repeat, I'm ready to help you turn suicidal again."

"Why do you apologize so much? You're disgusting."

"Fine, sir. Allow me to depart. Happy suicide!"

"Happy suicide to you too."

I turned my back on him and crossed the street. There were only a few inches between me and the far side when I sensed his shadow falling on me.

"Do you think the police will understand you and your accent?"

"Come on: let's give it a try. Climb on that bridge and throw yourself off."

"Deal."

I took his hand and led him toward the bridge. I asked him to remove his shoes. Then I told him what I thought of his shoes. I don't much like square-toed shoes, which remind me of the queen.

"Queen? The chess queen? Ha, ha, ha."

"Yes, how did you know? Listen: I was ready to enroll in the University of Baghdad. The night before, I went to sleep with headphones on, listening to religious programs broadcast from Iran. I'm Iraqi, by the way. From Iraq. Have you heard of it?"

"Yes, of course. I graduated from the 'Stanford University of Terrorism,' as the president says."

"No. Perhaps you mean Harvard."

"Exactly."

"Fine. Let me finish. I began pious. In those days, God existed. He existed almost everywhere. But later, he disappeared, in general . . ."

"How long is this story?"

"I won't keep you long. Listen. My father woke me up with a powerful punch to my shoulder. It took me a moment to grasp what was happening and to understand what my father said. 'They're here for you. They are at the door asking for you. They are summoning you for five minutes at the headquarters of the Baath Brigade. Do you understand what five minutes means? It means five years, not to mention entering dark holes and dungeons of scabies, hunger, and disease. In Saddam's reckoning, time is multiplied by ten.' Before I rose and met them, my father ordered me to hide the book he had bought for me. My father had taken money from his salary and from the household budget and had borrowed from a colleague at school in order to give me the amount I requested to buy a book. He had told me that the family wouldn't serve me dinner for an entire month. I immediately agreed because I thought he was kidding. But during the ten days after I bought the book, that's what happened. To be precise, I was denied supper the first day, and after that, I voluntarily abstained from eating. That spiritual book—*The Collector of Felicities*—was packed with

stories about people who devoted themselves to God, piety, and absti-
nence. It mesmerized me and helped me dominate my desire. I lost a lot
of weight. A Shi'i scholar named Naraqi wrote it approximately seven
hundred years ago, drawing on the works of Aristotle, Socrates, Zeno,
Marcus Aurelius, and other Roman Stoic philosophers. But he tinted
their ideas with a glaze of Shi'i Islam, combining Greek categories with
those of imams from the Arab Desert. The first logical assumption
used by ancient scholars of logic and philosophy appealed to me: man is
a rational animal and belongs to the genus of predatory animals. Thus,
he must master his own hyena, lion, tiger, serpent, hoopoe, parrot,
fox, swine, and dog, which all live inside him and seize control of his
organs. Man's vices can be attributed to the parts he shares with other
animals: the anger of lions, the ignobility of hyenas, the cunning of
foxes, the slander and whispering of serpents, the sexual depravity and
deviant desires of swine, and the squalidness of dogs. The swine raging
within me sustained my vile desire for men. It had become domesti-
cated but masturbated by itself, launching mental fantasies that recalled
actors in Indian films with rippling muscles and handsome heroes with
dubbed Syrian voices in Mexican serials shown on the TV channel run
by the president's son. These were pirated from television programming
broadcast by neighboring states. Even so, masturbation orgies associ-
ated with the brown boar inside me would result in my burning my
hand occasionally or holding it too near hell's flame, because masturbation is strictly taboo."

"Hey! I don't understand this story. Why should I listen to it? I
don't want to."

"I know that, but do you? That book had a thick binding. It was
a used copy but, all the same, wasn't cheap. From ten centimeters
away, you could smell the fragrance of its vintage pages, which dis-
seminated an attractive smell of paper and caused birds on the wing to
fall prostrate from the intoxicating spirit of words. I used that binding
a lot and treated it as the quills of a hedgehog, hiding other forbidden

books inside it and carrying it with me to work. I went overboard on this and purchased gold nail polish to camouflage the cover by writing one of the sayings of the Warrior Commander President. This granted me astonishing freedom to spy on detectives on the street and the bus and to prevent them from harassing me, because no one thought that starting a conversation about the president's sayings was a good idea. The important point is that this all came to an end. It was the zero hour, and my father ordered me to bury the book beneath the barhi palm tree in our house's small garden, which resembled a cat cemetery.

"To tell you the truth, the security men entered the room where my bed was and dragged me out while my mother silently slapped her cheek. They were gentle with me, except for the pressure on my wrist when they dragged me to their vehicle, which was tethered outside. On the whole, though, their treatment of me was fine. They may have taken into consideration that my father was the dignified principal of an elementary school where some of their children studied. I don't know. I didn't feel demeaned until they opened the cell door and tossed me inside. My foot slammed into a metal box, and I stumbled into pools of urine, which smelled of ammonium chloride that stung the nose and closed the pores of my face. As I gradually adjusted to the darkness, I noticed I wasn't the only person in the cell; a woman was cowering inside her abaya and singing.

"Why she was singing with such a deep voice I learned only two days later, but from the first hour, I realized she was Mahiya! Why did they put me in women's wards in hospitals and in the women's section of prisons of the party's Brigade? That was my question, but Mahiya curtailed that dark moment by asking, 'Why do you think this is a women's cell?' Before I could reply, she rose, and her lanky form stood as tall as the wall itself. She removed her abaya, raised her tunic, and planted her hand deep under her cotton underpants. I did not feel there was any call for such a gesture—why would she thrust her hand that far, as if poking it into a box to clutch a shrinking pigeon?

"I did understand, however, once Mahiya pulled out her dormant, serpentine thing and remarked, 'What about this? All this time, have you never noticed?'

"I wasn't surprised she had a penis. What surprised me more was her singing voice. I did not regret that I hadn't discovered this the day I met her in the desert of al-Faw. That was why kids in the desert called her the three-legged woman! What a dunce I was!

"Her melodious voice rose from some fissure in her soul. It was moist and resonated with a trace of desperate weeping—the type of tears the wind dries because there is no one present to wipe them from the cheeks, tears that ride the face like a cross and adhere to it, trickling here and there in search of someone to wipe them away but drying before anyone appears.

"The gist of the story is that Mahiya, who had two vocal ranges, had betrayed me after being tortured. She had been arrested when she persisted in disclosing the future to her customers. She had been reported by jealous fortune-tellers who were also informants for the police. No divorced women, widows, or young men with hearts broken by unrequited passion sought them out while Mahiya's renown increased. Mahiya—that strange lady who was moored on the banks of the Shatt al-Arab and who had a hoarse, virile voice—not even the president's novels could help her. No, her situation was all the worse because she had used them. She was treated and punished as a person who had defiled the words of the president and his sparkling, pithy stories.

"Mahiya's head had retained nothing but my name and the name of her true love. I wasn't angry she had blurted out my name when staked to the ground from four directions as they dripped hot wax on her fingernails. To the contrary—I was proud and boastful that Mahiya remembered me and recalled my name, treasuring it together with her lover's. What was hard was seeing the faces of my mother, father, and brothers gaze at me through the police car window. That was also a relatively happy moment, because the security forces had apparently arrested me on charges unrelated to my being a sodomite. This was a great feeling and a reason for delight, because I finally had an ordinary arrest story like thousands of other Iraqis who had been detained, persecuted, and disappeared for political resistance. What a blessing!

"I dozed repeatedly on the lap of Mahiya, who had retained the equanimity of mothers and the breath of their perfume on scorching hot summer days. We were waiting to be brought before the judge or sent to the security forces' offices. They had jailed us in a local brigade's facility, without any judgment being rendered or charge made. Even Mahiya's case hadn't been reviewed by higher authorities or registered in the courts. To be more precise, we were waiting for nothing but the Lord, and that was exactly like waiting for Godot.

"Mahiya told me the story of her true love, as she called him. She used dozens of names for him. At times, she gestured with her fingers in the air to sketch his appearance for me. She told me she had been catching flies on the shore. The beach was separated from the sea, and he was slithering on his belly between the palm trees, myrtles, and banana plants. He was a medium-sized youth whose mustache was so virile and brawny that he could have stood upside down on it. He had to catch a hundred flies every day to sell to the fishermen who lined the length of the riverbank—as bait for river fish to swallow along with the hook.

"Her true love wasn't a real fisherman; instead, he was a fly whole-saler, and this was a level above selling flies to fishermen. He had invented this profession. A recent graduate of the College of Business Administration and Economics, he had wanted to use his academic expertise to create a career for himself. He ended up becoming an excellent middleman between the fishermen and the fly catchers. His banter, which influenced both sides, made his presence a prerequisite for both the fly evaluation and deal making. But after his career took off, he grew very stubborn and treated one fly catcher poorly. This fly catcher would later become known as Mahiya. Before then, they quarreled and envied each other. They butted heads like rams, grappled like cocks, and kissed each other, man to man. A kiss like that is normally preceded by a bite to the neck.

"As nights and days passed, we watched not the sun but, through the slit beneath the door, the shoes of Baath Party men coming and going. Some shoes reminded us of the sun and others of the moon. The red shoes belonging to the man who headed the group, the Brigade's secretary, represented the sun. When we heard them clatter on the floor tiles in the morning, they signaled that day was dawning. The athletic shoes of the tea vendor who traversed the corridor at sunset indicated that the moon was rising.

"One day, after a violent torture session, during which I lost feeling in my face and in my tail, too—yes, I had a tail—a policeman entered, kicked my head, and asked me to give him my shoes. He did the same thing to Mahiya. I had a literal tail, which I treated as part of my body. It was Mahiya who referred to it as a tail. This was a piece of cloth that dangled from my waistband, and by which they strung me up every day. If I tried to loosen it, they tortured me even more, because strapping it back on took time, and these men were short on time. So I had to live with that cloth tail to save them time.

"The policeman collected our shoes without our grasping his goal or intention. After the moon rose, we heard a wave of chortles, yells, and general pandemonium. We could not learn much from the gap beneath the door. (It was less than a centimeter high.) What we could see was a line of shoes, more precisely their heels. At first, we thought that men were lining up, one after the other. Then we saw bare feet moving among the shoes, and we grasped that the shoes had taken their places in some sort of arrangement—like a chessboard. The commanding secretary was ordering his men to move them about and carry them from one place to another. I explained to Mahiya the game of chess, which they were playing with shoes and army boots, outside our room. She made no comment. Instead, she turned her face toward the wall and crooned a bluesy country ballad."

Twelve

"In the room next to ours, we heard a man praying very loudly. Mahiya feared the Baath Party men might think the voice, which was offering supererogatory prayers and supplicating God, came from our cell. Offering the Shi'ah denomination's prayer out loud was risky for everyone, especially in this city. I heard my father's voice carry from the executive secretary's office every day after sunset as he pleaded for my release solicitously and sympathetically. After one night when there was loud shouting, I stopped hearing his voice. Apparently, they had rebuffed and scolded him and ordered him not to return. They also seemed to have swiped his sandal, because I saw it playing the bishop on the hallway chessboard visible from beneath the door.

"They would get drunk at night and drag out the man who was always saying his prayers to place him among the shoes. They would order him to advance one step forward, as if he were a pawn. The only living being on the chessboard among the slippers and shoes, the man showed me his face when they put him on the floor and trod on his face after he killed the queen—or more precisely the 'vizier,' because there's no queen in Arab chess. He was handsome and had light-colored eyes. He sported a bushy ginger mustache, and his thick neck reminded me of a Roman emperor's.

"Off the chessboard, he had no such royal assignment, for he was accused of being related to someone who had thrown a hand grenade at the Baath Brigade. That assailant had been arrested and was killed together with his immediate family. The praying man was merely a cousin. After his head had been pressed to the floor for two hours one evening, the chessboard was packed with women's shoes, because his family—his mother and three sisters—had been arrested to keep him company. Then his cell began to broadcast communal prayers accented by the sounds of an elderly woman blowing her nose and cursing Saddam. Instead of frightening Mahiya, these developments strengthened her markedly. As for me, this was the first time in my life I had encountered a person who felt strong enough to insult Saddam, except for once when my father did so when I was alone with him. But he hadn't dared repeat it for fear I would grow accustomed to such outbursts and follow his example outside our house. Like him, I watched the episodes of *Science for Everyone*, but they were suddenly replaced on television with the president's tours and multiple activities. The music accompanying the fourth segment of videos was by Bach. The president, who wore his olive uniform with its thick belt and brandished his Cuban cigar, would stride forward as his companions shuffled behind him and majestic baroque music framed the scene. This abuse of music delayed for a long time my ability to enjoy Bach, Beethoven, Tchaikovsky, and Wagner, because in my childhood their music was stored in the same section of my brain as the president's tours. My father was upset the science program had been canceled, and the image of the president upset him even more. Once the music stopped or started to die away, the announcer would comment on the president's visit, saying, 'His Excellency the Commander President received . . .' Then my father would interrupt: 'A bullet to his chest.'

144

"He said that as if expressing a cherished wish hidden deep inside his heart. Simple as that: the president would receive a bullet in his chest, and we would be rid of him. But, of course, this did not happen. I learned from my father that long-held wishes curdle and calcify, becoming impossible, so it's best if we don't hope for anything and don't cheer ourselves with hopes, or that we at least use special protective gear when we handle them. Some hopes are harmful and detrimental. They teach us not to hope, because hopes transform what we wish to achieve into impossibilities, into a fourth impossibility over and above the three things Arabs typically say are impossible. They say something is the fourth impossible matter when they want to describe something that will never occur, connecting it to these three impossible items: a ghoul, a phoenix, and a faithful friend.

"The supererogatory prayers we heard through the cracks in the walls inspired Mahiya to believe that a bright voice had illuminated the stone and made the spiders flee. Mahiya saw them dry up, die, and eat their own webs. Perhaps this was the moment when Mahiya turned into a true believer and asked me to tell her about 'the' Sayyid.

"Al-Sayyid al-Sadr, his religious-political movement, and his followers were at the peak of their influence in those days. He was a very problematic person and an amalgam of riddles. He was the only person who played chess with the authorities barefoot, but the authorities killed him the next week, and many of his followers rioted, causing a security crisis like the one created by the family of the man in the adjoining cell. The Sayyid's name was Muhammad al-Sadr, and he belonged to a family that had a troubled history with Saddam. During the five years before his assassination, he was able to capture the hearts of large masses in all the cities. He launched an offensive against his fellow religious leaders and delivered advisories known as fatwas. These outlawed kissing sayyids' hands, permitted smoking during Ramadan, the Muslim month of fasting, and made communal prayer on Friday obligatory for everyone. He also announced that a few Christian families had joined Islam because of their admiration of its morals and piety. Some of his colleagues, who were major religious leaders, had accused him of being Saddam's man and his surrogate who hypnotized people emotionally, because he referred to Saddam's speeches. As his crowds screamed at him, he would shout, 'No, no to America! No, no to Israel!' All the same, he would insinuate, in symbolic, allusive, and coded language, that Saddam himself was an agent of America and Israel! He accused his clerical opponents of being tools of Saddam's secret service, which had for decades conspired to destroy Shi'ism and Islam. A rumor circulated from them that he asked his enemies to remove their turbans and rewind them themselves, betting they couldn't, because he believed these religious leaders were phonies—foreigners and Jewish agents—not authentic scholars capable of winding their own turbans, since winding a turban is an advanced skill mastered only by those who devote years to religious study.

"The man and his two sons were slain in a Mitsubishi sedan, when he was driving them home following the communal prayer service, thus sparing one young son, who was known to be an intellectual lightweight and childish. Saddam's regime ordered the boy to stay in his house and not leave it, but the masses wouldn't keep still, because they assumed the killing of al-Sadr was a momentous sign that the world would soon end. They never grasped the horror of the incident or its bloodiness and could not conceive that God would keep silent about Saddam's tyranny. Like me at that time, they assumed that God still existed.

"Some of them spread out through the cities and suburbs, and others fled the country. Many were attacked that week from various Baath Party headquarters, and arrests multiplied in the ranks of his followers. The man praying in the next room wasn't the last of them. Without meaning to, he became involved in a strange dialogue with Mahiya, who would knock once on the wall. Then he would answer her with two knocks. She would knock three times, and he would reply with six. When she rubbed the wall, he began rubbing it too. This was her complete repertory. He, for his part, increased the volume of his personal and supererogatory prayers, which reached her, muffled and incomprehensible. Mahiya gradually lost herself in her dialogue with the man and began to imagine, interpret, and philosophize about his knocks until in the last of those murky colloquies, she said he was asking her to wear the veil! I have no idea how she was able to translate those raps of his fingers into comprehensible language. What I am sure of is her cleverness, which was displayed when she replied to him with taps as her lips murmured, 'But I do wear the veil!' The man stopped knocking then. When he resumed the next morning, he snarled and struck the wall. From that, Mahiya decided he thought her way of wearing the veil did not conform to the sound dictates of Islam.

"'Boy! Boy, how can I inform him with knocks on a wall that I have one of these?' she asked me, pointing disdainfully to her penis.

"I can date to those days the beginning of Mahiya's spiritual states and her psychological change. Her face contracted, and her sleeves grew longer. I found she was starting to hide her bangs and the hair descending over her temples. She asked me to teach her how to pray, and I did. She, however, improvised, betrayed my instruction, and added some of her own gestures—as if she didn't trust me to be a responsible guide to the movements and words of the prayer ritual. Something within her made her doubt whether I was fit to undertake a task like this, and I envied the man tapping through the walls, because he, apparently, was an exemplary person, whom Mahiya hoped would begin to instruct her.

"I once heard her beseech God that they press the man's face down with the shoes when they were playing chess so she could see it. When that didn't happen, she repeatedly asked me to describe him to her. To make it seem I was being very cooperative—overcoming my despicable feelings of jealousy—I set about drawing him on the wall with a piece of stone. I drew a man I had never seen properly. As soon as the policeman noticed this drawing, he made me wash his underwear as a bribe to keep him from informing on me. Then Mahiya quickly rubbed out the portrait with her hand, line by line. She wasn't so much erasing his face as recording it in her imagination, erasing to confirm, erasing to remember it clearly."

"Why do you think I need to listen to this?" the suicidal man asked.

"I need to be going," I told him. "Please be careful not to fall on a bird when you kill yourself."

I descended the elevated stairway and, at the bottom, encountered a man and a woman who were laughing together. They had clearly been watching us—me and the man who was determined to kill himself. When I approached, they turned to look the other way, pretending they weren't interested. I walked by them and quickened my step, but as soon as I had passed, I heard the woman ask me, "What were you saying to him? You're the first person to spend so much time talking to him."

I turned back toward them and stared at them without uttering a word. They were in their thirties. Both were filthy and almost completely wrapped up in a dirty blanket. In front of them were a six-pack of beer and some pastries that I surmised they had stolen from the nearby store.

I ignored them and walked back toward the man who wanted to kill himself. I saw from the distance another man standing before him—someone who seemed to be a tourist. This tourist was pleading with him to come back down and abandon the idea of ending his life. Then I understood what the homeless couple meant. This man had no intention of killing himself; he was trying to arouse the sympathy of passersby and gain some spiritual or material support, looking for an appropriate patsy each time. I had been his previous victim.

All the same, my pouch of memories had opened. He had helped fill it but had failed to close its mouth. At times, a memory pouch resembles the cross of a Sufi who binds himself to it and then looks for someone to crucify him. We shouldn't abandon an outpouring of stories in the middle of their being told. I repeated out loud, "Where is someone who would like to hear a story? We have stories!" I sang out—like a vendor hawking his wares: "Where can I find half-empty heads that seek to be topped up?"

I set my course toward the three monkeys' house because I would never find a better listener than Heraclitus.

The dog was dozing; a trail of saliva drooled from his mouth. There was a small leaf on his chin. Heraclitus had turned into a vegetarian canine some years earlier.

For this reason, I told him, "Listen, Vegetarian: Mahiya's heart had no handles. It was impossible to get a grip on it or to place it somewhere. It was gelatinous and took the shape of any container holding it. You could find that it resembled a jug of vinegar or an old shoe. It was difficult to prevent her from falling in love with whomever she wanted, but the man she loved had certainly been led off to execution. We didn't witness that, but it was difficult to imagine any other destiny for him. The taps on the wall had ceased, and the mysterious colloquy between these two ended. All that could be heard from his room was women's keening. We all felt depressed after he disappeared. I was sad because I had grown used to hearing his voice; Mahiya because of her passion for him; and the executive secretary of the Baath Brigade was bored now that he no longer had a praying man on his chessboard.

"Mahiya recalled the man's face and was able to discern it amid the dampness of the walls and the salt circles corroding their paint and plaster. Some days after his departure, she stood up and passed her hand over his imaginary face, which time had sketched on the wall. It took me quite a while before I could see his face the way Mahiya did.

"They refused Mahiya's request that they provide her a prayer rug. They refused my father's request to give me the Qur'an he'd purchased for me. He brought it with him every week. All the guards did was kiss it, place it on their foreheads, and then hand it back to him. Eventually, my father discovered a new ploy, which was to grease the tracks. That meant giving the guards currency folded up small enough to be thrust in a pocket. After a wait of four months, I received my copy of the Qur'an, and my father was able to glimpse me through the door's small metal window, which had its own little door, locked from the outside. I didn't see his face, but he saw me, and I heard him wonder aloud, 'Is this Mortada?'

"I didn't know why my father was surprised by my appearance, and wondered about that till I left the jail. I seized this Qur'an and lay down, eager to leaf through and read from it. I know I had seen copies of the Qur'an hundreds of times, many times more than Mahiya, but it was the only book in this small, dark, cubical world of a prison cell. The moment my belly touched the cold ground, Mahiya imitated me. I began to turn the pages, only to find that the book contained no surahs, verses, or ornamentation. A different book was concealed inside the Qur'an's covers. The problem was that the title page had been torn out, and we found only a book with no foreword or preface. After she realized that I was entirely consumed by reading and paying no attention to her, Mahiya asked me to give her part of the book to read. She jumped up and stuck her head to the window, which they had left open that day, to air out the foul odors we released, as they explained. She shouted to them, begging them for a metal saw or a knife. She intended to cut the book in two, horizontally. She would not yield to my suggestion to pull out half the book and insisted on her idea of cutting it in half. I would read the top half of a page while she read the bottom, and then we would exchange top for bottom. It was a compromise solution and one that seemed weird to me. Once she despaired of getting hold of a saw, she agreed to my plan. I decided to tear out the pages I had read, and that was what we did. I read the entire book in a day and a half. Once we finished it, we decided to read it again, after giving it a title that Mahiya couldn't quibble about, because I didn't let her. I told her that the book was named *Injured Manhood*, because the story was about an Arab Sudanese student who travels to Britain, works as a university instructor, and indulges in sexual pleasures, sleeping with white women as a way of avenging his wounded, narcissistic culture and earning a victory for the people of his homeland over their colonial invaders. Years later, I learned that this novel's actual title is *Season of Migration to the North* and that it is a very famous Sudanese novel.

"My father realized that I would grasp the game of fake copies of the Qur'an. The following week, he arrived with a second Qur'an, which Mahiya and I grabbed quickly and used exactly the way we had the first. It was another novel, and the hero was a man who challenges the ocean's waves to pursue a whale. Even so, Mahiya insisted on winning the honor of giving this coverless novel a title. She called it *The Pillow My Head Doesn't Like*, because she didn't finish this novel, which she thought was very heavy and thick enough to use as a pillow, as she explained. But my father had thought of everything. He knew he wouldn't be able to return for a long time, so he smuggled to me that lengthy novel, which I would later learn was entitled *Moby-Dick*. This was like filling your refrigerator with daily necessities and packing it with supplies—the best types of food and drink—because you know you'll be away a long time while your son is confined to the house. The third Qur'an was a book that told a bitter love story. I decided to name it *Cholera in a Time of Love*, because a lover, who is on a ship with his true love, convinces people that a cholera epidemic is raging on the vessel. So people flee the ship, where a quarantine flag flies from the mast to warn people to stay away, leaving only the two lovers on board. They devise this scheme so they can stay together after a tortured love story that lasted decades.

"The last book was a genuine copy of the Qur'an, which we could not tear apart or divide, because such a deed would be dreadful. According to Mahiya, anyone who ripped apart a Qur'an would infuriate God, who would turn him into an ape or a bitch. Thus, we took turns reciting it, each in our own fashion. We devised melodic modulations unique to us and endeavored to recite the entire Qur'an each week or every week and a half. Then we would read it again from start to finish.

"Finally, they decided to release me—but not Mahiya. My mother came alone, because my father feared he couldn't bear to see me in such a condition. My mother hugged me and sniffed my neck, despite the foul odors emanating from my body. On the way home, I saw my face reflected in a stagnant, black pond and saw that I resembled a hedgehog whose quills had been ironed flat. I was a little taller, and my face was paler, with some sunburn I suffered on first being exposed to the sun's direct rays. My body resembled that of a pious man who has repeatedly prostrated himself in prayer and developed a small dark bump on his forehead from planting it in the dust while praying. Perhaps this was what made it difficult for my father to recognize me in prison.

"That evening, my father seized my hand and took me out for a walk. We had a silent, weird, wordless dialogue as if we truly believed that words were worthless, but our silence was also out of concern for our safety. I was proud to walk with him, even though this situation

seemed to call for a display of humility and a determination to mend my ways. Instead, I was proud and happy to be walking around free after being charged with an offense unrelated to any love for men. For the first time I had been implicated in a typical case like those of many other Iraqis. This was something that bore no relationship to my nature or to deviant, libertine thought.

"Truth be told, my father was attempting to console me for a loss I would not feel till some hours later. This concerned my departure to Baghdad to study there. My family had been notified that I was no longer eligible to enroll that year because I was too late in matriculating. This had happened despite my father's mediation attempts and his liberal expenditure of money to free me so I could enroll in the College of Engineering to study petroleum engineering.

"Are you still awake, Heraclitus?

"I want to tell you about Baghdad.

"For me, Baghdad means Morise, because I met him there. The problem is that to me, Seattle also means Morise. Fine. I'll let you sleep. I know I've worn you out and burdened your head with stories that aren't about you."

"Never mind," he replied. "You can tell the rest of the story to that cup over there. Cups never sleep."

"An excellent solution! Sleep well, Philosopher."

"Hello, Cup. My father warned me not to become a recluse in Baghdad and counseled me to mingle with people as much as I could. He told me, 'Don't let them think you're a loner and an introvert. Don't write or draw in front of them. It would be better if you didn't write or draw at all. We have no idea what disaster will flow from your fingers, which even you can't control. People will doubt you and suspect that you read books and aren't a real Saddam supporter.' I took that advice to heart and attempted to follow it as best as I could, except the part about worrying what impression I made on other people. Any effort I made to feel comfortable among others was a lost cause, out of reach, and beyond reasonable expectation. Then I discovered that Baghdad is different—quite unlike Basra. Most important, my father's security concerns about Baghdad weren't accurate, because people in Baghdad were less frightened of the authorities and less concerned about them. This was part of the regime's plan to control the South and North with terror and intimidation, while allowing the capital breathing space, because people there were less likely to foment civil unrest and there was far more diversity in Baghdad than in the southern cities. This fact diminished the opportunities for groups to unite against the government or for opposition Shi'i thought to spread.

"I stood in a line, waiting my turn to receive the key to a room in the university dormitory complex where I would live. An entire year had passed, and I had a new opportunity. This meant I had to be diligent, because I had only one year; other new students would have two years to complete the syllabus. When my turn came, the housing director turned and fiddled with a pile of junk behind him. This key distribution took place in the courtyard of the housing bureau, when the sun was straight overhead the queue of young brown men arriving from rural areas, bags filled with sweets, cheeses, and rice and testicles filled with ripe sperm ready for masturbation before the shadowy beauty of Baghdad women. It was a special moment of drudgery fraught with many implications.

"The housing officer leaned over and picked up a wooden door, which he placed on his head. Looking at me, he said, 'Take this.' I was expecting a key like any other student—not a door—but, even so, I did not hesitate to accept the door and place it on my head, as if it were a tray of fish carried by fishwives in the countryside. I tried to relieve myself of the door's weight, setting it aside so I could complete the room-assignment process, but he ordered me to leave, indicating that he would sign for me. He did, however, mention the room number and the building where I would live, once I installed the door.

"As I walked away with the door on my head, I could hear snickers and sarcastic remarks from the windows. The student-housing complex was a large group of buildings like dominoes. My building was the last one. Before I reached its entry, the front of the door bumped into another student. From the cut of his trousers, I guessed he was from the South, like me, because this style, not fashionable in Baghdad, said a lot about a person who wore such trousers. He didn't complain when he received a blow to the back of his head. Instead, he offered to help. Then he took the whole door, which he carried like a professional porter. On the third floor, we found the room, which was at the end of the corridor. It was the only one with a gaping mouth and no door to hide its contents. What was adorable was that this fellow showed me his papers so I would know he had been assigned the same room.

"'They told me it's the bathroom. This is the bathroom, isn't it?'

"The student doubtless was referring to this room, and, not just from him but also from the room's features, I learned we would be living in a bathroom. It had been recently and hastily painted. Some remnants of the dividers between toilets, which had been removed, were visible, and the bad paint job hadn't managed to conceal them. In corners and cracks, the wall's paint had mixed with the students' pubic hair and solidified, making the wall appear to be covered with fur or the belly of a sleeping animal. In the floor, there were filled-in holes where the sewer pipes had once been. You might not realize at first glance that this room had once been a bathroom, but you would reach that conclusion after a few minutes in it.

"The student, whose name was Khishan, started to install the door but didn't succeed in securing it with hinge pins. So we had to lift the door down and put it back up whenever we wanted to leave or return.

But it was a door, like any other door, and performed its duties as a door perfectly, except for the subset related to opening and closing.

"The first night, the cockroaches and ladybugs were another matter. They crept around, celebrating our presence with special sounds, like spectators trying to prompt actors to come onstage for a spectacular evening. The next morning, Khishan and I realized that we were studying in the same engineering department. I learned that we were the only two engineering students in our cohort. The others were divided between the faculties of education, literature, religious studies, and agricultural husbandry. I was forced to lie to my father that first week and commence a sequence of lies that would last a lifetime. He called to ask about everything, using the phone at a nearby grocery store. I fed him less than truthful answers to all his questions about the most specific matters, beginning with my clothing, what I ate, and how much money and food I consumed. I naturally avoided providing any information about my repeated visits to the book market. I affirmed to him something that I definitely hadn't done—attend Saddam's Baath Party meetings—to ensure that I was perceived to be an upright, unproblematic student. When he asked me about Khishan, his clan and his family, his accent, and whether he snored in his sleep, I replied fully except about Khishan's family, for whom I invented a different surname. I never talked to Khishan about his family, because just by hearing the surname, I realized he belonged to the family that was implicated in an assassination attempt against the president's son—an attempt that left the president's son partially paralyzed and incapacitated for the remainder of his life. The mere mention of the name of Khishan's grandfather was enough to stir trepidation in every soul; at the same time, however, it made them respect him and try to avoid upsetting him, because it was widely thought that the entire story had been fabricated and that Saddam himself was responsible for the attack, which he had orchestrated to discipline his son, who had been kidnapping coeds and raping them. Therefore, Khishan's family was protected to some degree. Nothing was known for certain. There were just suspicion and speculation about what might have happened and what might be investigated."

Thirteen

"Baghdad, in the center of the country, was an area to which Sudanese, Egyptians, Palestinians, Kurds, and Turkmen flocked during the war with Iran in the 1980s. They settled here, learned the difficult local Iraqi dialect, and worked in bakeries, hotels, and low-cost restaurants that catered to visitors from Iraq's southern cities. The style of the houses and apartment buildings in this area recalled the magnificent villas of Jews whom the Republican regime deported in the 1960s. Thus, although the district appeared impoverished, it concealed a heritage of grandeur and ancient charm. The Ministry of Education, as part of some weird scheme, built dormitories for students in this wretched neighborhood, which had been a vibrant area in the past but had since changed into a suspect area and a relatively secure refuge for individuals on the lam.

"After noon, the place's true face was disclosed as veils lifted and queues of men took possession of the street, creeping through the alleys like long worms, because the houses of prostitution opened their doors to customers at that hour, offering adolescent girls and blondes—thanks to dye or heredity, as Greek logic would put it. What the sex workers needed most here were the arts of disguise, to hide from their families and kinsmen, who went searching for their lost girls. They might wear sunglasses as a disguise, and so forth. In short, this place was hardly ideal for student housing. At night, many student boarders witnessed from their windows troubling incidents of street sex, because the rear of the dormitories overlooked whorehouses, wineshops, and quiet corners that accommodated patrons seeking a quick blow job.

"It was totally different inside the building, because southern students during the last days of the 1990s and the beginning of the new century were influenced by Shiʻi movements and disturbances in Najaf, which was regarded as the capital of Shiʻism because it was the headquarters of this Muslim denomination's religious leadership. This leadership, however, was fractured and divided by the assassinations of major spiritual figures, whose brains were spattered down lanes and alleys, thanks to these individuals' troubled relationship with the government.

"The spiritual path of puritanical purification was becoming popular and dominated the souls of many students. The academic program was difficult, and curricular requirements were rigidly upheld. In my first year, I had to adjust to the Baghdadis' prejudice against and disdain for southerners. At the university, I was shielded from that prejudice during my first months, because many people believed, on the basis on my appearance, that I was a Yemeni who had come directly from Yemen. This assumption made sense because the ruling Baath Party had recruited many Yemeni, Palestinian, and Jordanian students to study at the party's expense. Normally, these students were treated circumspectly, and no one harmed them, because they were 'the Commander's guests.' For their part, they signaled their satisfaction with the Baath Party's behavior and embraced its Arab nationalist principles, which held that Arabs are distinctively brave, heroic, and victorious—together with a bundle of other emblematic slogans that an ordinary Iraqi citizen deemed boring and repulsive, although he would not express such thoughts openly and kept them to himself. I am referring to slogans like 'Free Palestine,' 'Down with America,' 'Crush the Pagan Persians,' and 'End the Existence of Israel.'

"I first realized that people thought I was Yemeni when I was late handing in a homework assignment for Engineering Drawing, due to my noticeable lack of preparation in techniques of representation of mechanical appliances, levers, and inorganic shapes. This shocked me, especially when I saw the rest of my cohort execute this drawing skillfully and hand in drafts that were so clean and precise, you couldn't detect a spot where lines met in the corner or any bumps caused by the pencil. I had not anticipated this failure and still don't understand it, because I am a draftsman and am skilled in the use of drawing instruments and all the various types of compasses. At least, that's what I assumed! It took me a number of weeks to realize that this wasn't true and to grasp that disciplined drawing is separate from the aesthetics I observed in paintings and in Arabic calligraphy. There were strict principles from which I deviated and used more as amulets than strictures, because effort, concentration, and care in drawing are not merely desirable but mandatory. I do not claim that I later became first rate but can assert that some modicum of orderly discipline penetrated me, and I have since been able to utilize it not only in engineering but in other arts I practice.

"Art must incorporate some amount of discipline and inner regulation, and this was a lesson in juxtaposing and adjusting things with each other and experimenting with reference to what the engineer can learn from the draftsman and vice versa.

"The female supervisor for the drafting room told me not to worry about submitting the drawing, 'Because we understand the difficult circumstances of Arab students who aren't Iraqi,' referring to Yemenis. This was the first time I realized I could play the skin-tone/ethnicity game to my advantage. But this worked only inside the university and when I kept my mouth shut. The dialect of Arabic I spoke blew my cover and disabused other people of the notion that I had come from Yemen as a guest of the Commander. I remember that during the next month, I set out to buy some things, which I needed in order to take notes during lectures, from an office supply store near the university. Wearing a white tank top under my regular shirt with buttons, I stood there in a short line of only a few individuals. The cleanliness and fit of my tank top did not placate the clerk, who came out from behind the counter and grabbed me by the collar. He said, 'It's obvious you're a backward southerner, because who else would wear an undershirt? Tell me what you want.' I don't know how I was able to secrete a considerable amount of saliva and spit in his face before I fled. This conduct was somewhat counterproductive, because he had already taken my money before he spewed out that sentence. Thus I lost the money I needed to buy the requisite supplies.

"Yes, dear cup, my journey combatting racism starts with collecting saliva and ends with me talking to cups.

"The Baghdadis' racism didn't trouble me too much because I was able to mimic their accent and mastered it early on. Speaking like them saved me a lot of time and unnecessary conversations that strangers initiated on hearing me speak with a southern, Basra accent.

"My greatest obstacle was living like a worm in a poorly equipped dormitory that not only lacked basic services and windows but swarmed with half-naked male students whose tongues spat out nasty words about libertine men. I say 'worm,' because that was the term customarily used for homosexual men in those days. [Seven years later, people started to refer to 'puppies' instead of 'worms.'] The word's use may have been derived from an outrageous belief in ancient culture that a certain worm in the large intestine was responsible for a man's attraction to men. But I was a worm, disciplined and very secretive, because even when I noticed another worm, I would avoid wrangling or mingling with him. I saw many worms outed and beaten in the dormitory.

I recognized a bunch of them when they stood outside in an alley looking for paid sex. They were somewhat disguised and would stop passersby, cabbies, or laborers who lived in that corner of Baghdad. When they returned to the dorm, they tried to look as if nothing had happened and melted into the general mix, which was pious and somewhat spiritual.

"I lived with Khishan in the bathroom for two whole years. He was a diligent student, but in a strange way. I was diligent, like him, and read voraciously. But I doubt that I matched the effort he gave or his utter exhaustion, which made him whinny like a horse when snoring at dawn. I also discovered that, like me, he read books with fake covers. He would obtain Shi'i religious books and replace their covers with one that wouldn't excite anyone's suspicion. Khishan jerked off daily, or every other day, and made no secret of it, as one might suppose. He would abandon all his religious and tribal indoctrination when a conversation strayed to topics like women and sex. I frequently heard him recite the Cow Prayer when a coed student passed. This is a prayer that begins with the phrase 'May God make her appear like a cow to my eye.' In other words, he was asking God to turn this beautiful woman into a cow so she wouldn't tempt him and awaken his lust. With the goal of training his spirit and cleansing it of lust for women, he memorized many strange prayers and performed different rituals to diminish his sense of guilt and his weakness vis-à-vis sex—which he seemed to combat successfully, if not verbally. Moreover, Khishan didn't succeed in hiding his intense fear of a certain type of student, especially students belonging to the Student Union, which was personally supervised by the president's son. Perhaps because we studied daily near the Department of Civil Engineering, where the president's son was enrolled, Khishan did not appear at ease during class hours, especially because the university had erected a wall around the Department of Civil Engineering to separate it from the other departments and to shield the president's son, guarding him with concrete and cement from other students.

"One day, Khishan asked me to serve as his imam for the Friday prayer. Muslim ritual prayer consists of a sequence of set words and gestures. To keep everyone in the congregation together, one pious Muslim is chosen to stand in front and to serve as 'imam' for the other congregants to imitate. Each of us knew what the Shi'i denomination's religious books say about the legal preconditions for a person to serve as imam in communal prayer. I repeated these to him and emphasized that the first precondition—'adala—is mandatory. This term means 'justice' and stipulates that the man behind whom you wish to pray must be free of sins and major offenses. I did not think myself sinful, since I did not consider homosexual desire something that would sever my tie to God. Instead, I thought it was a special tribulation God imposed on an elect group of his worshippers whom he loved and wished to test continuously, because he loves them even more than they love him. Thus, he isn't concerned by how difficult his challenge is for them. It is not a distinction; it is a special, extremely secret matter between me and God, whom I had begun to address while I prostrated myself humbly for long periods in subservience to him. Spiritual attributes and insights developed within me on the basis of books of Qur'anic exegesis, jurisprudence, scholastic theology, and logic, which are topics that popular religious culture does not treat but that turban-wearing students of religion study. For these reasons and based on my many conversations with Khishan, he was keen to have me serve as his imam for prayers, because I seemed well informed and well trained in religious studies. Besides, no one would know we were offering prayers as an imam and a congregant, respectively, because we would close the door of our bathroom and pray alone. If someone knocked on the door, we would know how to pretend we were doing something else.

"This situation placed an enormous responsibility on me, and whenever I masturbated in the bathroom or enjoyed looking at the naked bodies of male students, Khishan's face would pop into my imagination. Then I would feel I was spoiling his prayer, worship, and link to God. That feeling would quickly evaporate, though, because I would explain to myself that Khishan was buttressed by the strength of his intention and his belief. As long as he continued to believe that I was pure and a true believer, God would judge Khishan by what he knew of me, not by what he didn't. For as long as Khishan did not consider me a sinner, God would not punish him by invalidating his prayers for performing them behind an imam like me.

"The problems began when our prayer circle expanded, because Khishan opened the door to other worshippers, beginning with someone from his village. This tall, lanky young man wore glasses with thick black frames and was a good example of a bright person who concentrated on his studies and ignored the wider world. Then another young man arrived; he would weep fervently whenever I recited the special prayer for prostration and dusting the forehead with dirt.

"One day when I was genuflecting during prayer, and they were repeating after me what I said, the door, which was suspended in place by its own weight, moved. We hadn't worried about the door during prayer and had let the person closest to it push against it. This intrusion was a stern trial that caused pious young Khishan to become terrified and pee on himself involuntarily. The sight of us praying communally would excite fear, because in general it was a strange adventure. I had long thought that, for me to live peacefully, the spirit of adventure that leads to destruction needed to be reined in.

"It was my father, who had spent the previous night on the long road from Basra to Baghdad, sleeping in the bus and riding through the night. He had reached Baghdad at dawn, eaten breakfast at the bus station, and then headed to the dormitory to see me. He did not come bearing presents, rice, frozen soup, or sweets. Before he stuck his head through the opening of the door, we had dispersed throughout the room. He greeted us one by one, sporting an embarrassed smile. I don't think he had discovered we were praying. Perhaps he never knew that.

"After he met my prayer-mates, inquired about their health, and observed the hair mixed with paint in the corners of the room, he took my hand, asked the other students to excuse us, and drew me out of the building. He took me to a nearby restaurant, saying, 'They make superb kubbeh here.' Then he began to talk. 'I don't want you to come to Basra. Stay here. I'll send you as much money as you need to cover your expenses for food, drink, and clothes. Talk about you and what you do has begun to spread among our family and kinsfolk. What's important to us is your safety, because I can't guarantee that even your closest relatives won't harm you. I don't want to find your corpse in a dump heap. I also don't want our reputation harmed. You have sisters who are looking for good husbands. No one may step forward if people learn about your behavior. Your presence in Baghdad protects and shields you and safeguards all of us. This is a telephone number you can use to contact us when you need something.'

"He kept his head bowed while he said these things, but I felt we were looking each other in the eye, because my head was also bowed. Faces looking in different directions see each other at some point in space, especially when these are harmonious faces or ones linked by a clear tie of sincere affection. He spoke while looking at the floor, and I listened to his every word while fleeing into my imagination and then returning to him, as I reflected on a non-Euclidean geometry lesson that said two straight, parallel lines meet at a point somewhere—even the rays from my glances and those from his tearful eyes. The professor explaining to us how parallel, straight lines may meet had referred to a verse by a heartsick ancient Arab lover, who described his separation from his beloved and his search for her visage in the sky:

I cast my gaze into the sky;
It may meet hers, up there, and die!

All downcast faces may meet at a single point one day, somewhere, even if they stare at the ground.

"He may have thought I didn't understand what he was saying, so he repeated it more than once, expressed in different ways. My only recourse then was to rise, pretend to be angry, and leave him to drink his tea, which was heavily sugared, while I embarked on an excursion through unfamiliar lanes as I penetrated the alleys of Old Baghdad. Suddenly, I found myself at a large mausoleum shrine. I think this moment ignited my attachment to the figure known as Sahib al-Zaman, the Master of Time, whose title suggests that he is connected to the mechanism of time and to the theory of relativity. According to adherents of Twelve-Imam Shi'ism, the largest denomination within Shi'i Islam, Hujjat Allah al-Mahdi ibn Hasan ibn Ali is the twelfth and final Shi'i imam, and he disappeared from human sight centuries ago into a mysterious Occultation. He isn't connected to any theories about time or physics, even though his title suggests this. According to accounts in Shi'i texts, he will be responsible for stopping time on Earth before history ends. He, like Jesus, never died, and none of his foes has ever vanquished him, over more than a thousand years. I believed in him and accepted the idea of his eternal existence—that he has lived longer than any other human being and that God provided him with biological cells that do not die or perish. This attribute may have allowed him to live through and participate in every age, including the reigns of the Abbasids, Seljuqs, Barmakids, Fatimids, Persians, Mamluks, Turks, and Byzantines, and through the Crusades, the wars in Andalusia, the Mongol and Tatar invasions, England's colonization, the fall of the monarchies, and the Free Officers' coups in the Middle East, which were followed by the dictatorships. He has experienced all of these, and our temporal tranche, in which we exist, is to him 'as insignificant as an armpit hair'—as the medieval Arab poet al-Mutanabbi put it.

"The Master of Time watches over me attentively. He knows even the moments when I engage in unseemly sexual practices, and I don't think he's angry with me. Who would be angry with a well-intentioned, industrious student who flunks an examination in a subject that even mountains would fail—the love of men? This is a trial for select souls and those with secret forms of spiritual communication.

"Historical stories and accounts I have read about the Master of Time when he announced his first, short, temporary Occultation say he entrusted the affairs of his followers to four envoys. They all lived in Baghdad and were buried there. When the last of them died, Sahib al-Zaman announced the age of the great Occultation, which will extend to the time of his reappearance, which all his followers anticipate, repeating a famous phrase, the gist of which is 'He appears and fills the earth with justice and righteousness after it was filled with tyranny and despotism,' attributable to tyrannical rulers, catastrophic poverty, and rampant misrule over the people. But, during his great Occultation, pious people may achieve moral, spiritual stations that entitle them to a special encounter with Sahib al-Zaman, after they have made a diligent effort to purify the soul and discipline it against the defects of conceit, arrogance, mendacity, and vanity. A worshipper may follow several paths to care for his soul and to scrutinize it while he isolates himself from human society and any consciousness of it. In addition to all this, he should disavow his ego. Naturally, this is a difficult and taxing balance that requires a mind that is extremely perceptive and a soul that is incredibly well disciplined.

"Many of the Shi'ah believe that the sepulcher to which I found my way contains a single grave for all four emissaries. According to my esoteric instruction, these men, although they did die, in some sense are also alive and still constitute a preliminary gateway for an encounter with the Twelfth Imam, the Sahib al-Zaman, the Master of Time. It is not easy to encounter him without first passing through these gateways and mastering personal trials through immersion in the ethical pathways of his four envoys.

"I spent many hours by these four graves, which are found in Baghdad's ancient alleyways. The government did not maintain these graves, because according to its point of view, they represent a deviant understanding of true—Sunni—Islam. I met many religion students who had removed their turbans to frequent the structures of those graves and worship clandestinely there, undetected by anyone because they disguised themselves by dressing like porters, merchants, and truckers.

"Khishan noticed the change in my conduct and what seemed to him to be many strange practices, because his knowledge of religion did not extend beyond externals like performing duties such as ritual prayer and fasting. He may have considered what I was doing to be an exaggerated, inept transgression. Even though all these extraordinary measures were very pacific and amicable, they rubbed him the wrong way. When he saw me walk barefoot all the time, even when we went out to purchase necessities, he would scold me, even after I told him I was imitating the humility of the prophet Moses after God chastised him. I really considered myself inferior to everyone else and struggled to combat any feeling of superiority over other people. This wasn't merely to convince myself. Reading the lives of saints and pious people from my spiritual perspective, I concluded some things many others did not. When stinky cats congregated at the door of my room, looking for the food I doled out to them liberally, Khishan grumbled and usually left the room. He considered cats impure, but that idea is contrary to basic Islamic law. Dogs are impure, and in Shi'i Islam, you are not allowed to pray (and your prayer is not accepted) if you touch dogs while you are wet, since moisture transfers contamination. There is no disagreement about that. It is okay to touch dogs or cats, but your body during prayer should be clean from their hair. So don't touch them when you are wet and want to pray. Therefore, Khishan went berserk when he found me sheltering stray dogs in our 'bath' room and letting them lap milk from my hand, in defiance of the ruling of impurity against them. I assumed that Islamic law and principles could not contradict the principle of compassion and tenderness toward others, and that dogs are fellow beings, too, just as much as we are. We shouldn't feel we are superior to them. At this point, Khishan lost his temper and decided to look for another place to live.

"Some droll students were happy to call our room the shrine for spinster cats, pushing a satirical, apocryphal story, the gist of which was that cats converged on our room to seek my blessing and that each cat asked me to pray she would meet success in finding herself a husband. I didn't blame them, because they did not dare advance those claims to my face. Instead, they pretended to be extremely reverential when they were in my presence, and I never saw them cut in front of me when we were walking. They stood aside and waited for me to pass. Many of them, on seeing my bare feet, would fetch a pair of sandals and race to set them before me humbly. Then I would bow and return the sandals to them. In fact, a sizable number of students didn't disdain my practice. Despite the gravity of our circumstances, we organized spiritual lessons on ethics and creedal logic once a week in a large clean room—not my room. Eventually, Khishan lodged a complaint against me, and I found myself evicted from our room. I didn't criticize him for that, because I was guided by the demands of the extraordinary tolerance I embraced and preached. I simply took turns sleeping in other crowded rooms. Many friends surprised me by refusing to let me sleep with them, and I concluded that their refusal was related to my reputation as an extremely pious person. Yes, these fellows did not understand the type of piety I believed in. They would not easily attain an exemplary spiritual plateau or that of the calcified, Jurassic-era homosexual worm inside my brain.

"Then, finally, I was offered a space beneath the bed of a Turkmen student who spoke broken Arabic and sheltered beneath his nose an enormous mustache that did not match his suave, short form. His name was Tayf, which in Arabic means 'all the colors of the spectrum.' I doubt that this name is related to the gay pride flag. The Turkmen and Kurds, like other ethnic minorities in Baghdad, had long ago succumbed to a wave of Arabization of their names and the suppression of their languages and accents, because they feared being accused by the government of belonging to opposition Kurdish or Iranian political parties. In fact, you would find that some of them exaggerated their pronunciation of Arabic consonants and read the Qur'an aloud with great accuracy. On the other hand, among themselves, they were keen to speak their own native languages, especially when an Arab student, someone not affiliated with the state, was with them, perhaps in order to show off their language.

"The sperm percolating in Tayf's testicles caused him many problems. Our room was the venue for trysts between Tayf and a Baghdad girl who managed a whorehouse next to the dorm. It seems that his affair was discovered and that his relationship was revealed to the top pimp, who ran three houses of prostitution in the area. So we were surprised one evening when the pimp entered the building and locked the door behind him. He became rowdy and screamed in everyone's face, as more than two hundred male students became the target of this pimp's filthy curses. When he realized that no one would come forward to combat him, he invoked the name of our 'President and Commander,' saying he was a friend of the president. In those days the expression 'friends of the president' was in wide circulation, and thousands of people claimed this sobriquet. Most had never met the president or shaken his hand, but the label was awarded to them as an honorific in recognition of special missions they had (or had not) undertaken. Falsification of titles and spurious claims to honorary distinctions were also common.

"When he shouted his assertion of friendship with the president, we formed a circle around him, feeling clueless, with faces blanched by fright and despair. After the pimp humiliated dozens of men from both the South and the North of Iraq—village men who boasted of their heroism as virile men and their legendary courage—Tayf himself turned the tables on this man. If he hadn't, everyone would have been swept into history's dustbin. Tayf stepped forward, though, seized the huge pimp by the collar, and shouted at him, 'I'm one of the president's friends too. And here's more news for you: my father is the chauffeur for Mr. Qusay, the president's second son.' The pimp quickly de-escalated his threats and gradually withdrew every word he had said about Tayf and about his molesting the girl.

"I knew full well that Tayf was lying and that he did that to quell the Saddamite pimp's false threats, which Tayf's strategy easily exposed.

"Tayf prayed according to the Sunni denomination's version of Islam, and his ritual prayer differed in certain particular respects from Shi'ah practice. He loved to listen to the songs of the Lebanese diva Fairuz, whom most Arabs ranked second only to Sabah. As a result of his attack on the pimp, his status changed significantly, and many people showed him respect. This situation did not last long, however, because during the forty-eight hours that US president George W. Bush granted Saddam to leave power along with his sons, while recently dug oil-filled trenches blocked various areas of the capital, a group of Kurds entered our room and dragged Tayf from his bed. They tied him to a light pole and stripped off his clothes. They beat him with their shoes, because they thought he was a vile Saddamite and a friend of the president. I knew full well that he had used those lies only for self-protection.

"Those hours were incredible—beyond any expectation and our greatest hopes. Getting rid of the president and his sons had long been merely a dream. Even when we saw with our own eyes American soldiers roll Saddam's carved head around, we didn't believe what we saw on our television screens, which had broadcast lies for the past forty years.

"*Et tu*, Cup? Even you could not have convinced me if you had been with me then and told me, 'Saddam has fallen.' Cup?

"Hey! Cup?"

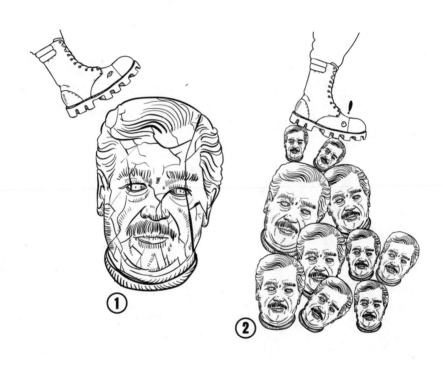

① ②

Fourteen

The house of the three monkeys resounded with my footsteps and the creak of wood on the stairs. Liao was drinking coffee with his legs crossed, watching a drop of rainwater slowly slide down the window-pane. He would read a little and then close the book and yawn. Erick seemed to have dropped the Christmas sweater, with its yarn trailing on his lap, and his expressionless face gazed into the void. Josie, for his part, seemed frozen as he silently flipped through television chan-nels. He said nothing when I appeared before them and attempted to excite their interest and draw their attention. Their stillness, though, was more profound than I had imagined. I went to fetch spoons and knives as noisemakers, but—even then—none of them protested the random din I was making. So I sat on the steps to wait for one of their stony faces to come to life. That happened. Erick rose and asked me to fetch my drawing materials and follow him. I didn't jump to obey him till Josie stirred and repeated the request. I responded once all three of them asked me. Trying to appear contagiously charming, I got my drawing supplies, climbed the steps, and headed to the room they had all entered quietly. I found them waiting for me beside Heraclitus.

"Have you attempted this before?" Erick asked. "We want you to draw a dead dog."

Then I realized that Heraclitus had died. I approached him, following the scent. He reeked of Indian cologne, and an orange ribbon surrounded his neck. His head looked larger than before, and his eyes were half-closed. His mouth and nose were very clean and extremely handsome. He was almost dancing—like Keith Haring's red, yellow, and blue dogs. His expression was easily captured on paper, and his eyes seemed to be glass globes. His face made a sound as it printed itself on the sheet of paper. The noise wasn't barking or snoring. The living dogs I had drawn had extended their faces meekly and hadn't made this beautiful clamor while they spread over my white page.

My portrait took its place in the basket where Heraclitus usually slept. The philosopher had died, leaving his caretakers with no guide or caliph.

Here I am—accompanying Erick to a pet cemetery in the southernmost part of the city. We walk among the trees as our footsteps create a duet. I sense that we are walking twice or that someone else is walking with us. Erick is experiencing an extremely pure state of clarity, and an all-embracing peace radiates from his spirit's pores. Perhaps, for this reason, he is inspired to launch into an unusual conversation with me, for the first time.

"Are you still waiting for Morise? I want to ask something of you. It's true that I shirked my responsibility to help you find him. Allow me to postpone that now. I ask you to learn about Seattle—to read it like a book and study it—to investigate it yourself as if it were a lesson, assignment, or on the school curriculum. Learn how people live, about their lifestyles and complexions, about that thick layer of things that no one discusses but that are present—about matters that do not seem to exist but they arise, burgeon, and disclose themselves intensely. I want

you to 'learn' America, and Seattle in particular. I hope you understand me. I am also asking you *not* to understand me. You need to forget Morise. You mustn't shut down your life for the sake of someone you met during the Iraq War. Soldiers lead a troubled life and may not be the same people when they return home. Morise in Seattle is not the same as Morise in Baghdad. He has surely spotted you, gazed at you, or looked stealthily at your face somewhere here, and then turned and fled. This means he does not want to see you. He does not wish to meet you. My friend, you need to respect this wish. You're educated and know the very spirit of the law and of ethics is to respect the wishes of any person who does not wish to see you. Heraclitus, whom we buried today, Heraclitus, if he had spoken, would have told you: It doesn't do for you to insist on picturing yourself in only one situation or with only one person. It isn't right for your moments to collapse beneath the feet of some other person or for you to refuse to see yourself without him. It is a massive error for us to put our lives on hold for one individual and to deny ourselves any worth without him—for us to be unable to imagine ourselves without him. Imagine yourself after him. Re-create your Self beyond that forbidding barrier, and cross over with us to life. Leap on board the ship. You won't find some land of security awaiting you. Instead, you will discover worlds lined up, anticipating the touch of your feet on them, as you start all over again. I know this is easy to say—very easy. When we want to construct moralizing sentences, all we need is air, some brain cells, and a chattering tongue. This is true. What is even truer is that we should imbibe this statement no matter how bitter it is and take a leap. Your head must be stuffed with a verbal mishmash. Spilling from it come wise maxims and good advice that thousands of human beings have vomited at your head from books and screens and in real life—as I am doing now. This is life. Our heads are congeries of communicating vessels that draw from here and spill out there. You yourself have practiced this role and repeatedly placed on your head a sage's skullcap. But the physician won't recover from the disease by merely mouthing the prescription. He must swallow the medicine itself. The prescription is nothing but a piece of paper. Many people swallow paper, on which their intestines ruminate, but they don't recuperate. We mustn't recite a prescription. Instead, we must prepare the medicine and drink it at the prescribed time. We watch over the body of our spirit while we recover. The medicine doesn't prevent us from becoming reinfected. Immunity means remaining disease resistant. Your problem may be that too much knowledge is crammed inside you and that too many voices and fluids mingle together in your head. Please take note: I want you to pay careful attention to my voice, to what you hear in my voice. There is a slight rasp, which I've had for thirty years. It is caused by a small swelling that obstructs my words as they emerge from my mouth and makes them sound bloody and filled with pus. I want to share with you a little secret. It's something I've never told anyone. Neither Josie nor Liao knows it, although these two men are closer to me than anyone else and are my best friends. You may have noticed that we rarely speak to one another. But, by my life, ours is a firm friendship that does not depend on words or the ordinary means of human interaction. I beg you to conceal what I am going to tell you beneath your tongue and not share it with anyone. Can you do that? I beg you. I don't want anyone else to hear what I am going to tell you.

"I don't know exactly how old I was, but what I am going to tell you happened when I was a young man. I think I stopped keeping track of my age after that. This slight, careless process, which is lodged in some brain tissue responsible for reckoning ages and keeping track of birthdays, hasn't worked since then. I was raising my children and carrying them on my shoulders like slender glass flasks. When they walked, I watched their heels land and rise, to keep them from stepping on anything rough. When we walked along the sidewalk, I positioned myself like a guardrail to keep them on track: a girl of five and a boy two years older. I transported sand in my dump truck between two points separated by a bridge, a river, and a hill. I would return home before sunset. Just before that, I would pick them up from their grandmother's house. That morning when I started the vehicle's engine, Heraclitus I leaped up beside me and began to poke me in the gut. I gave him some stale cheese, and he calmed down a little. Then he started jumping around again and landed in my lap. He kept bugging me and making it hard for me to see on that foggy morning, which was haunted by folk songs. I had the radio turned up loud and was listening and repeating the words of the songs while Heraclitus I continued to fidget. He wouldn't stop butting my chest with his head and licking my neck. When I reached the point where I planned to load the sand, Heraclitus jumped out before I could. Then he got into the bed of the truck. I had to scold him and chase him away. I was away from the vehicle, and another truck was about to empty its load in my truck. But Heraclitus was back and didn't want to leave the bed of the truck. Finally, the dog jumped out, and we dropped a load of sand in my truck. When I got behind the wheel and called Heraclitus to climb in the cab with me, the dog refused and fled. I told myself he wouldn't disappear and that I would get him on the next round, because I had five round trips to make that day. As you know, dogs can find their way home and rarely act that crazy. Heraclitus, whose grandson we buried today, isn't the hero of this story as you might think. There were two heroes, whom I discovered, Mortada, when we dumped the load of sand at the site. I found my two children beneath the load of sand. I had dumped a load of sand on top of them that day without knowing it. Heraclitus knew, and I think he told his son that, and his son told his son in turn—the dog we buried today. He was the only one who knew this secret. It seems I have needed to transmit it to you. I can't carry on unless I feel that someone still living knows. But always remember that we did not bury only a dog today; we buried a dog and a secret.

"What I want to tell you is that there are people who have suffered on this earth exactly like you, but the passing years are always capable of opening a clean, white page for you to start again. I remind you of this so you will know that I'm referencing more than the ugly, empty, sermonizing sentences that everyone recites. I know firsthand what I am saying and have experienced survivor's guilt too. I know the delight of being content with what you have and not demanding too much, of not questing for what cannot be achieved. Button it up—the vast shirt of hopes. You must button it tight and zip it up occasionally. Morise, Morise—every day Morise! You parted years ago. Why should Morise suddenly bounce back into your life like this? How can you permit him to upset your daily life and fill every hour with misery? My words may upset you. But, please, allow me to tell you . . . that Morise is over, that Morise here is not the Morise you knew there. The Morise of Seattle isn't the Morise of Baghdad. Please stop, I beg you. Focus on your life here. I've heard you talk of wanting to learn AI coding. Well, I think it is an excellent idea. I can help you apply to the university. Perhaps I'll introduce you to the group of programmers I know here. I've also heard you've distinguished yourself in your current employment. These are all excellent choices. I know you spent some time in Seattle without any work, almost like a homeless person. The shelter we've provided you won't last forever. You can work sincerely and hard and obtain a real job. You wear more than one cap on your head. I know things have been rough for you, but that's true for others as well. You will attain some special distinction, one that doesn't depend on Morise. When people free themselves from sorrow, they become light and grow wings. They become radiant, and their selves become more powerful and fresher. I beg you: take the prescription. Close your eyes and drink a spoonful of the medicine, my boy."

I watched Erick's face as he ran through his advice. Without saying so, I was preparing myself to cut the last, painful knot and turn Morise's page forever. I had been thinking about that and had promised myself that the moment when we got out of the car after burying Heraclitus would be the start of my life without Morise.

I found a letter from the woman who owned the Akita waiting for me back at the monkeys' house. She was inviting me to a dinner at her house. A sentence in the invitation added that I could bring one of the wise monkeys with me. It was easy to pluck Liao from his window, place him on the commuter train, and then draw him into a conversation, en route, about his Norwegian husband's rare skill in using words. When Liao was angry at me, he would deplore my limited English vocabulary. I think he developed this feeling by watching me contort my jaw resentfully, while his genius would elaborate on his husband's fluency and eloquence in writing letters. Liao had his own special ways of taking revenge for little slips. He had a set of these no bigger than the head of a match—or even a little smaller. When he felt some error had been made, he wouldn't forgive it but saved that urge for suitably timed revenge. His discussion on the bus about language and vocabulary was related to a slight offense I had committed against him. For the past month, I had begged off accompanying him to concerts by a homosexual chorale. I had apologized, saying I was busy. This was his chance, and he found me an easy target, as if I were sitting in the garden. All I could do was stare at the palm of my hand.

Once we reached our destination, the Akita lady, our hostess, watched me stroke the surface of a postmodernist painting. It was circular and looked like a round smudge. My hand had caressed it, to the frame, and then had continued stroking empty space till, without my being conscious of this, my hand touched a copy of the Torah, which was near the painting. I didn't realize this was the Torah until she interrupted my reverie by saying, "I'm Jewish. Did you know?" I stammered, and said, "Ah, that's beautiful." I don't know whether that was a stupid response. I was trying to appear as affectionate as possible, even if that meant seeming simpleminded. Avoiding overly blunt speech is like walking through a desert planted with mines. Restraining the tongue and controlling facial expressions are like walking on two ropes in a circus of flattery, when caution proves the sure route to disaster.

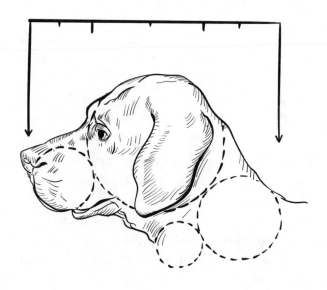

Even so, I had imbued my head with a special sensitivity to talk about color, ethnic group, and religion—even about different breeds of dogs and any preference for one over the other. Because people cannot reach inside you and examine all your opinions about these matters, and because you cannot raise the permanent billboard, you say instead, "I'm very affectionate and love all of you." You need to grasp the stick by its middle and press your weight onto the rope you're traversing.

A joke paused in my throat long enough for me to suppress it, because it would no doubt have proved a disastrous pleasantry. I wanted to say, "Oh! You're Jewish. I don't believe it. Why don't you speak with your mouth, then?" This joke is very offensive and extremely repulsive. Besides, she wouldn't have understood it, and I would have seemed like a total idiot. In any case, my plan amounted to seeming somewhat of a fool. This would be a safe guiding principle for the evening.

She wouldn't have gotten that joke, because it requires a brief introduction, and jokes that require explanations die in the mouth before they're born, when they may become tragedies. What would have happened if I had explained to her that Jewish characters in Egyptian Arabic-language television serials, to which we Iraqis are addicted, speak with a special, extremely nasal accent, as if speaking through their nostrils instead of their mouths? An Arab actor given the role of a Jew must learn to close his mouth and expel air through his nostrils. I don't know the origin of this stereotype. Probably it originated with an actor who had a supporting role in the 1980s in a serial about an Egyptian spy in Israel, and then it carried over to other actors' roles on different programs. When Saddam, in the 1990s, wanted to produce a political drama about an Israeli spy in Iraq, they made the Jewish Israeli character a homosexual and used makeup so the actor would look quite ugly. He played a gay, Jewish character. In fact, he was typically a homosexual and thus open to various satanic temptations—one of them being Jewish.

We prepared the food together, and our moments of relaxation and congeniality allowed her dog with the large head to jump at me and, without warning, to bite me in the groin again. She looked very embarrassed. I was relaxed about this and not upset, and a carpet of goodwill spread between me and that lady. When the wine flowed in our veins, she commented that she had noticed my teeth hurt and that she would take me to her special dentist.

I won't deny that I allowed myself to provoke her after the wine had filled my veins, especially once she asked how I had learned to draw dogs with such precision. I told her I used to collect anatomical representations of dissected dogs, to scrutinize their bones, muscles, and layers of fat. While I was explaining this, I succumbed to a bout of hiccups, which I subdued only by downing a big gulp of water. She then said, "You seem to have examined human corpses carefully to improve your drawing skills . . . That's not very nice."

My face froze when I heard her sudden and demeaning comment, but then she began to laugh. "Your hiccups are gone. Sorry, but fear and outrage are a quick cure for hiccups."

Even though I realized she had made that comment with a noble goal, for which I thanked her, I replied, "Yes, on my computer I scrutinized a special archive of anatomical drawings of the human body. Many of these came from a book by Dr. Pernkopf, who is famous among scholars of anatomy and surgeons as well as artists and sculptors. It's the best source for details of the human body. He relied on cadavers and the actual faces of homosexuals and Jews exterminated by the Nazis. The science of anatomy and art are indebted to those victims." I said this, even though I realized I was becoming tedious and intemperate, despite her silent, focused gaze at my face.

Meanwhile, Liao seemed to be watching this encounter carefully. I had not previously noticed that he was this sensitive or was interested enough to sit and observe us as if he were watching a film with great enjoyment.

When I freed myself from her dog's head, which it had planted between my legs for a third time, Liao approached and said, "I've never seen your tears flow so freely."

I replied, "I'm not weeping. This is an attack of a cold and nerves."

He laughed and turned toward her to say goodbye.

On the bus, I explained the reason for my emotion but told him, falsely, that the Eustachian tube connects the nose and the eye—if only to make him laugh again and reveal my lie, because the Eustachian tube connects the ear and the nose. But he managed to find another name for that tube once I told him what the woman had done for me.

"While you filled your glass with wine and appeared to be having a successful conversation with her husband," I said, "the Akita lady took me on a tour of her sumptuous house. I admired the carpets, paintings, small pictures, and portraits of her dogs through several generations in black and white. Then she took me to a lower floor and told me she was fixing a room for me there. She said, 'This is a secure room; you can hide here if you want. Truly, I'm not kidding. You can hide out there if evil circumstances should make that necessary.'"

"We'll call it the 'Invisibility tube,'" Liao suggested, referring to my new bunker.

He may have grasped the riddle effortlessly. The lady was compassionate and had handed me a letter, the gist of which was "I know what it means for a person to need to hide as a result of political statements or governmental decisions or a war or a holocaust." The context was clear to me and Liao. At that time, the media was shouting about a ban on Muslims entering the country. But the lady's statement went way beyond this. I sensed that it emanated from a million mouths of people who had been pursued or placed in an underground cell, hidden from sight during World War II, and that she had told me in a single sentence—which said far more than it stated—her own family's story.

That night, Liao restrained his excessive excitement about Morise and embraced me before we entered that house of simian sorrows. He told me he had news that was both happy and sad. I asked him to repeat his sentence. He said, "My news is both happy and sad." I didn't understand this equation and didn't ask him to explain. When he saw that my enthusiasm was fading, he hugged me again and yelled in my ear that he had found Morise and that we could go the next day at dawn to observe him "through the glass."

"Through the glass?"

"You may change your mind when you see him. This is merely a precautionary step."

"Listen. I've stopped looking for him. I ask you to forget the subject."

"I'll wait for you at the door at six o'clock, and we'll see Morise."

"Fine! At dawn. Dawn, I'll be ready here at five a.m. Don't break your promise."

Fifteen

Liao said that Morise worked in Seattle as a volunteer at an institute for deaf, mute, and blind children. This idea made sense to me, and I welcomed it, because I knew Morise excelled at sign language, which he considered as sacred a language as Sumerian, Mandean, and Aramaic. He would get angry if I mentioned this comparison, though, because these languages are dead, and sign language isn't. Signing is the oldest language and the longest lived, because it lacks the curses of eloquence, verbal embellishment, and grammar. In fact, it is filled with life's clamor and expresses, in his opinion, things the tongue cannot. For this reason, I did not doubt Liao and, setting out at dawn, followed him breathlessly till we reached the place, a one-story building with windows filled with drawings and clever comments by children. Liao said additionally that he had launched a new search via a friend—a former soldier—who said he had attended an Easter dinner where he had met a young Black man who spoke Arabic. Because Liao's friend bore an Arabic inscription on his upper arm, he had shown it to the young man and asked him to translate it. That Arabic speaker had refused to ascribe any meaning to the inscription, which he termed a decorative cluster of tree leaves that looked like Arabic script but wasn't and thus didn't spell a word. This brief discussion led them to an interesting conversation, he had said. The former soldier learned that the young man had visited the Middle East many times and now worked in an institute for special-needs individuals in Seattle. The second step that Liao had taken was to search for that institute. We sat opposite it now, afraid to enter and hesitant to approach any closer. I naturally had a reasonable excuse, because I was beside myself with fear, and Liao didn't dare force me. Liao's only excuse was, perhaps, concern for me or fear I had concealed something he didn't know about my relationship with Morise. The virus of fear spread to his face, and we sat glumly by the entrance, waiting for Morise to turn up, in compliance with the theory of chance or some other common theory no one believes in. At an hour like that, my intellect becomes so brittle, it's ready to believe gray squirrels can fly, and fear triumphs over belief.

Finally, Liao summoned up his courage and asked me to position myself behind a large tree near the building—right beside a small playground. He left me there and walked confidently toward the glass-doored entrance. His shadow disappeared first and then his entire body. The sun's rays created a shadow for him that made him look less scary as he moved away, leaving me alone, and that's an excellent role for a shadow to play. Morise once whispered to me that people in Seattle have no shadows—as if implying that they shed their shadows at the city's limits. The matter wasn't related to the limited amount of sunshine or the frequency of rain, which is hostile to shadows and wipes away the footsteps of travelers. But that day, the sun proved Morise a liar and positioned a shadow behind Morise to encourage and assist him. On that day, I would have welcomed anything that gave the lie to Morise and cut him down to size as he gradually faded from my heart.

Even so, he had always been small, despite a late growth spurt.

Some fifteen minutes passed—fifteen of the world's minutes, but perhaps five years by my internal clock. Time's progression changes once you move inside my head. Even though I was very vigilant, and my eyes remained trained on the entrance, while I watched for Liao to emerge with Morise, soft grains of sand were falling with amazing languor in the hourglass of my mind. Every part of my body was alive and readied the way a defeated hero prepares by bowing before the guillotine, but all this did not prevent me from searching diligently in all directions for something to use to continue my story—anything. I asked myself aloud, "How about an upside-down shoe?" as I looked at a child's shoe lying in the small outdoor playground. I remembered the extremely short story attributed to Hemingway, "For sale: baby shoes, never worn," and recalled other stories about the shoes of drowned children from Mosul and Damascus washed ashore, upside down on Mediterranean beaches. I stood, grasped the shoe, and placed it in front of me, near enough for it to hear me clearly.

"Hello, Shoe. I'll meet Morise soon, now, in a few moments. I don't know exactly when. He'll probably look out here at any moment. Can you picture that? Let me first tell you how I met Morise.

"Baghdad fell—that's what they said on the TV placed on top of a refrigerator in a grocery store near the dorm. It was the only store that had enough electric power to run this appliance. The statue the Americans dragged to the ground was only half an hour on foot from the dorm, but we preferred to watch on the screen. That meant the president had fallen, but only inside the screen. We felt we had to touch each other to assure ourselves that this was true. Tayf found someone to untie him from the pole. The dorm's aged guard, whose cheeks protruded on both sides, sat frozen in front of the television as he pressed his eyes and squeezed them. Beyond the windows danced pillars of smoke and an all-embracing calm—a calm like that after someone asks you a question you can't answer and then stares at you. I was wondering whether people were motionless and silent, or if the inanimate world had lost its voices. Someone had detached the audio stream from the monstrous video inside which we lived and had dropped a ceiling of silence over our bodies. To be fair, one sound finally broke out from the rear of our group around the TV: the elderly guard farted while all eyes were preoccupied by that momentous, dramatic scene of people tossing shoes at the president's head—at the statue that would later be termed an idol.

"Brothels weren't a good setting for student lodgings. For this reason, the university decided to house students inside its own campus, in newly vacated dorm rooms, departments, and halls that had been used for assemblies of Baathist students. We carried our possessions on our backs and headed to the campus on foot. The trip took approximately two hours, during which we watched Baghdad burn on one side and glow with delight on the other. People were still uncertain how to greet their new life. During our trip, we passed a tall and well-built multistory building behind which swarms of people were congregating. They were circling it and plundering windows and doors that they took turns ripping out. Gradually, religious leaders' fatwas made their way to the street and forbade people from plundering assets that belonged to the public, the state, and the people. Although the fatwas, which were edicts from important scholars, came too late for this building, it still contained some tables, chairs, and air conditioners. We left our belongings with a classmate, who was limping because his legs were tired, and followed the people traipsing through the unidentified building like blood circulating through the body. It is worth noting that they all asked everyone following them to keep quiet and walk on tiptoe. Some moments after I joined them, I learned that they were listening intently and using all their senses in hopes of hearing the voices of prisoners, somewhere behind the walls or underground. Someone had spread the rumor that the building had been used as a prison. Minutes after I began following them, I grew bored and lost interest. Unlike me, they became increasingly excited. We left them as they continued searching and calling to their lost sons in the skeleton of that vacant building. As a matter of fact, this scene was replicated all along our route: people searched for mass graves and clandestine prisons where their sons had been held during the last thirty years. Reports of newly discovered skeletons became common in newspapers and magazines and on screens and tongues.

"While we were crossing a street, our building's guard stopped suddenly—like a single bead plucked from a rosary—and stood alone in the middle of the street. We saw him sink down and sit on his buttocks. He didn't respond when we shouted to him, not even when some fools among us laughed at him. I went back and tried to drag him away, to keep him from being crushed by crazed vehicles crammed full of treasures and valuables looted from the presidential palaces located near the university. But he asked me to leave him. Then he leaned forward, covering his eyes with both hands. He couldn't see—that's what he said before he assumed the fetal position. Five of us volunteered to carry him. We comforted him, saying that this was just a transitory affliction caused by the terror of events and the atrocities we were witnessing in the streets. For his part, he started saying it was a curse. 'God doesn't want me to see my son, who will return after the fall of the regime.' We learned from this that his son had fled to Iran in the 1990s and had worked with the opposition forces there. Since caravans of opponents of the regime had begun to return to Iraq after an absence of many decades, Mr. Hirjis expected to see his son. Yes, the man who lost his sight was named Hirjis, which means 'fox cub.' It was an unusual name, but this meant every student knew it.

"With his radiant face and fair treatment of everyone, Hirjis was able to facilitate the opening of the university's gate for us. Then students entered, like ants attacking their prey. There was no order or registration, and many students' housing files were lost. This fact may have helped many suspect individuals, and people who had escaped from prison, infiltrate our ranks. I finally found a room with a door.

It was meant to house two students, which meant by our reckoning it was big enough for seven. We left Hirjis weeping and praying in a small kiosk near the main gate.

"That first night, unlike subsequent ones, was calm and undisturbed. Since security was lax at the entrance, the university soon became a theater for assorted ghosts from political and religious factions. During the first months after the allied forces entered, we found that the campus became a basic target for many of the new political parties, which 'arrived on the back of an American tank.' We heard this phrase used frequently in reference to their endeavors. The person I heard employ it most often was Uncle Hirjis, who used it about almost everything. Everything and everyone he didn't like had 'arrived on the back of an American tank.' For this reason, people kidded him a lot when students gave him bread, tea, and rice. He would snatch the grain and relief supplies from the students and banter with them, imitating the voice of the former Iraqi Minister of Information to amuse and entertain them so they would continue giving him presents. Hirjis also used the resemblance between him and that former government minister, who had fled, when he groped his way to the American checkpoint, where he would also imitate the minister's voice. This performance entertained the students but not the soldiers, who didn't understand what Hirjis was saying—especially not the word *'uluj*, or 'white barbarians,' which the minister had used in his last speeches to the Iraqi people when he threatened that the allied and American forces would try to intimidate them when approaching Baghdad by calling the Iraqis *'uluj*. This was before that minister disappeared and melted into the capital's districts in a matter of minutes after the defeat of the Iraqi army and the entrance of the American forces into the heart of the capital. The word he had used, *'uluj*, extracted from the womb of dusty, historical chronicles, became a joke and a word used for comedic effect. The *'uluj* were white 'page boys' enslaved by Arabs during their ancient conquests of lands with light-complexioned and blond inhabitants in outlying areas of Europe and northern parts of West Asia.

"It seemed clear that this man was gradually becoming demented, and everyone—students and soldiers—understood he was experiencing a special crisis. Therefore, when he acted in strange and puzzling ways, as his condition continued to deteriorate, no one held him accountable.

"This played out at the entrance to the university as incidents of violence increased all around with booby-trapped vehicles and suicide bombers. On the campus, there were attacks to purge former members of the Student Union and those close to the president's son, who would later die with his brother while resisting American troops.

"We saw the names of members of the former Student Union written on the pavement and then found them written over, crossed out, and replaced with alternative expressions that friends of the president's son, members of the former Student Union, would write clandestinely. All this made the university and its environs a clamorous place that was totally unsafe. The initial war of words and phrases written on the walls developed into combat with projectiles and hand grenades.

"For this reason, when a bomb exploded in front of the printshop opposite the entrance to the university, I found myself thrown to the ground and totally covered with pebbles as bullets and sheets of paper flew through the air above me. I had seen Uncle Hirjis stroke the walls a bomb had pockmarked. These terrorists filled their bombs with small shot in order to fell as many victims as possible. As the bomb disintegrated, small metal pellets and bullets would fly out of it, causing more casualties than an ordinary bomb. They announced on television they were targeting white barbarians, the *'uluj*, but they were exploding bombs in the markets and among students, far from any Americans. After they took me to the hospital and Hirjis heard I had been hit, he decided to donate blood, even though my injuries were superficial and minor. All the same, he wanted to participate in helping me recover, because volunteering would be a blessing for him, as he said. Like many people during that period, he knew I served as the imam for prayers at the college's mosque.

"Uncle Hirjis was observed more than once stroking the walls, especially walls damaged by shrapnel and singed by sparks from bombs. Most often, those walls lined a place frequented by civilians whose blood and flesh splattered the facades of those walls until the concrete became embedded with teeth, hair, and small fragments of bone.

"He would come to me after I finished praying in the college mosque, sliding slowly till he reached me. Then he grasped my hand and asked me about very private matters and his new relationship with God—or, as he would say, 'the God that arrived on the back of an American tank.' He would say that so softly no one else could hear, because it was clearly a blasphemous phrase that would have outraged many of the men praying there and caused him palpable harm. Occasionally, the music of the phrase would grip him, and he would expand on it: 'The Americans placed God in a blue balloon, transported him by Apache helicopter from Texas to the as-Sayliyah army base in Qatar, and then pulled him with naval frigates across the ocean to the Arab Gulf. Then they divided him into pieces they placed in boxes for transport from the South of Iraq to Baghdad, in buses. Here they are trying to reassemble God. All these shocks and explosions result from their failures to piece God back together again.'

"One day, I was delighted to discover that he was learning braille and could read some books and that his son finally had visited him. He was able to touch the faces of his Persian grandchildren, who could not speak Arabic properly. 'These are my grandchildren who sprang not from my loins but from the loins of an American tank,' he said, suppressing what might have been ringing laughter between his jaws, where it turned instead into a mighty coughing fit.

"He continued to practice his hobby of probing walls' protrusions and pits caused by bombs and booby traps, and I surmised that he was reading the walls the way he read braille. I guessed that, and my hunch

proved accurate, but why did he read the crevices? Could they say anything? If they could, who had written that message? I asked him these
questions after the sunset prayer during Ramadan when some wealthy
families from the affluent neighborhood close to the university sent us
food so we could break our daily fast and dine. Hirjis was blissfully
delighted by the food, and that's what encouraged me to ask whether
he was using his knowledge of braille to decipher the crevices left from
suicide bombings on Baghdad's walls.

"I didn't get any answer from him. Instead, he affirmed that he
had stopped reading crevices in the walls, because it wasn't entertaining. He no longer found that creative, because to pursue this hobby, he
was forced to follow explosions throughout the capital and plead with
taxi drivers to take him toward each new explosion. Thus, according
to what he said, he had decided to stop reading the cracks that bombs
wrote, because they all said the same things. He had seen fit to adopt
a new profession, which was to write words in braille on those walls.
He was no longer a consumer of what the walls said; he had become a
producer. Indeed, he now carried a pick and a hammer in his pocket
and tapped existential questions into walls for the terrorists.

"The import of those questions has only become clear to me now.
It is obvious that they were ambiguous, remedial sentences he wished
to use to eradicate their raison d'être. They were braille inscriptions
to vent his grief and an attempt to envision what might happen. He
wanted to delete what was, according to his conscience, a reckoning
with words. That was before he himself was terminated and his body
was turned into crevices in a giant, nightmare blast that occurred in
the large market near the university just at a time when pupils were
getting out of nearby primary and middle schools. Hirjis died and was
dispersed into the air. His splendid vision and his merry spirit, which
his darkened eyesight did not suppress, did not die nor did his sarcasm
about everything.

"We organized a small funeral procession, which not many other students cared to join. They argued that since people died by the dozens around us, there was no point in mourning just Hirjis. We offered no rebuttal and responded to our own emotions. I was pleased with the scene of a limited number of individuals carrying his remains or walking in a procession behind. These mourners included one American soldier, who placed the coffin on his shoulder exactly the way Iraqis do and who wept exactly like us. As he wept, he gazed at my face.

"Have I kept you too long, Shoe?

"I apologize and ask your forgiveness. Like you, I'm suffering from waiting so long. Liao is still inside. I hope he doesn't emerge till I've told you how I first met Morise. That soldier was Morise. But we did not consider that meeting our first. Our second meeting counted as the first, because the first was merely a drill, a rehearsal, and preparation for field readiness, as Morise said."

Sixteen

I noticed Liao's face through a window of the deaf and dumb institute. He was smiling and chatting with an individual in front of him. *Could that person be Morise?* I needed to move closer. First, I had to stand up. All I could see of the other man was the edge of his shoulder. The temple of a pair of glasses seemed to rest on his ear. I asked leave of the shoe, gathered my strength, and managed to rise. Then I found myself walking toward the window. As I did, Liao noticed me and smiled more broadly. His expression was sunny, and his eyes sparkled. That's the way he looked when he felt he had scored a victory and wished to take revenge on anyone who doubted his ability and mistrusted his social skills and network of contacts. Here his eyes were telling me, "Come. Come. I have resolved the situation, and you need to bow down thankfully and gratefully before me."

Liao's smile frightened me even more, though, and warning bells rang in my spirit. As a precaution, I stopped halfway there, intending to go no farther. I didn't want to feel disappointed. I didn't want to feel triumphant either! Both these clearly defined endings were suspect. I did not want to believe anyone. Then I wouldn't rue the hour I discovered the truth. I was very stoic at that moment, bowing to the teachings of the Roman soldiers and Caesars. I did not want to expect overwhelming happiness for fear of feeling remorse. I would not build a cage for the bird of delight only to find it had flown away. Instead, I was content to watch it circle in the air and admire its brilliant colors. Not advancing meant not experiencing sorrows. Saying no to anticipation meant saying no to disappointment. This is the gist of the teachings recorded in my heart. But I can be disloyal to teachings, oblivious to counsels, and occasionally resent the "best practices" found in volumes of sage advice and philosophical musings—as if they were medicines.

The man's neck and shoulder came into view as though to apologize for not letting me see him or blocking my view of him. Before I reached them, the man turned his entire neck toward me, revealing a polite laugh with very white large molars and a bald head. He sported a small black mustache, which clearly had been recently dyed, and a silver nose ring. After turning halfway around, he took my outstretched hand and shook it, while introducing himself. "I am Thomas." I froze momentarily before him and then regained my breath and balance. Liao had apparently told him something about me. He had obviously also fabricated a little story as an excuse to meet the man, telling him he had heard about the program for volunteers in this establishment and desired to join it soon. Then Liao had pivoted to a few personal questions, because he doubted this man was Morise.

When I appeared, Liao's face began to contract and lost its shine of delight once he felt sure that I didn't believe this extraordinarily gracious and clearly refined young man was Morise. Typically, though, he was unwilling to accept blame and wanted to hand all the censure to me. As we were leaving, Liao turned to me and attempted to repair his defeat with a bitter joke. "Oh! Not so fast. What kind of Morise do you want? What complexion? Without a ring in his nostril? We can order him for you with blue hair if you want. We can provide you with a sparring partner. We can give him colored contact lenses to provide a different eye color to your taste."

This bout of sarcasm lasted about fifteen minutes while we walked toward Capitol Hill.

Once we entered a gay bar, to which he accepted my invitation, even as he repeated, "But I don't drink," I found myself face-to-face with the three priests. One of them was quite tipsy, and the man hugged me longer than I felt was appropriate. I failed to integrate Liao into this group, and after less than ten minutes, he whispered to me that he wanted to leave. That was an awkward moment, which I interpreted according to my rudimentary knowledge of Liao's eccentric personality. As he walked out of the place, he stared at the faces of the three priests, as if he knew them only too well. I felt embarrassed by his conduct and turned toward them, apologizing with a broad smile.

These three priests were the exact opposite of my three monkeys. The holy men were better educated than the monkeys and read a lot. Besides that, some sarcastic whispers escaped them about other patrons there in the bar. They released these inside their bubble, into which they gradually drew me, glass by glass, one joke at a time.

"Was that your boyfriend?" one of them asked me.

"No, he's my friend Liao. He's always preoccupied. We'll let him go tend to his affairs." While I said that, I watched them suppress a huge laugh and button their mouths.

Then one priest turned to me and remarked, "You know, we're all monks." A second one seemed to contradict him, saying, "Actually, we're all priests." The third one explained, "We are all priests and monks: we live monastically but have been ordained as priests and can celebrate Mass."

The season of strange encounters between monkeys and monks was about to commence.

From their conversation, I grasped that they were waiting for someone. All three of them admired the same person, and this was how they treated relationships. It was the first time I had met a trio who were united in their desires and searched for one and the same partner for all of them. The three monkeys were bachelors. They would date for a time, marry, divorce, and remarry. Then they would return to their headquarters, safe and sound—and crowned with bachelorhood again.

I grasped that I would need to depart once the person they were all waiting for appeared. And, that's what I did. I had expected to leave quietly with a quick greeting and a light hug, but that wasn't how it played out. My whole body shuddered when I said goodbye to them and started to leave hurriedly, just as a wave of people appeared, wearing leather dog masks on their faces and dangling rubber tails from their haunches. I was trapped in a discussion that flared up among the priests about homosexuals who like to celebrate being gay, those who refuse to, and a third bunch who celebrate merely for the sake of celebrating. The three of them didn't agree. I told myself that perhaps my presence had encouraged them to express a balanced and diplomatic opinion. When they realized that I was listening intently to their conversation, one of them asked me, "What do you think?"

But they left me no opportunity to reply, because one of them dusted off his leather briefcase, which resembled a Russian doll with many cases inside it, and pulled out a dog mask, which he donned delightedly. When the entering pack saw this, they burst into applause and whistled.

Morise's look-alike, the dancer who had left me angrily some time ago, appeared again, inside the priests' bubble. A place was made for him among them, and he successfully inserted himself into their conversation. "The world seems to be smaller than the eye of a needle," my mother used to say. But it returns to its normal, infinite size when we aren't crazy in love with anyone, because love is a minimizing glass that collects and reduces the size of the whole world until it fits into the palm of one hand.

Seattle is smaller than the eye of an ant.

Taking my drink with me, I found an empty seat at the bar, near the door, and hid my face between my shoulders, as if I were incognito, to keep the dancer from seeing me and to avoid roiling the trio's serenity as they welcomed their new lover. At this moment, a white palm with chubby fingers appeared before me and greeted me. Palms don't usually speak like this while reaching toward my face. This means merely that this thick hand moved. When I looked to the right, I found a happy person gazing at me. "Hello! My name is K.G.! This is my first day here! I came out today! Will you let me buy you a drink?" He was a young fellow, even though he looked huge. It took me a few seconds to discern that this celebrant of his own homosexuality was a young man in his early twenties. He picked up two thick books that lay before him and then put them back down. He was delighted and enthusiastic about what he was doing. I grasped the two books after I returned his greeting politely. Both concerned homosexuality. I harbored a mean feeling inside me. I was tipsy and had trouble uttering my congratulatory and supportive comments. I wasn't able to control my discomfort at that time. I extended my hand toward his face and removed his glasses. He smiled, displaying his gentle temperament and his innocence, which resembled that of a docile child who had just entered a utopia of good, nonpredatory people, and for whom the bar's door resembled the magical portal between two worlds. Here was his peaceable kingdom, and before he entered, he had needed to buy two books to use as a catalog or guide to the strange creation we call homosexuality. These thoughts crossed my mind at that time.

I needed to return the glasses to their owner, who never stopped laughing and glancing around, unconscious then of my wickedness. His feet danced under his chair, he was so relaxed and delighted, in a cartoonlike fashion. His body was so massive that I was almost invisible beside him. He rubbed his eyes to try to encourage me to return his glasses. But I didn't. I dropped off the chair and sped away as I had done when I saw the dancer.

I went to the bathroom, where I put the glasses on my face and looked in the mirror for a time. Two men urinating became conscious of my presence, and one drew back his hand, which had been reaching for the penis of other man, who turned slightly to show me his penis to discover whether I was interested in touching the small red, coquettish creature hanging dormant from the opening of his trousers. I would have liked to tell the man that I wasn't Israfil, the angel charged with breathing life back into dead things. But he wouldn't have understood this dirty joke. When one of the stalls became free, I shut myself up in it. My bowels didn't need evacuating, but my mind did.

I placed the boy's glasses before me and began to speak to them softly in Arabic.

"Do you have my glasses? Please give them back to me. I need to go home." I heard the young man's voice from the other side of the stall door. I was surprised by how mean I had been. I didn't listen to him implore me to return what was his. I was busy returning glasses to another person who had asked me that same question more than ten years earlier.

"That was also the day I met Morise. I was outside the university's mosque after performing the prayer service there with a dozen students praying behind me. I was walking toward the river barefoot. That was my strange habit, for which many people condemned me, even though I was imitating God's prophets Hud, Salih, and Moses. Among the willow trees, I heard someone ask me this same question: 'Do you have my glasses?'

"It wasn't exactly the same. He said it in Arabic, and the voice's source descended from on high. It wasn't God or one of his angels, messengers, or saints, to whom I was praying and whom I was addressing. Even so, I thought that was the case initially but then changed my mind. Why would saintly beings ask where their spectacles had landed on the earth? When the voice was followed by a drop of blood, which fell on my neck, I realized that the questioner was an inhabitant of the earth. I raised my head to find a young man bound by his back to a tree trunk in a small grove of trees that separated the university from a large man-made lake. The grass was hot and parched, and the trees looked dry and poorly cared for. The wind twisting through the empty branches created the atmosphere of a nightmare scene in a bad horror movie. A large strip of skin on the face of the young man had been flayed and was bleeding profusely. It formed something like a veil that was partially lifted from his face. But it was his actual face, which had been pulverized by shoes and punches. His left leg was twisted back, and his dangling arm didn't seem connected to his elbow. From the dirt matted in his hair, I could tell that the torture-and-dragging party he had endured had lasted a long time. I was too short to try to get him down, because his body was fastened to a section of the trunk that resembled a grappling hook.

"The question wasn't repeated, and he appeared to be lapsing into a coma his glasses wouldn't help. In that deep part of the Self inside, where everything seems clear and comprehensible without lenses, in that happy, secure place, once you have left your body at the door and are pursuing rare, happy moments of your life—as if they were butterflies—you might remember your mother's face, a holiday gift, or a moment when you drew a palm tree and a boat in school. Those are neutral moments that don't cause other people to hang you up by a hole in your back and don't make it necessary for your face to be stripped from your skull. These are simple moments that disturb absolutely no one.

"Even though I knew he wouldn't reply, I asked him his name, attempting to extract information that might lead me to his companions or kinsfolk. I grasped his cold foot, which was coated with salty dirt and thorns, and recited some special prayers for forgiveness and healing, because I thought that was what he needed. I assumed he was already dead then, but he moved a little and opened his mouth. 'My name is there,' he said, pointing deliberately to a piece of paper that had fallen, upside down, on the ground. He could have whispered his name, all three parts of it, and even his address, but preferred to point toward the paper. His name didn't seem to suffice. He felt he needed the piece of paper that his executioners had left on his corpse to identify him. The wind must have blown it a few meters away, where it lay in the gray grass.

"I found his name elegantly inscribed in Arabic on the paper with fine ink along with the phrase 'The disgraceful sodomite.'

"Going by the blue lines and the circular hole on the side, I guessed the sheet of paper had been torn from a student's spiral notebook. I thought this likely because most of the religious parties had quickly infiltrated the university and begun to spread their activities, exploiting the students' fiery emotional proclivities toward religion to perpetrate violent acts and cleanse the world of sinners. The American troops camped at the university's entrance paid no heed to this threat and weren't conscious of it.

"I went to search for anyone nearby to help me lift the young man's body down from the tree. Then I heard footsteps fading away and the clamor of vehicles in the distance. I ran toward the street where I found a group of students in dirt-covered clothes, panting from fatigue. I felt a strong hunch that these were the perpetrators who had punished that young man according to their understanding of religious law. When I caught up with them, I saw that the young fellow walking in front was Shaheen. Glasses, you should know that this Shaheen was an acquaintance and fellow student who had seized every opportunity to chastise and mock me for what he called my 'eccentric practices.' Accompanied by his associates, he had made a point of visiting the mosque where I prayed and telling the other students they should quit the place. He convinced many not to pray behind me, because—in his opinion—I was a depraved imam. Most likely he didn't know about my homosexual tendencies, which I concealed completely by waging a ferocious war inside myself to suppress and reject them. What upset Shaheen about me was his belief that I didn't accept the primacy of any of the leading religious figures. His people believed you had to follow a major scholar, a *marjaʿ taqlid*, and imitate his conduct and actions, because he was nearer to God. Every person needed a human model to guide him to God. As far as he was concerned, I was misguided and blind and lacked a guide.

"What made all this even more complicated was that Shaheen and his group did not lack competition. There were a few other cliques with leaders like Shaheen, and each of them followed a certain religious scholar. This created true anarchy, in which even the most attentive people were lost, and a maelstrom that destroyed anyone who thought he understood.

"One afternoon, we heard that a hand grenade had been lobbed at an American soldier from the window of a room inhabited by students, very near the balcony of the small room I shared with eight others. All hell broke loose as soldiers shouted and students fled in terror. I rushed downstairs to attempt to calm the others. Suddenly, all the floors of the building fell silent as students began to whisper to each other to warn against going outside, because the situation was very dangerous. Then I decided to walk slowly to avoid upsetting anyone—to keep anyone from thinking I was up to mischief. But, as I proceeded slowly and cautiously down the steps, I noticed, on my chest, a red spot of light that slowly descended to my belly and then rose to stop at my neck. I froze in place, feeling rattled and anxious. Should I continue downstairs or return to my room, wrap myself inside a heavy blanket, and hide completely from view? The point of light, which came from the weapon of an American soldier who was surveilling the place, came to rest on my mouth. Then it started to dance like a crystalline fly on my nose. After that, it returned to my mouth, and I think it vanished and became lost in my beard.

"I guess the soldier felt he had toyed enough with my body and decided to direct the beam of light beyond me. Perhaps he had discovered another body nearby, because I had gone on my way, walking without hesitation through campus. I was barefoot and held in my hand a rosary of a hundred and one clay beads. I was very pious at that time, and my mind was attempting to focus with great attentiveness on God and only God. For this reason, my face was pale and looked extremely submissive and calm. I wasn't concerned with anything or interested in what people around me were doing.

"While I was walking, my foot touched a piece of paper on the ground. I picked it up and placed it in my pocket without reading it, because I was dominated by a sense of being so involved with God and his saints that I had to ignore anything that would divert me from them. But then I reflected that this might be a spiritual missive from a sacred source, because I believed that all of existence thinks, is telepathic, and sends messages and signs. The contents of this paper might guide me to a new station.

"'We will blow up the American checkpoint at the entrance. Be cautious and stay in your rooms.' I couldn't ignore this paper, which I'd opened, this warning designed to make students feel they needed to be on the lookout and cautious. I was near the entry gate where American tanks and armored vehicles were stationed. So I decided to head there and inform the soldiers about the broadside, so they would do something to guard the students.

"On my way there, I heard whispering behind me and footsteps. I was trailed by three students who prayed at the mosque every day and who consulted me for advice on personal matters. They had opened a spiritual dialogue with me, thinking the best of me and trusting me in an exaggerated way. When I turned toward them, they stopped shyly, because they didn't want to disturb me or interrupt my devotions.

They realized that all moments for me were potentially devotional, even walking and studying. But that was an exaggerated idea. I resumed walking and heard them whispering. One said to another, 'I'm sure he's the one, the Awaited Imam, the Master of Time.' These fellows were fascinated by stories about the arrival of the Expected Imam, the Master of Time, who was comparable to Jesus in some respects. There are many stories about his arrival, when he will meet with a number of people or be incarnated in human bodies. These students nurtured such suspicions about me, believing the Imam's spirit had entered mine. When I drew near an American armored personnel vehicle, I was aware that the students were whispering to each other again. Then I felt even more uncomfortable. I would not be surprised if these fellows informed on me to leaders of other student groups, even though they loved me, because even disciples can do stupid things. So I decided to slow down and wait for them, wishing to speak frankly to them about the matter, because an accusation of cooperating with the Americans could destroy a person and totally ruin his reputation. I wasn't ready for that or prepared to suffer isolation and exclusion.

"I told them I was heading to the Americans at the gate to tell them about the broadsides so they would provide us extra security, investigate the matter, and arrest the group responsible. They exchanged glances, trying to think of a suitable response. I added that seeking assistance from the Americans in such circumstances wasn't prohibited by religion and that we needed to be smart and protect ourselves.

"I didn't leave them before being reassured by tentative smiles on their faces. As I approached the armored personnel vehicle, that red point of light struck me, but it was naughty and focused on my groin. Then it gradually slipped up toward my chest. Morise was on top of the vehicle, pointing his beam at me, toying with my body and addressing me in his own special way.

"That was the decisive moment when the alarm bell rang inside me—about him."

Seventeen

"That soldier wasn't the real Morise. Morise was hidden inside him, concealed behind a heavy machine gun and beneath a camouflage army uniform, a helmet, face scarf, and silver-tinted goggles. All these protective layers separated the real Morise from the alien, rowdy world—teeming with contradictions—that surrounded him. Half his body protruded from the opening of an armored military transport vehicle, which resembled an ancient tortoise that had lost its way in Baghdad. All his senses were clouded by fear, apprehension, and astonishment, except for a new one he had gained the first day he entered the land of Iraq. It was that red point of light he beamed from his weapon to touch moving things he encountered.

"After he realized I was heading toward him, he had to ascertain that I wasn't booby-trapped, that my body wasn't decked out in bombs, and that I wouldn't explode into thousands of bits of metal. His military unit, stationed at the university entrance, tried to treat students properly, to garner their satisfaction and understanding, and to avoid angering them, because upsetting people would drive them to withhold vital information about security threats and attempts to cow civilians. This was the operative theory that Morise's unit adopted as it tried to control the situation, but it wasn't enough to make the soldiers trust all those who approached. Each visitor had to be searched—even a dove holding an olive branch in its beak.

"Behind me, the students who thought I might be a reincarnation of the Twelfth Imam, who lived for thirteen hundred years, began to titter as they compared Morise's complexion to black coal and to a popular type of Iraqi candy, which, because its logo was a drawing of a Black boy, Iraqis commonly called 'slave's head.' My acolytes whispered in my ear, 'Be careful! Today is Thursday!' At first, I didn't understand what they meant. Then I remembered that many people joke that Black Iraqis go berserk Thursday evenings and practice healing trances and spirit possession while invoking African deities. They are alleged to turn into psychotic spastics who act with uncontrollable fury and emotion. Morise didn't understand their Arabic, and that was lucky for all of us. So many things happened during the few meters I traversed to Morise that they seemed to last more than a few minutes. Sensing that time had become viscous and dense, I had trouble transiting the remaining seconds that separated me from Morise, whose name I had not yet learned.

"I turned toward the curious students and gestured for them to move away. I was thrilled that they obeyed me. This was the first time I had ordered them to do anything. They seemed to like being ordered around and for me to play the role of their forbidding commander. They loved being obedient and treated like followers.

"Morise welcomed me in Arabic: *'Marhaba.'* Then he took a small pad from his pocket and began to flip through it, glancing at a list of words he seemed to have learned from passersby, recording them during his brigade's long journey north to Baghdad, because these words, which he pronounced in a very original manner, came from many Iraqi dialects. He was researching how to ask 'How are you?' but before he

215

found that, he uttered the Arabic equivalents of dirty words like 'cunt' and phrases like 'son of a bitch' and 'let me fuck your sister.' He concluded this string of foul expressions with the Arabic for 'I am honored to make your acquaintance.'

"For my part, I chose to remain totally silent until he had concluded the rituals of greeting and searching me. He began by touching my chest and gently poking my waist. Then he sat down to reach toward my thigh, exactly the way his light beam had. He began to move his hands slowly. Then he quickly stood back up as if suddenly remembering something.

"He asked in Arabic, 'Where are you hiding your bomb?' He laughed softly as he said this, his laughter screened by the thick scarf that covered the lower half of his face.

"I had trouble answering him clearly, because my English was broken and ill-suited for kidding around or expressing goodwill. But I understood the gist of what he was saying and confined myself to replying, 'No, no, no.'

"'Do you have something you want to offer us?'

"'Yes, yes, yes,' I responded.

"'No and yes—this is a beautiful little dictionary. I wish all dictionaries were limited to these two words.'

"I handed him the flyer and used both hands to demonstrate that the explosion would occur here, that students would die, and that we needed help.

"He took the paper from me with great interest and began to turn it over. Then he disappeared. In less than a minute, he returned, took my hand, and drew me inside the armored vehicle. Immediately, his questions rained down on me. I didn't notice that I was enclosed in a narrow khaki space inside his tortoise's shell, which smelled of gunpowder. That smell drew me deep into my mind, and I recalled the days when I collected spent shell casings in the desert and took liberties with military detritus. I needed to pay attention to his voice, the sound of his steps, and the way he stared at me. These insalubrious matters took place in insalubrious moments and would make my coming days problematic. It was that one moment out of a lifetime when the protective coating is stripped off our spirits, forcing us to spend the rest of our lives in a state of chronic inflammation. Put another way, we become emotionally vulnerable and may fall in love with all of creation.

"He told me he would take the flyer to his superior officer and explain everything. 'Have no fear. Don't be anxious,' he told me as he removed his goggles and freed himself from the thick coverings over his face, which was revealed bit by bit. This scene resembled discovering a silver coin on the riverbank—the coin glinting among the pebbles and enchanting every eye with its gleam.

"A green twig protruded from under his collar. It was a bright tattoo that seemed to move, sprout, and climb his neck, which was pulsing with muscles.

"At that moment, I sensed that he was shy—no longer the determined man I had just met, the one who kept spelling out dirty words in Arabic. He told me with his eyes that he wasn't that man, or at least that he wasn't anymore. He gestured to me with his index finger to stay put and that he would return shortly. And that was what happened. He returned, though, with a long bag that he placed in my lap, telling me it was my supper. Without hesitating or even inspecting it, I picked up the bag and placed it apologetically beside me. He then put it back on my lap. That didn't surprise me. What did was the way his face seemed to grow angry when he returned the bag of food to my lap. That made me laugh, and I laughed out loud, because the soldier had evidently absorbed some Arab traits and behaviors: when an Arab offers you food or a gift to welcome you and demonstrate his affection for you, you mustn't hand it back; otherwise he will pretend to be angry and announce his categorical rejection of your rejection of his present, because such a rejection insults him. Morise must have learned this from Arab tribes he met on those long, desolate roads from the South.

"As far as I was concerned, my excuse was that I couldn't return to the other students with a bag of food from the Americans. That would be injudicious. Besides, such foods were considered impure, according to the beliefs of many students, especially those waiting for me outside. They would be shocked to see their holy imam carrying a dinner from the 'Crusader Occupation.'

"Morise disappeared again and returned, carrying a few more bags as an expression of his newly acquired grasp of Arab hospitality and of his fondness for receiving security information from a young, holy spy. I was obliged to express my stern rejection of what he was doing. I used my hand to explain that these foods did not meet our religious standards and that I couldn't eat them—that he needed to respect my views and beliefs. I threw in some words of English to clarify my last statement, but didn't know whether he understood, because when words leave the tongue, they assume responsibility for themselves and may betray us after we utter them.

"I said a lot, using words that I thought were English while making a major effort to convey my meaning with my hands, and he followed my attempts with interest. When I readied myself to leave and headed for the door, he quickly locked it. It was now almost dark inside the tortoise.

"I didn't feel at all threatened by him. Fright didn't appear on the list of possible emotions at that time. What I felt was dépaysé. I told myself, This may be the dumbest thing I've done in my whole life. Time had stopped. I heard the giant hands of the hours come to a grinding halt, like Arabian steeds stopping abruptly.

"'I've been watching you for some time from the tower on the hill,' he said, gesturing at the inside of the military vehicle, because we couldn't see outside.

"'When I'm on duty, I use binoculars to watch you slip to the riverbank where you sit, watching ripples in the river for hours. Are you praying? Muslims don't pray like that.'

"'What's your name?' I asked.

"'Morise.'

"'Do you want to know my name?'

"'Your name is Mortada. Everyone in the unit here knows your name. I mean . . . they know your name because of me. I've told them about you.' Then he laughed out loud.

"He seemed to have acquired a lot of information about me by watching me from the tower. I suspect it wouldn't have been hard to learn my name. It would have been easy to ask about the student who led the prayers in the College of Engineering mosque. What was difficult was pronouncing my name, and he did that brilliantly.

"I remembered the students who were waiting for news outside and told him I needed to leave. I never expected him to prevent me from leaving again. He went so far as to stretch out a hand in front of my face to stop me from moving. Then we heard a commotion outside. He asked me to be calm, even though he looked concerned and nervous. It would have been easy for him to make room for me to leave, but he didn't. Those awkward minutes were not of our world. Those moments defied comprehension, because I myself wasn't thinking of leaving. Besides, I was confident he would do whatever he needed to prevent me from quitting the vehicle. That was why I insisted he should let me depart. When I began to speak louder and started to push against his chest to shove his hand away, he threw himself against my body and pressed me against the wall. I pretended that my head had struck the edge of the window and claimed he had hurt me. At that point, he went crazy and seized my head. He began to gently pass his fingers along the alleged site of the nonexistent injury.

"I found my lips were pressed against his lips and discovered the tip of his tongue between his teeth. I closed my eyes, because I realized he had closed his. I sensed that we didn't need sight. The world became quiet and stiller than at any moment in the past. Eventually, time started progressing again, perhaps merely to inform us that this might have been the longest kiss in history. It may have lasted an hour, or a little less. When our lips parted, our lower limbs met and united, only to draw apart and repel each other in a dance of embrace, attraction, and avoidance. Morise was trembling with embarrassment, fear, terror, or happiness—I don't know which. All those were possible, because what he was doing was dangerous and would expose him to a stiff penalty. What I was doing would solicit a bloody death and a catastrophic slaying.

"Our bodies began to shake when intense lust overcame us, and the tortoise made a racket, as the Humvee began to rock noisily. I heard the students waiting outside exclaim, 'Allahu Akbar! God bless Muhammad and his family!' These are expressions of delight Muslims use when they perceive that some charism or miracle has occurred. I think the students believed that their imam had imposed his holy authority over the American infidels, whom he had begun to chastise and counsel so forcefully that their armored vehicle had started to shake. Their minds were completely prepared for me to perform a miracle. Even a half-baked one would have completely satisfied their wishes and desires.

"I asked Morise for permission to leave immediately. He was exhausted and reveling in pleasure, as if he hadn't had sex in a thousand years. He moved his limbs with difficulty, averse to leaving the land atop which he had experienced so much rapture. I asked to leave once more, and he complied with my request, but only after he had kissed my neck, apologized, thanked me, and grabbed the sacks of food to move them away from me, because he now realized that they posed a risk to me. Then he opened the door and gestured how to get out. As I shoved half my body outside, he didn't forget to kiss my hand.

"I left Morise's tortoise, feeling beset by sins. His fiery kiss had incinerated several years' worth of spiritual refinement and progress on the road to God. That's what I was thinking. My whole body—not just my head—was slammed with perplexity. I was searching for suitable phrases to use with the saints and people of God who suddenly appeared in my head, asking me, 'What just happened?' The assembled students had increased in number and curiosity. I wasn't concerned about them and wasn't troubled by their intrusive questions about what had happened inside. I myself did not comprehend what had occurred between me and Morise. These were things a man had to delve into by himself, without help from anyone else. Rare, courageous things take time to understand fully—unlike communal activities in which everyone participates—like riding on a train, invoking God, or going on pilgrimage.

"I walked away, and the students followed me, whispering to one another and offering whatever explanations and commentaries their imaginations suggested. Their numbers doubled, and their chatter grew louder. I could hear its angry tone and their grumbling and abuse. The number of those who thought that a miracle had occurred inside the tank or that some religious victory had been scored began to diminish and dwindle as my former disciples left to spread glad tidings to students who trusted me about how the university's imam had defeated the Americans.

"I was surrounded by the hostile, insolent eyes of those who intended to raise doubts about me. Those who believed in me were far outnumbered by those who couldn't stand me.

"I could not return to my little room that day. I was too scared of the demands for explanations and the questions that would explode from the students' imaginations. Late that night, I slipped in to get my books and lecture notes so I could prepare for the exam on the engineering of drilling oil wells. Then I cast myself on the grass among some short myrtle bushes to read, my feet stretched casually toward the sky. I felt I was an indecent, filthy person who needed to submerge himself completely in running water. That was just what I did later, forgetting that, although I was in a place I usually had all to myself near the river, Morise could see me clearly. I didn't remember that until I had stripped naked and plunged my entire body into the water, feeling the little nibbles of fish on the tips of my toes and hearing the murmur of the rippling water as it embraced me.

"After the exam, I quit the lecture hall abruptly. I needed to be alone and didn't feel like talking to anyone. Silence proved my protective armor against the curiosity of the others. But my silence was broken suddenly when I heard them say, 'They killed him.'

"A troupe of frightened female students had gathered in front of the cafeteria, afraid to make their way through the throng of male students. I heard them repeat, 'They killed him, an American soldier . . . They beheaded him. No, they didn't behead him. They merely put a bullet through his head . . . We saw him dragged across the ground . . . We saw a line of blood left by his feet . . . The poor guy . . . A criminal . . . a barbarian . . . handsome . . . very handsome . . . red like a tomato . . . white like cotton . . . a Crusader . . . friendly . . . not dangerous . . . He came to liberate us . . . He came to seize our oil and to destroy our way of life. To elevate us. To rid us of the current mentality.'

"Voices collided with each other, and people made statements that contradicted each other. But I felt certain that the explosion hadn't happened, that vengeance hadn't been wreaked."

Eighteen

"That night, walking down the corridor that led to my room in the dormitory, I stumbled over a pillow and a pile of books. I felt my little toe slam into a large volume, behind which other books were piled. That tome looked like a dictionary of philosophical terms, but I knew the cover camouflaged a book about lovers' deaths. I knew this because it was my book, which I was reading to learn about the lives of the most famous lovers in Arab cultural history. Most of their tales ended with the phrase 'Then he took one final breath and died.' I won't deny that I was looking in it for homosexual stories, which typically blaze with the most extreme conditions of heartbreak and insane passion. Its fake cover made the book thick and awkward. They must have tossed it out of my room. Here, too, was my belt. That was my box of pens. Here was my pillow, and this was my blanket. A bunch of shirts were stuffed into pant legs. This signaled that they were evicting me. Apparently, the story of my entry into the American tortoise had reached Shaheen and his gang of zealots. That's what I assumed, but my assumption changed when I learned that Shaheen wasn't the only one behind my eviction. Most of my roommates had been looking for an excuse to throw me out because the murder of the American soldier had caused the Americans to enter the dorm, search everywhere, and turn everything upside down. For this reason, many students wanted nothing more than to distance themselves from such dangers.

"I woke when I heard girls' heels clattering near my head. Lifting the blanket, I realized that I had been sleeping in the middle of the campus, where the large fountain's spray dampened my feet. Male and female students walked around me, showing no interest in my presence there. They didn't start laughing until I rose and collected my blanket, my quilt, and my toothbrush. I naturally had to wrap my bedding around me as I walked, especially since I needed to pee badly and my hard, erect penis pushed against my pants. I ran, looking for a place to conceal myself from the students' eyes. I was acting like a wet dog trying to find a hole to hide in. As if that weren't enough, I needed to avoid falling into the hands of the Committee for the Promulgation of Righteousness and the Prohibition of Deviance. Some students had established it to pursue dating couples and coeds whose dresses were too short or who violated its standards of modest attire and behavior. These were all new trends that had appeared at the university with the arrival of the Americans, and that phrase always made me think of Hirjis, who had said, but only to me, 'They brought God with them in an Apache,' which was clearly a phrase that would provoke accusations of blasphemy against anyone who said it.

"Moreover, the map of Baghdad had begun to fill with red scars on Google, each demarcating the location of an explosion. These began to spread over the map's face because of the resistance movement's initiatives, which morphed into sectarian warfare that did not kill nearly so many Americans as it did civilians in the streets, markets, and schools. God, who had arrived by air, as the late Hirjis put it, had begun to flex all his muscles, like a plastic monster doll. I think that was the day I stopped going to the mosque and decided I would never set foot in a place of communal worship again—but not because I didn't feel pure enough to pray, for this was a foregone conclusion. Instead, I was brooding about the meaning of prayer and about its value in its typical form, which I had practiced. Then I began to postpone its set times a lot and plunge more into reflection, contemplation, and a hearkening to the movement of things around me. This was like placing yourself inside an invisible monastery you carry around with you as you circulate among people, feeling both a profound isolation and a happy, positive solitude—while surrounded by throngs of people.

"'Have you seen my slave? Our Excellency has heard you were playing with him.' I wasn't surprised to hear that voice. What dismayed me was her use of the word 'slave.' Iraqis on the street refer to African Americans as slaves and use the same word—'abd—for Arab slaves. Even though the term is frequently used without any reference to slavery, language can often overcome thought. On the other hand, *Abd* is frequently an extremely beautiful part of the name of many Iraqis of different complexions—as in *Abd Allah*. Usually when Iraqis want to refer to a person from the Black minority population in the South, they will say, 'This is a slave,' using the word 'abd, and then add the traditional caveat, 'But we are all slaves of God.'

"I thought she was exaggerating, because my 'play' with the American soldier inside the military vehicle hadn't been witnessed by anyone else and was an event I myself tried not to remember, because I didn't want to believe it had happened.

"There was no need for me to wonder about the source of the voice or ask myself who had spoken, because the voice of Queen Aliya was known to everyone at the university. She was a woman in her thirties who wore elegant garments typical of the 1950s or 1960s and pretended she was Queen Aliya, mother of the late king, who had ruled before the appearance of Republican regimes in Iraq. When that young king was killed in a coup in 1958 along with numerous members of his family (his mother had already died in 1950), his body was dragged over the pavement, and his fingers were hung like garlands from the windows and balconies. Decades later, the 'new' Queen Aliya conducted herself like the late queen, treating people with exaggerated condescension. Her appearance made one think she had just stepped offstage after performing in a tragedy or had slipped out of a scene from a historical film about the decline of the eras of the kings and their monarchies. All the students thought she was batty and ignored her, avoiding any contact with her.

"Before the Americans arrived, people feared the deranged, homeless people who wandered the streets, because the prevailing assumption was that such people worked for the authorities, who sent them throughout the city to spy on citizens and inform on anyone who harbored negative feelings about the president. Such miscreants, once identified, would be tortured in the cells of the Ministry of Security. After the Americans arrived, there were many fewer such crazed beggars, but people were still scared of these madmen, who tried to provoke people by mocking conditions and impersonating historical figures or by using political expressions that seemed off base but contained elevated wisdom. Some would misbehave and use unwholesome language, picking this vocabulary from the depths of society's vocabulary and behavior or inspired by suppressed traits rising from deep within our society's unconscious essence.

"I did not answer her because I was preoccupied by looking for a safe spot where I could set up camp far from the eyes of the students. That was what I intended to do as I walked in the shadow along the walls, shielding myself, till I reached my favorite spot on the riverbank. I could be safe here, as I suspected Morise might see me from the distant hill through his binoculars.

"I fashioned a small tent from some clothes and arranged my books inside it before submerging myself completely in the river. When I left the water, I found Queen Aliya reclining inside my little tent, totally naked, and turning with some difficulty to stay in the shade because her corpulent body did not fit. Her feet and head poked out of opposite ends of the tent, which concealed her belly and massive breasts. Because my eyes still were well trained and habituated to avoid looking at women's forbidden regions—training that did not extend to nude men—I turned my face away and asked her to draw her legs in and cower inside the tent because I feared looking at her would expose me to dangers. When she ignored me, I was obliged to shove her feet inside.

"In the distance, on the far side of the river, a column of gray smoke rose into the sky, disrupting the V shape of a flock of cormorants in flight.

"'My God, shield us! My Lord, my Preserver, if the number seven is disturbed, something major will occur,' Queen Aliya said, pointing to the birds' formation, which had been shaped like the Arabic number seven—a large V. She seemed to think this development was a bad sign and an evil omen.

"The queen's body disappeared entirely into the tent while she rifled through my possessions. Minutes later, she emerged, carrying my rosary and prayer rug.

"'Here! I'll pray behind you. Let's pray. I want to repent before the army enters and kills my son and our family.' She was referring to the Iraqi army storming the royal palace in 1958, killing the king and much of his family.

"I complied with her request and spread out my prayer rug and began to pray, oblivious to her standing naked behind me. She ran her fingers through her long, dyed hair, making a sound like leaves rustling.

"Morise had certainly never observed a sight like this. He must have been up there on top of that hill, watching through his binoculars as a young man prayed and a naked woman imitated him, while he served as her imam for prayer. She prostrated herself, kneeled, and moved her head when he did to show her piety and devotion.

"But we did not complete our prayer because we heard a drumbeat of footsteps drawing nearer and some shots. A unit of American soldiers arrived to occupy our favorite place on the riverbank. They encircled us and quickly dismantled my tent. They placed a sack over my head and slipped a gown over Queen Aliya. We walked a few paces with them, only to find ourselves inside an armored transport vehicle. I knew from the smell of gunpowder, gear, and the laughter of the gung ho soldiers.

"We didn't drive far, because they deposited me and the queen near the university campus and quickly removed our blindfolds. Before they undid my fetters, I found myself walking in a spear-shaped phalanx of soldiers. The first soldier kept his right hand stretched before me, as if to protect and shield me from the eyes of the grim-faced students who watched while I was led to my room, from which I had been evicted.

"The soldier kicked open the door, pulled me inside the room by my hand, and sat me down on my bed. Before he turned to leave, he lifted his goggles above his kerchief just enough for me to see he was Morise. He left me staring at the walls and asking myself whether what he had done was normal protocol or whether it should be chalked up to the stupidity of people who wished to demonstrate their honorable intentions. I wasn't even thinking of the possible consequences or whether a truly courageous person would take risks without considering the dangers. What had Morise told himself when he returned me to the room from which I had been evicted along with my toothbrush, books, clothing, and what was left of my tarnished honor? Had he considered what the student militias would do to me as they became ever more daring and vicious? I did not reach any satisfactory conclusion, because events began to accelerate, eliminating any opportunity for reflection. I spent a few hours almost rigid in my room, which Morise had liberated from my hostile roommates. The other students were too anxious or shocked to enter, and I was hesitant to go out, for fear of verbal or physical abuse.

"At sunset, Shaheen entered. I avoided looking him in the eye and limited myself to pretending to look at the fly shit sticking to the blades of the ceiling fan. Eventually, after he gave up trying to engage me in conversation, he launched into a one-sided diatribe.

"'Just as I expected! Do you know? I've never hesitated for a moment to doubt you. What really stuns me is the way these praying asses trusted you, placed their confidence in you, followed your example. Is anything more outrageous than such contempt for prayer? Don't think I'm referring to the entertaining books you read to pass the time or the naked bodies you sketch in the margins of books— showing women's breasts and naked men with rippling muscles. Nor should you think this is criticism of how affable you are with everyone, smiling grotesquely at everyone, even if they are filthy infidels or sinners. You put them all into one basket. You're fond of them all and love them all, and they love you. You have never once dared display a surly face to deviants to remind them of their sins. No, I'm not referring to any of this. If you think I mean the way you exchange greetings with Americans and sit with them, you are mistaken too. Many pimps do that nowadays. We live in a time when fraternizing with the Crusader Occupation is considered normal. My God! I don't mean any of this. But you know exactly what I do mean.'

"As Shaheen spoke, he perspired profusely and followed my pupils, which moved around the room and focused on specific points, looking at everything except Shaheen's face. That may have unnerved him, but I do not doubt that it also emboldened him in the choice of his words. This was the first time that Shaheen had been able to level some clear charge against me. It was also the first time he seemed capable of speaking to me without stammering. Shaheen had a stentorian voice and a religious diction that deliberately added a musical coda to the ends of sentences. He had long been awkward around me and had had trouble producing a meaningful sentence in my presence.

"I had met Shaheen in the heavy crude oil laboratory at the department. He used his right leg to walk and move around, totally ignoring his left. Students assumed he had suffered an accident and broken a leg while he still had classes to attend and exams to take. This wasn't true. At the time, Shaheen belonged to a secret spiritual society. I knew some of its other members from the time when I lived in the dormitory complex that was surrounded by whorehouses. Based on leaks from those students, I learned that Shaheen had committed some sin for which his spiritual mentor punished him by forbidding him the use of one leg for a week. Sins for such people were simple matters, like having sexual thoughts about a woman's body or imagining an incredibly beautiful girl's face. Caressing a woman rose to the level of major sins, and such actions belonged to an unthinkable category. After that one week, Shaheen appeared with a paralyzed hand. The pretend bandage on his hand was strapped to his neck, and I learned that he had committed quite a minor sin and that his punishment was not to use his hand for the allotted time. Shaheen apparently revolted against his teacher after he heard about me, met me, and spent time with me. Then Shaheen found another way to refine and train his ego and raft over the white waters of his spirituality!

"My goal was to affirm that what they were doing made no sense and defied logic and the teachings of ethics. Shaheen had come to me submissively, fed up with his former group, and my analysis of his condition was that he was booby-trapped by psychological burdens and concerns. He told me about his father's pattern of domestic violence. The man had constantly beaten Shaheen's mother, who paid him back twofold when he lost a leg in the war. She then became the man of the family and started to beat him, humiliate him, and burden him with household chores. One day, Shaheen felt he needed to share a deep secret he had been keeping to himself. He admitted he brooded a lot about the band of men his mother received in their house, within sight and hearing of his father. I tried to help him think the best of the situation and shed those negative, obsessive thoughts about his mother. But he began to bawl and wail as he placed his head in my lap. That proved an excellent opportunity for me to delve deep with him and demolish his weird former religious ideas and the training he had received with his former mentor.

"After two continuous months with me, Shaheen recovered his equilibrium and returned to his senses. After the fall of the regime, he joined a group affiliated with Muqtada al-Sadr, the son of the Sadr who was killed by Saddam. Muqtada al-Sadr created a militia to combat the Americans and to prepare for the appearance of the Prophet Muhammad's offspring, who would rule the world and dominate the terrestrial sphere. His previous confessions to me disturbed him more than his indignation at my refusal to join their group. Shaheen was no longer as spiritual as he had been. He became prone to violence and enamored of domination and leadership. This totally contradicted the teachings of the previous spiritual paths he had pursued.

"I couldn't get him to stop haranguing me. I had bundled up my possessions to be ready to leave the dorm room. When I headed toward the door, he rose and blocked me. He shoved me back and shut the door. He fastened his arms around my body as if to embrace me, pressed hard against my chest, and when he noticed that I was preparing to knee him in the belly, he headbutted me and called to his companions, who were outside the door. Then the room filled with five members of his gang.

"It took them only a few minutes to tie me to the legs of the bed. All I could do was curse them, but I chose the best and most ferocious expletives I could muster—words as sharp as poison-tipped arrows that continue to wound their victim, no matter how long he lives. I dealt with them one by one, discussing their psychological flaws, social diseases, and major fears. In response, they started punching me with fists of steel, and I felt my face explode with sparks and words like ashes.

"The final scene that Shaheen staged for me was ordering his gang to untie my bonds to the bed. They merely pulled my arms together and joined my legs. Then I asked them for a pillow.

"They fetched a pillow from outside the room. It was one of those sold in the government-run markets in the 1980s. It had daffodils and the words 'Good Morning' embroidered on it. I ordered them to place the pillow beside me, near my head.

"'Sleep well,' Shaheen said as he left with his gang. They didn't forget to lock the door, from the outside.

"About two hours after they left, my body relaxed, and I stretched out on the pillow. Then I dozed off, surrendering to the sovereignty of a deep sleep. I didn't wake up till I heard pounding on the door and the shouts of Queen Aliya. To my surprise, Americans burst in, led by Morise. They succeeded in severing my bonds, but I didn't see Queen Aliya. I was sure I had heard her voice at the door, and that made me look around to search for her face in the spaces that the soldiers' bodies left as they crowded into the room.

"'Do you feel better now?' asked Queen Aliya, whose face I had searched for unsuccessfully.

"The voice came from a smiling American servicewoman who spoke colloquial Iraqi Arabic fluently.

"'Let me introduce G.M.,' Morise said, pointing to the woman, who clearly was also Queen Aliya, the batty vagrant.

"'G.M. is an Iraqi translator who works with us. She will help me . . . help us converse with you,' Morise added.

"The first thing G.M. told me in her capacity as translator, rather than Queen Aliya, was that the pillow embroidered with the phrase 'Good Morning' had been stuffed with hand grenades and bombs."

Nineteen

Josie excelled at something he called "the art of looking at art downtown." I substituted the following for his phrase: "Walking with Josie and the art of feeling that you are part of his wheelchair or a ring dangling from his ear." The murals along the narrow alleys looked different when I walked with him. His mouth was a fringe that framed the brushstrokes of the street artists—a fringe that stole the street art's gleam by describing it and thus creating a different artwork of comparable brilliance.

We were heading to a black tower that rose like a seal on the waterfront, because located inside it was a video game company that, Josie thought, needed a character designer like me. As we crossed the street to the entrance, he handed me a band of paper, asking me to place it around a coffee cup. "Put this on your cup and hold it up as you walk. Try to make this sign visible to anyone looking at you."

The logo on the band was registered to Starbucks. He had pulled it from beneath his vehicle, from a sack filled with bands bearing the logos of various brands. He placed one on his own coffee cup and handed me the other as if adding cream or sugar to the coffee. I felt he was pretending to be a barista, providing the finishing touches to my coffee.

We found the entrance closed and left without waiting. I didn't ask him why he wanted us to have the logo on our cups, but he told me anyway. "You can call this the art of preventing people from thinking you're a vagrant."

I got that and was able to understand him as I gazed at his face, which disclosed more to me each time. I was donning a new veil to safeguard me from being mistaken for a vagrant. A pebble was tossed into my memory, making ripples in it. Then I noticed that he was a few steps ahead of me. I raced to catch up, feeling I could allow my memory to bleed.

"Listen, Josie:

"Toward the end of the penultimate year of our BS program, there were fewer helmets and more turbans: 'Inverse Correlation: Oil Is Marines' Wine,' read the headline of a local newspaper. Images of imams were descried on the surfaces of ponds and on walls, and people created dozens of fantasy mausoleums. Arab and non-Arab militants began to slip into Iraq to resist the Americans, who had entered the country, leaving the door open behind them. People's tongues described strange creatures and beasts they claimed were starting to appear in the desert and outfitted them with special effects better suited to horror films. Fantasies reigned supreme in Baghdad, and the Baghdadis' fascination with the image of the American soldier began to fade. No longer regarded as incarnations of Nietzsche's Übermensch, the American soldier now seemed an ordinary person. Americans passing in the streets no longer possessed the magical characteristics, which Iraqis had initially attributed to them, of space pioneers. These Americans ate and drank like us and perhaps even defecated too.

"Companies in southern Iraq, where major oil fields were located, competed to recruit petroleum engineers subsequent to the arrival of flocks of large investors and small contractors affiliated with influential religious figures, months after the government announced it would award major contracts to dozens of Chinese, British, French, Dutch, Russian, and German firms for the extraction of Iraqi oil. For some unexpected and unknown reason, America did not receive any of these large contracts. That might come after the gradual withdrawal of America's forces.

"Morise believed that a new life was destined for me after the pillow incident. The phrase 'Good Morning,' which was embroidered on the pillow with linen thread and which Morise asked Aliya to translate, was revealed to be a terrifying, lethal expression. I had placed my cheek that day on a pillow filled with three bombs, in other words grenades, referred to in Arabic as 'pomegranates' because they resemble this sacred fruit, which is celebrated widely in our cultural heritage. For some unknown reason, the trigger on those grenades malfunctioned, even though they remained active. One of the soldiers had felt something rough on a side of the pillow at the American checkpoint to which Morise and his unit escorted me. With my sacks of clothes and a few other possessions, I began a new chapter during those days—a chapter entitled 'My Homeless Life as a Freeloader on the Riverbank, Where the Night Sounds of Insects Provide Background Music.'

"Morise frequently commented, as if he were of two minds about me: 'Part of me says that this is the courage of someone who is oblivious to danger and thinks every person should speak his truth and show himself, because what is life if not a collection of courageous hearts that do not cherish the truce on which everything humanity has achieved depends. Another part of me says this is sheer stupidity, because nothing is dearer than one's spirit, which should not be scorned by exposing it to fatal consequences.'

"I don't know what Morise would think if he heard what I am saying now. Part of me says to tell all. Another part says to tell nothing. The reckless part could care less about what other people say, hoping that my daring will open the way for thousands of suffering people and give them a voice they can rely on in their times of need, to make up for their voices that have been silenced. The other part of me is soaked in other people's acidic and injurious words, which ignore what it means to be crushed with pain and to live in a phony abyss.

"I told Morise, 'Other people's vinegary remarks are a blend of what they think of us and of what they want us to be. They are bacteria that coexist with values they don't support, except in so far as those values pertain to us. When we grow up, read, learn, and mingle with others, we find that even the cultured people and writers around us treat freedom of thought like a plastic cup they use once and throw in the trash—after *they* have utilized it to express *their* opinions. There is no room for my opinion or yours in this tumult and cacophony.' That's what I told Morise—or perhaps it's something I told myself. I'm not sure, because our minds began to respond to a single master and to perform the same dance.

"The remnants of a statue stood in front of the university's central library, where I daily spent many hours studying. The statue had been reduced to a concrete plinth on which stood two amputated legs—all that remained on the campus of the deposed president Saddam Hussein. The students had dressed the rest of the body in a graduation cap and gown and dragged it away, days after the Americans' entry. They had thrown it into the river like a sacrificial offering to expiate the sins of this earth, which had been defiled by idolatrous tyrants. For my part, I commemorated the incident with a cartoon that was published in the student newspaper, attracting a lot of attention from professors and students. I portrayed Saddam's statue falling to the ground and being dragged away by people and then breaking into tiny pieces, each of which turned into a new statue. It was a parable about how the character of a tyrant saturates the minds of many other people, transforming them into little Saddams, as a despot's evils are distributed to little spirits and then grow and multiply.

"I considered the congratulatory, appreciative card I received from the head of a strict Islamic party to be a thank-you and an expression of goodwill. These people considered me to be one of them, even after the news spread of the Americans' rescue, which cost me my reputation as a virtuous man behind whom one might pray. All the same, this affection and goodwill did not last long, because I submitted another drawing to the publication a week later. The new drawing depicted the same statue, standing upright in its original position. No one was dragging it away. No one was taking it down. It was Saddam, but this time he sported a black turban on his head. The message was that Islamists supporting Saddam were Saddam himself, but with a turban. Even if you removed his helmet or cap and replaced it with a turban, he remained the same crook. I don't know how this drawing found its way to internet sites, but that probably contributed a lot to undermining my personal security. This has been one of my longstanding traits—I have caused myself many problems, drawn unfavorable attention to myself, and raised questions. I would draw everything that popped into my head, defying my father's advice to restrain myself. He had seen the corpses of too many young men tossed onto dump heaps for having expressed themselves. I disobeyed my father—I don't know why—by writing, speaking out, and criticizing what I saw, without worrying about the consequences, regardless of being in a particular region or a time period when no one had a right to speak his truth. In such circumstances, you must become very duplicitous and as skillful as a chameleon at hiding amid the weeds. These weeds may crowd in upon you and crush you, but if that happens, you will not yourself have turned into a thorn that pursues peaceful people.

"Morise asked me to stand beside that broken statue at sunset every day and look at my wristwatch to signal that I was okay. I didn't ask him how he would see me. I knew it was pointless to ask, because his mighty binoculars could locate anything. He told me once how he saved the life of a dove when, with those binoculars, he saw a yellow snake slither toward it. He woke up the dove by shooting a bullet into the wall on which the bird had built its nest.

"'He saves a dove but wouldn't hesitate to kill me,' I said, flirting with him.

"Because he was quick-witted, he shot back, 'Warriors always call for peace.' It was years before I discovered he had borrowed this phrase from a book on the art of war.

"I found an opportunity to work in a small printshop near the neighborhood where our dormitory had been in the days of the president. Thus, I knew this district very well and remembered all its details. I recalled the faces of its prostitutes and pimps and even of the brothels' most famous patrons, because the dorm windows had acted as a cinema screen through which I viewed Baghdad's version of Hollywood and especially the dank alleyways through which wafted musty air and the terror of women fleeing from kinsfolk. Interestingly, the owner of the printshop was a rich man who liked to drape a traditional headcloth over his shoulder and let it flow down his back. He grew comfortable with my work ethic and, after two full months, decided I deserved to become his assistant. He may have felt he could trust me because I pretended to pray, and my beard had grown long. I don't think my gift for finding the right word, correcting advertisements, and proofreading proselytizing religious texts excited him or attracted his attention. His printshop hummed with special projects—printing religious booklets and election brochures—but he demonstrated no interest in ensuring that these publications looked attractive. He used to say, 'These are sorry faces we shouldn't harbor in our printshop for even one night.' His first concern was a quick turnaround with no interruption or fact-checking for election-campaign materials. Those were plastered with politicians' faces, which looked well tanned—thanks to Photoshop color correction. He confessed privately that he felt that the ads were bad omens, and joked about the election slogans. Even so, he wouldn't do that publicly. He would mutter those grumbling expressions only to me, blowing them up like balloons that only I could see.

"I told him my story and how I literally lived as a vagrant between the Americans' tank and my campsite on the riverbank, where I would fish but then throw each fish back because I felt sorry for it. My personal safety could not be guaranteed in the student dormitory, but I had a limited security clearance I could use to enter lecture halls to complete my studies and to take exams. He rolled up his sleeves and pursed his lips to demonstrate his intense concern about the matter. Then he asked me to give him a few weeks. During those days, Morise was trying to write to me in Arabic, assisted by Aliya, the translator and Her Royal Highness, who had stopped playing that role after some students found out about her. She had then decided to fabricate a story about the murder of the madwoman known as Queen Aliya, in order to practice her original profession as a translator embedded with the Americans—or, to be more precise, as an unofficial translator between me and Morise, even though I didn't have much difficulty conversing with him because my English was gradually improving. The real problem was his desire to speak Arabic to me. He found it immensely entertaining, even though it left me flat on my back, kicking my feet in the air as I was laughing so hard when he spoke a proper sentence in Arabic. In those days, I wore a light turban that one of the religious men I met at mausoleums bestowed on me, saying that the person who donned it would surpass hundreds of the students he himself had encountered. He said he felt I deserved that turban. He taught me how to wind it and explained to me that it was woven from pure camel hair. It was expensive and reserved for exceptional students of the religious sciences. I wore it stubbornly in the presence of Shaheen's gang. According to Morise, I wore it out of spite, not stubbornness. I didn't wear it all the time, however. I would put it on occasionally but usually didn't wear it. People who made a pretense of being religious shunned this practice, because they considered doffing one's turban disreputable and an affront to true religion.

"The printshop proprietor did eventually broach the possibility of my living in the little house adjoining the back of the shop. I accepted his offer immediately, raising my eyebrows, frozen with shock because I was so happy. It wasn't a house in the literal meaning of the word; it was more like a shipping container. But the printshop proprietor used a metonym instead of a metaphor to refer to it when he made the offer. 'I'll let you live for an entire year in the stork's nest,' he said, referring to the small tower that extended three meters above the tiny house's kitchen. Bird shit, straw, and string fell from the tower, and plastic bags fluttered off it like naval pennants. It did not serve as a stork's nest while I lived there but contained the remnants of a venerable, long-occupied nest that storks had vacated because they didn't like the war—explosions, the sound of artillery, and the whine of airplanes. The name had persisted, though, and Morise and I decided to use 'stork' to refer to the house.

"Morise wasn't satisfied with occupying Iraq with his buddies. I accused him in jest of 'liberating' my little house with them. At first, he would find some suitable excuse for a visit—like searching for suspects on my street, which was the last place fugitives from justice

would live back then. Most residents of that street were prostitutes, madams, or pimps, whose circumstances had changed dramatically since the occupation. They had announced their repentance and browned their foreheads with the bottoms of hot cups to simulate a prayer mark there. They made a point of praying as loudly as they had once shouted to attract johns. One day, while I was reading on my balcony, which resembled a coffin, I heard a penitent woman criticize her mistress for prostrating herself too much. Then the whole street erupted with the risqué laughter that whores excel at prolonging harmoniously. The street's dignified piety vanished for a few seconds, before its serenity returned.

"None of this prevented him from coming—inventing a new story every time. I won't deny that I began to watch for his arrival and listened attentively, with both ears, for the sound of a military vehicle stopping near my house—the stork's nest—even if he never succeeded in pronouncing the two instances of the Arabic letter *qaf* in the Arabic word for 'stork.' I suggested he just say *laklak* instead of *laqlaq*.

"The sight of three American armored vehicles in front of the stork's nest excited the curiosity of the niqab-wearing women, who would open the doors of their houses and release a shameless laugh. Because their faces were veiled, I never succeeded in tracing the laughter to the actual woman laughing, especially since she would cut short her laughter the moment she remembered she was no longer a whore at whose door men formed a queue, nor was she standing half-naked at her window, chewing gum and relentlessly rubbing her groin.

"While his companions treated my house like an archeological site for foreign tourists enraptured by the magic of the East and messed around with my pots, kettles, spoons, books, and pens, over which they ran their fingers with phony admiration, Morise would sit on the floor beside my bed, asking me any questions he wanted. It is a taxing situation when someone besieges you with his glances and scans you with the rays of his eyes, from the arch of your foot to the crown of your head, and you can't escape the scrutiny of his senses for even a few seconds. When he stops his investigation and allows you to be at ease, you exhale profoundly as if you have just escaped from a critical situation. All the same, you yearn for him and ask him to repeat that all over again. People who love us allow themselves to prowl around inside us, even when we're separated from them. When we're together, they play a role and focus on our forehead as if it were the diamond on a ring.

"He would ignore the other soldiers while they went through my cupboard. He would raise a hand to tap my nipple as if it were a cherry and then ask me to speak, to tell him the truth—what I was truly thinking about—and shove aside the solid rock that normally sat on my chest and prevented me from speaking.

"This proved an excellent incentive for me to speak and to tell him the truth. I would continue talking till he fell asleep with his head on my thigh. Then I felt that an entire orphanage was dozing on my body and that I shouldn't move for fear of waking the kids.

"There is no way for me to characterize this stage of our relationship. I don't remember having any plan in mind. The only thing I knew for sure was that I was experiencing an amazing adventure that encapsulated my life. I basked in the attention of his eyes as they devoured my face—its fat, flesh, and bones—without considering the future, perhaps because the morrow always arrived with Morise as part of it. He would knock on the door, and I would clasp his hand. Then he would kneel by the bed first, before he leaped on it and coupled with me. This brief pause was his way of apologizing for what had happened inside the armored military transport vehicle. We would draw out our lovemaking, turn it into a rite, repeat it, and squeeze the last drop of pleasure from it, to keep that day inside the tank from ever ending, to revive it and to reestablish it.

"When I bought a used TV from a flea market, Morise helped me pick shows and watched while I flipped channels. When recitation of the Qur'an came on, I started to change the channel and look for a foreign film. He immediately seized my hand and asked me to return to the Qur'an channel. When I did, his face lit up, and a strange force permeated his body. Seeing this disappointed me. I didn't like that aspect of Morise, who seemed soft and transparent when exposed to spirituality. That may have been because I wasn't ready for this difference: he was entering Islam just when I was leaving it entirely. What diluted my grumpiness was his immediate candor. He told me he wasn't thinking of becoming Muslim, but that religious music made his heart palpitate, and of course the whole Qur'an can be chanted. This one statement didn't convince me, and I felt he ought to press the candor button harder. Then he told me that for five years he had practiced an African faith that required him to become someone's disciple. Typically, the religion of the guru didn't matter. To make successful contact with his guide, Morise needed to understand him better, to research his circumstances, and to understand his culture. Chance had made his mentor a Muslim.

"This made sense to me and caused me to be less suspicious about Morise's infatuation with Islamic texts.

"Letting him revel in the sound of the Qur'an reciter, I went to make cardamom tea. In a few minutes, I heard the soldiers shouting at each other. Apparently, one of them had seized the remote control and begun to switch channels. They had ruined Morise's enjoyment, and I couldn't do anything about that. After I returned with the tea, Morise's huge white comrade, whose every word defied my comprehension, tormented Morise by changing channels every thirty seconds. Morise chased him through the house, trying to wrest the controller from him. That made me leap frantically and grab it. I noticed that they all calmed down then and began to act like soldiers. Apparently, my frantic leap had disconcerted them, and they felt cowed by my anger. It was hard for me to explain what had come over me. I spouted words in Arabic without completing any sentences. The calm that reigned in the house made the announcer's voice seem louder than usual. He was an old man who could barely complete a sentence without sighing between words. He threatened, castigated, and menaced deviants, evildoers, and those who violated customs and traditions—as he put it. Such a person would have his head cut off and his body crucified if he so much as touched an unveiled woman or a profligate young man.

"The other soldiers were downcast. Morise grasped my foot and squeezed it. He didn't want to try to calm me in an overt way his comrades would notice, because he did not wish to reveal his homosexuality to them. When we were with people, we were just friends, and that continued for some time. Morise was gay but continued to conceal his body's secrets, keeping them hidden from other people, especially from his soldier pals, who apparently weren't comfortable with homosexuality.

"'You didn't succeed in cutting it, Morise,' I said, finally concocting an entire English sentence that was grammatically sound.

"'Who? Cutting what? Are you okay, *habibi*?' He used this Arabic word, because he was sure his comrades didn't understand its meaning—'my love'—but, as usual, he had picked the wrong *h* sound.

"'That's Mahiya! That politician on the screen is Mahiya! I know that woman very well, Morise.'

"'Woman?'

"The politician looked like a man. The line at the bottom of the screen said this man headed the Religious Virtue Party in my hometown, but the line supplied no other information. I had heard the man's voice before but hadn't watched him speak. I had seen him hundreds of times while printing politicians' election posters, which passed before me on the printshop tables and rollers, with decorative elements in green, which was the color held sacred by Mahiya's party—Mahiya, who was no longer Mahiya, but, no more and no less, Mahiya. I told Morise the story without any marginal comments or details, because that would have required me to dig deep with him into a boy's days and nights of gathering spent shell casings from a peninsula of scorched palm trees.

"Before that night ended, Morise gave me a book approximately the size of my hand but rather thick. On its cover was the picture of a man kneeling and holding his cross. That was my introduction to James Baldwin and his book *Go Tell It on the Mountain*, the first book I read all the way through in English. It opened the door for me to Morise's imaginative world, the world from which he had sprung and where he had lingered more than anywhere else. It was an opening: Baldwin poured a lot of light into the stork's nest, and his light continued to expand and extend until it opened the door completely and I found myself madly in love."

Twenty

In the three monkeys' house, no one believed in mailboxes. Josie was responsible for this. He felt a special attraction for mail carriers. Liao also felt they possessed an attractive magic. To explain Josie's peculiar infatuation with everything related to the mail, Erick used Pavlov's theory about dogs that were trained to eat when a bell rang and then became hungry every time they heard the bell ring.

Thus, Josie was responsible for the mail, which occupied a major part of his day, and that chore made him his happiest. He would overflow with an enthusiasm that filled his body. His hands would dance as he guided his wheels between our rooms to distribute the mail.

When he knocked on my door, I was busy drawing. I had received a grant to create a moving picture called *Language*. It was based entirely on the story of Hirjis, the blind man who read the braille of crevices. When I draw, I retreat entirely into myself, and my perception of the world grows weaker. He had to go to some effort to rouse me and extract me from my solitude. Because the smells and look of multiple packages delight me, I couldn't restrain myself from immediately opening the large envelope he placed before my eyes. It was clearly a book, but the sender had wrapped it inside so many layers of bags that it resembled a cabbage.

I must admit that I wept when I touched the book, smelled its fragrance, and read its cover. It was *Go Tell It on the Mountain*—the book Morise had given me. Wasn't that enough to explain my panic and shock? These emotions lingered for some minutes as hope's light flooded over me again. I turned the pages, one at a time, searching for the stains of salty tears and remembering that we had opened the book repeatedly to search for stains from dried tears, which we circled in black ink. We treated tears like precious ruins and encouragements. Therefore, Baldwin's book was filled with little circles, the meaning of which only Morise and I knew.

With Baldwin's book before me, I started to feel again that somewhere on this planet another person existed. This may seem a strange way for my relationship with Morise to manifest itself, but I saw only him then and not the other people and creatures around me. This may therefore seem an infirmity. I would tell myself that my intense belief that I was special lubricated my spiritual engines and that each person has his own special spiritual oil, for which he can't substitute any other.

"I found this book on the bus with a bank envelope containing receipts inside it. Your address was on the envelope. I hope this is your correct address." I found this note on a slip of paper inside the package. Then I realized that someone had found the book on the bus and generously and kindheartedly returned it to me. I had forgotten that I lost the book. Here was a stranger finding it and returning it to me. My happiness did not last long—or let's say my artificial happiness, which

I had inflated and created with my hand to deceive myself. The stranger who had found the book had included her name and address.

So I sent her a letter: "Thank you. You made me very happy for five minutes. I draw dogs. Do you have a dog I can draw free of charge?"

Two days later, I received her response: "My husband loves raccoons, and his fortieth birthday is next week. It would be really sweet of you to draw him a cute raccoon as a surprise."

I drew an innocent raccoon that held a sign reading "I'm in Seattle, where are you?" and sent it to the lady. I didn't forget to add salty little circles falling from the sign. She might think they were leaves or just spots on the body of the raccoon, which had to be laughing since this was a birthday present. She would never know the meaning of those circles, but Morise and I did.

A week earlier, the three monkeys had arranged an event for me at the benevolent organization where they worked. Erick had suggested I give a talk there, and Josie had placed it at the top of his list of priorities. I even saw he had tucked a note about it beneath his armpit. He brought that out to excite my enthusiasm, because Josie believed I was very shy—a young man who was bashful and limited in his words and language. Liao, for his part, sat with me briefly while he told me about the organization, which helped many people; it wasn't limited to HIV-positive people. Many needs were met there. I won't claim that I did much to prepare for this talk, perhaps because I wanted to speak about Mahiya, her story, her long struggle, and how her life ended. In addition to her story, I wished to discuss people whose lives resembled hers, those who live in an alien body, surrounded by a very problematic society with inhibitions and complexes about people with fluid gender identities. That meant I would speed like an arrow to recounting a story to the audience, because I was talking about matters I had experienced myself and had considered from every direction. Even today, I don't know whether I did a good job or not. The people's eyes in the audience helped me find the right expressions and keep the sequence of events in order. During my talk, I became conscious of the profound boundary that separates people here in Seattle from people back there in Iraq. I noticed in their eyes that everyone expected me to present myself as a refugee who was grateful for being saved from certain destruction, not because those present wanted to feel proud of the praiseworthy boons this country affords them, shielding them from annihilation, torture, and violence, but because the language of gratitude is more easily understood than other tongues. Imprecise simplification was preferable to using complicated and precise ideas. I was expected to don the cloak of a refugee whom the white man had freed (with democracy and respect for human rights) from the bestial third world, which overflows with injustices, atrocities, and terror. Besides, I wouldn't be understood otherwise, although I don't mean I would have been shunned by the audience. Moreover, I didn't know anything about the nature of the audience. I might as well have been speaking in the dark and delivering my opinion inside a well—a well with its own special vocabulary and ways of understanding things and strangers. The matter was perplexing.

Mahiya's story and accounts of people like her stirred the hearts of many of those present. They heard all my words and understood some of them. I noticed the three priests in the back row. They gazed at my face with interest, which they showed with their eyebrows and fingers, pumping out the lubrication I needed. But I, for my part, was a special puppet that could be lubricated only by Morise.

"You're a traitor!" shouted someone who stood up in the next-to-last row. He was an old man, seventy or slightly younger. He raised his voice and bellowed at me that I was a traitor, a *kha'in*. This conduct was not what I had anticipated as a possible reaction to my words. His conduct stirred the rancor of the audience members, who urged him to put his butt back on the chair and listen politely. That didn't succeed in calming him. My problem was that I had trouble understanding his dialect, which I didn't know. Consequently, I lost much of what he said, so I didn't attempt to respond. After the event concluded and members of the audience scattered, many people came up and apologized for this individual, whom they didn't know. One person volunteered that he did know him and that this old man had suffered from difficult circumstances. What lingered in my mind was his word *kha'in*, "traitor"—that one word. It was all I had understood of his verbose torrent. The audience members' faces indicated that he had said much worse things. Some people found the presentation enlightening. That proved what I meant about the barrier separating two worlds that do not blend easily, like oil and water. This may be because America, as Morise says, is like an idea. Liquids that normally don't mix are placed in one vessel. They resist blending and even love the idea that they cannot blend. If a new liquid arrives, the others must prepare themselves for this idea and delete from their plans any dream of a complete merger. The problem is that this new liquid wastes time, till it perceives the reality of that idea and surrenders to it in order to live happily. I don't know. We debated this while I explained to him how to make a sweet confection Iraqis love from date syrup and sesame. You pour into a container a half circle of that thick black syrup and place beside it another half circle of sesame syrup. The circle is complete, according to the law of the golden mean, with a clear separation between the two liquids. We dip bread into both liquids, once in the date syrup and once in the sesame syrup, keeping them separate and not blended. They blend inside the mouth to create a delicious taste. If the two liquids are blended in advance, the sweet is spoiled.

In the elevator, squeezed between the three monks and the three monkeys, I lost my balance. They thought the elderly man's remarks had upset me so much that my muscles had gone limp as I leaned against the wall of the elevator, feeling hopeless. Words are the only murderers that walk scot-free without anyone apprehending them. This word "traitor" was no doubt a daring assassin. Even I surrendered to it as it buzzed inside my head like a fly while I tried to expel it and silence its buzz.

I slumped to the floor outside the elevator, trying to cling to what I saw before me: the astonished heels of the priests tapping around me. At the same time, I sensed that what ailed my body was much more than an injurious word. Faced by this turn of events, one of the priests placed me by the wall and leaned me against a table. The other two priests stood in front of me, restraining the man, whom they had detained as if they were policemen. They then took me and the man into a small alley behind the building. I could barely see or breathe. They thought the word had harmed me. They didn't know I was the one harming the word—together with all the other words in my head—because the pain in my body wasn't merely from a hurtful word. It was much more severe than that. Its causes seemed purely physiological, not spiritual or psychological.

Two of the monks seized the man by his collar and pressed their hands against his head. He started to apologize and to express words of sorrow and remorse for his conduct. His apology did not halt the priests from pressing on his head. As for me, I didn't understand what was happening and didn't grasp what my eyes saw. I felt a bitter pain near my waist together with dizziness and a desire to vomit. The man uttered a sentence that may have had no relationship to his conduct, but it stopped the monks from torturing him: "My mother renounced me because I was homosexual." The two priests stopped restraining him then and hugged him in a surreal moment that caused the pain in my body to proclaim a truce.

I wasn't totally unconscious when they placed me in a wheelchair at the entrance to the hospital and severed my tie to their confusion and anxiety. My face was turning right and left, searching for something in my breast. All my words were disassembled into units shorter than their component letters. My ears were giving off sparks, and my nose loitered before a mass of pure air it could not inhale. I lost consciousness and regained it as I opened my eyes to feel Erick's hand circling my forehead while the shadows of the priests surrounded me like angels' wings. Something startled me then, but I didn't notice it at the time. I only remembered it after I left the hospital three days later. One of the priests was talking to Josie as if he knew him—dispensing with the polite expressions and etiquette people use when they first meet someone.

I heard them whispering together, and some were cursing the others. One priest, whom everyone else seemed to blame, said to defend himself, "I swear I never opened my mouth. Liao, please, you've known me for eight years. You know I'm not that stupid."

This was a fine, clear sign that something I did not know tied Morise to the priests.

"I have sad news and happy news," the physician announced after she opened the door of the room and entered. All the men rose and looked up expectantly to encourage her to complete her comment.

She came toward me and stopped by my head. Then she said, "The sad news is that you have appendicitis and require immediate surgery. You'll be staying a few hours with us in the hospital. The happy news is that you have cancer."

It took me, "the traitor," a long time to learn how being diagnosed with cancer could be good news.

While I searched for a listener, so I could finish telling my story, all I found was the tip of my nose, which I could see only with certain visual limitations. Part of it seemed to be the whole, if I opened one eye and closed the other. To see it from both sides, I took turns opening one eye and closing the other.

"Greetings, Tip of My Nose. I will finish my story for you. Staying in hospitals is boring. Are you ready?

"The neighborhood women who had recently repented their sins became even more talkative. I would walk by them, carrying books, which I began to purchase avidly. They would stop me in the middle of the street and ask me about all the copies of the Qur'an I carried on my head and my shoulders as I staggered slowly like a tipsy snail. They claimed I bought nothing but Qur'ans. As far as they were concerned, any book was a Qur'an. In fact, all these books were Marxist philosophies, commentaries on Heidegger, and everything that Nietzsche had said and that had been translated into Arabic. With all my books, I looked like a saint to them. This was a good sign, because I was tired of wandering around, shunned like a pregnant cat. Now I started visiting the homes of these chaste, penitent, pious women, hearing their views and their religious pundits' counsels, which filled the ears and then sealed them with the wax of their advice and teachings— 'cover the body completely; don't heed what a female says'—and dozens of rules about how a menstruating person fasts, how a woman in childbirth prays, together with stern guidance about the temporary (mut'a) marriages, which the Shi'ah denomination of Islam allows. When done properly, a time-limited Shi'i marriage allows men to pay women to surrender their bodies and their enormous, pleasure-packed breasts without any feeling of sin or of rebellion against the Creator. Instead, they may experience a sense of completing and perfecting their belief, because the grandsons of the Prophet practiced this type of time-limited marriage.

"I would find Morise waiting for me during the exam period. He would cook rice with broad beans, carrots, and eggs for me. He never let me cook dinner. He wanted to do that himself. For Morise, cooking was as much a spiritual discipline as praying. Those days passed quickly, because they were so happy. We conducted ourselves like a married couple. We never debated the clauses, paragraphs, and conditions of our relationship. Everything arranged itself by itself, like hyacinth bean vines climbing a trellis and embracing each other on cold nights without any preexisting contract.

"He heard me quarrel once with an old man at the door. That penitent pimp voiced his resentment about the visits the Americans paid me. He thought that the opposition forces hiding out among the residents would soon learn about this and burn down the entire neighborhood. Usually these people didn't have the courage to challenge the Americans. Instead, they vented their anger on anyone who collaborated with the occupation. The term 'pockets of resistance' was frequently used in those days to refer to men who hid among ordinary citizens and attacked American military vehicles while rarely harming them. Those who suffered were the civilians, and dozens of people perished daily for this reason. What the penitent pimp meant was that those skirmishes might erupt here because of me. The entire neighborhood would be blown up, and the roofs of our empty houses would be leveled to the ground. These houses would collapse at the outset of any attack. What the man said wasn't far from the truth, because those houses were older than their residents. Their Jewish residents had left them in the 1950s after the demonization of Jews by rulers who accused them of treason after World War II. They were stripped of their possessions and evicted from their homes. Many were crucified on wooden poles in the squares. Then the houses changed hands many times till they ended up in those of pimps. Finally, their inhabitants repented their lives in the sex trade and became patriotic true believers who feared being tarred with any accusation of collaboration with the Americans.

"Morise, who was hiding behind the door, heard the man say, 'You have chattered with the Americans! How is this our fault?' He waited for the man to leave before asking me about the word *laqlaq*, which he had heard the man utter. Was the word related to a return of the storks?

"I postponed my explanation of the term until after I poured him the surprise that I had prepared for him. I had learned from a fellow student from Iraq's North, where there are vineyards and wineries, how to make arak—the most famous alcoholic beverage in the country. Even though it was difficult to distribute, many people obtained and drank it, thus gaining access to the high heavens of inebriation. I got the recipe from my friend and followed the directions step by step. I failed repeatedly, even though I was as careful about following the instructions as if I had been walking a tightrope. Then I asked that friend to procure some arak for me. That was the first time I had ever touched a bottle of booze, and just sniffing it was almost more than I could bear. That evening, I poured Morise a glass of distilled, grape-based, anise-flavored arak. A few drops were enough for me. Then I explained to Morise how people used the word *laqlaq* here. It symbolizes *tamalluq* or flattery. For me to live in a house in which storks nested was unusual and perhaps a chance twist of fate. This was why my neighbors had become convinced that I deliberately, with premeditation, had chattered like a stork!

"To call a person a stork is to insinuate that he toadies up to the authorities, especially if the authorities are powerful foreigners. The frequently told story says that a sexton noticed a stork land on the tower of his church and shit mercilessly, covering the church's large metal bell with excrement. Whenever he chimed the bell, the sexton was showered with guano. Then he went to the monk to ask him how to solve this problem. He advised the sexton to take a piece of camel liver, which

Jews won't eat, and place it on the tower beside a glass of wine, which is forbidden to Muslims. The stork would then eat the camel liver, feel full, and sip the alcohol till its body was unsteady, and then it would be easy to kill the bird. The sexton followed the monk's advice and trapped the stork. Seizing it by the beak, he scolded it. 'You reprobate, you have neither a religion nor a community, and you eat camel flesh and drink wine. So you're not Jewish or Muslim. You shit on the church, and this shows you're not Christian. I'll be forced to slay you unless you adopt a religion!'

"'The moral of the joke is that the stork ingratiates itself with some people by demeaning what is sacred to others and can slip from one religion to another gracefully because it is unprincipled. It flatters people to advance its own interests, even if this leaves the stork bereft of religion and honor.'

"Morise laughed, and the dimples in his cheeks appeared, creating a straight line toward his eyes. It was the route across his face and a signpost for people traveling to his smile. People watching him were taken on a trip toward his thick eyebrows and his bright forehead.

"Not all 'storks' slander their people to the Americans. Some enjoy slandering each other, complaining about offenses hearts commit—since the heart is a muscle that does not believe in religion—and of all the disasters, risky ventures, and wars that transform the earth into a spirit crying for mercy, a place where nothing grows save thornlike memories.

"Morise would wake on my chest and remember he was a soldier sent here with his country's army to liberate the land of Iraq from the dictatorship of a madman who possessed weapons of mass destruction, which no one ever discovered. When he said that, he would burst into laughter that shook his entire head, as if it were a glass filled with wine. He needed more time than usual to recover from a night he had spent in the arms of the traitorous stork while he heard dozens of stories, jokes, and poems poorly translated into English—even as his head spilled over with little stories about his mother, father, and two sisters. He would say that my chest had an excellent influence on his memory, causing small forgotten tales to suddenly announce their presence. 'Your chest, Stork, is a good remedy for Alzheimer's,' he murmured in a soft, melodious voice.

"He wouldn't plant a kiss and leave. He wouldn't crush my ribs with an embrace. He wouldn't offer a farewell smile as a promise we would meet again. No! He would disappear like a grain of salt that dissolves.

"This delight didn't last long. The exams concluded, and Morise's duties happened to change at the same time. So we rarely found an opportunity to meet. For his part, in keeping with his temperament, which loved to devise novel tricks, he discovered a creative way for us to stay in touch."

Twenty-one

"The first package I received in the mail contained a bullet. There wasn't a single word inside the package nor a threat. The sender may have been a lazy person who knew that someone like me would scare easily. What caught my attention was the beautiful appearance of the bullet. It was the color of gold, and a thin red line of lipstick had been drawn on it. Morise commented, 'Makeup has been applied to this bullet in your honor.' I was paying a quick visit to him at noon on that scorching hot day and stopped only momentarily at the university wall's rear gate, where their armored military vehicles crouched. I heard him grouse that his comrades were quarreling with him. They no doubt felt that a suspect liaison linked Morise to a brown Iraqi student. What he most feared was that he would become so angry, he would 'come out' to them. He said he adored his homosexuality and loved his body, no matter what it loved. He often used defamatory curses to conclude his confessions, which were flavored by his hostility toward the inhabitants of the entire planet and frequently threatened this world in my presence with a scream that lurked, ever ready, behind his tongue. But this time he didn't. During all the days we were together, he pretended to be straight and went to great pains to keep people from learning he was homosexual.

"Perhaps the people who sent the bullet were my neighbors whose orders I had been slow to obey. They reinforced the first message with another envelope that contained three bullets and a brief handwritten note, which contained a Qur'anic verse threatening infidels and libertines. That same week, Morise informed me that Queen Aliya had disappeared and hadn't contacted the base for twenty-seven days. Her fifty-year-old father, who had gray hair and wavy bangs, sat on the sidewalk opposite the Americans' headquarters, drying his tears, spreading his arms toward the heavens, conversing with God in broken English, and asking him about his daughter. When female students approached to console him and pat his back, he would lower his head, fold his arms, and speak to them in Arabic. While I watched him, I almost believed the heavens speak only English.

"All the other translators thought Aliya had been kidnapped, because most of them received envelopes containing bullets. They believed that Aliya, under torture, after being suspended upside down by her limbs, had provided the kidnappers with a list of people collaborating with the occupation. That list was subsequently known as 'the Queen's List.' Aliya's father persisted in his vigil opposite the Americans, imploring the heavens and criticizing the soldiers, who pretended not to notice him. Then he suddenly stopped coming. That wasn't because he despaired of their ever helping him. What happened was that when he was eating breakfast one morning, someone kicked open his door, and the morsel he was swallowing got stuck momentarily in his throat. Then the people who attacked his house dragged Aliya inside by her hair and dropped her before him. They warned him against collaborating with the Americans, cursed him, punched his forehead, and left. He was happy despite this demeaning scene, because he thought they had returned her to him. Nothing mattered if she was safe and healthy. But when he approached her to examine her body and turned her face, which was covered with wet locks of her hair, he didn't find it. He could not locate her face. Aliya had died after being disfigured.

"At three o'clock in the morning, while roosters in the neighborhood yawned and before the mosque's call to prayer, I left my house while trying to create as big a ruckus as possible. I wanted to inform residents that I was leaving with my possessions, my books, and the Americans' stink. This might come as good news to many. They gathered to gape from the doorsteps of their houses. Some, though, would lose the free English lessons soldiers offered here. It was a very taxing course of instruction. The curriculum focused on one sentence: 'God save America! Water! Water!' Whenever anyone came close to uttering this—saying, for example, 'Gad seive amreeka. Watar, watar!'—an American soldier would throw a bottle of water to demonstrate he had understood the sentence. That the student could have understood was almost impossible because the student didn't know that the sentence was in English or that he was praying for God to preserve America before adding that he needed water: *'Ma': Water!'* People paid little attention to protocol when they chased after Americans. A soldier might throw them water and candy in response to curses, too, because people cursed while smiling and racing after armored military transport vehicles.

"Approximately three hours after I departed, a young lady in her twenties entered the neighborhood. She wore a gleaming black abaya, and the morning light accented the eye-catching sheen of its soft fabric, which slew the hearts of passersby and penitent pimps. Her heavily powdered face seemed spread with a primarily cosmetic charm, as if a handful of flour had been sprinkled on her face. Her eyebrows arched like a Mongol warrior's sword. The bright red of her lips was a story all to itself. Her earrings, which dangled to her shoulders, resembled keys—as if to say, 'The key to your hearts swings below my ear.'

Women, whose eyes did not welcome her, sent her a spiritual message to cover herself if she wanted to live in this neighborhood and join the elite women in it. Their envy and their fear that their men would fall captive to such extravagant charms were obvious. The young woman opened the door of my former house, the deserted stork's nest, and settled in it. Within minutes a taxi arrived, bringing the rest of her possessions and necessities. Over the course of the next three days, this young lady greeted guests at the door—good people who welcomed her and asked if they could help her in any way or if she needed something. They all told her the same thing: 'We are happy you have come to live here with us. The previous tenant was a shady, shameless young man who fraternized with the Americans.'

"She told them her name was Enki but didn't leave it at that. To reinforce the joke and to identify with the comedy of the street, she added, 'My name is Enki, which was also the name of the Sumerian god of wisdom.' She was naturally prepared for them to make fun of her and mock her bizarre statement, because these people knew nothing about Enki, that Iraqi god of centuries ago, but she wanted to enjoy the show, because every aspect of her body resembled a shop window. She was the only lady who wore a nose ring and whose perfume filled the street, which needed freshening. She failed to display the quivering breasts women flaunt when they walk and had resorted to stuffing a sponge over her chest and another over her rump. She was an Iraqi drag queen—employing one of the homosexual arts to protect herself and to hide from the eyes of people lying in wait for her. Morise had deployed all his skills in applying powder and makeup, in making my eyes look larger, and in drawing eyebrows. I had never imagined I could look like that. This suggestion drew me into a loud debate with him when he proposed the idea to me as an unavoidable solution, which I countered scornfully. He was quite serious about the matter, but I objected that I didn't know at all how to act like a woman and that I had never even tried imitating a female. They had put a wig on

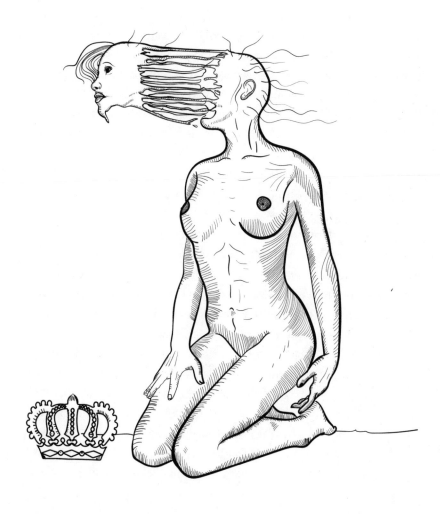

my head once and forced me to wear a woman's shift to humiliate me and make me feel guilty. That was meant to correct my behavior. In my childhood, acting like a woman was beyond the pale. I watched my body develop for many months the way someone might watch a rabbit in a cage and was keen to suppress even any typical masculine gestures that might not look manly. I measured my body precisely based on a scale of the six thousand masculine units by which I measured virility. 'I refer to these as MU,' I teased Morise.

"'Thus, I grew up with this dialectic, which didn't make me hate being homosexual, because I began to love being virile—very virile as defined by homosexuality!' Morise didn't like this phrase. It had taken me a long time to understand what being queer really meant for me. Morise's argument was that a man can't really see himself as a whole—no mirror could show all his features that don't exist yet. There are some bodily gestures that occasionally leap from me, disclosing remnants of femininity—hidden remnants from the past. 'These are features that only someone who comes really close to you notices.' I told him that men—all men—have a woman hidden in some fissure inside their egos.

"This Enki, who attracted the stares and jealousy of women wherever she walked, was naturally not able to receive strange men. The presence of American men would have been like someone pouring oil on a fire. So I only saw Morise when I left the university, and that meant I had to walk a long way to reach the new checkpoint. I tried to convince him to visit me disguised as a Sudanese servant, in clothes coated with paint. The Sudanese were the only Africans one saw there. Therefore, his presence wouldn't arouse suspicion. He rejected this proposal, because, like most of the soldiers, he didn't feel safe setting foot outside a base here in Iraq without his uniform. When I told him the joke people recount about the soldier who fainted in a working-class area here, he did not laugh. He didn't even smile. Such a scenario was a nightmare and not a joking matter for him. This frequently repeated joke says that an elderly woman who lived alone took in and cared for a white soldier, who had fainted. She stayed up nights nursing him and shielded him from prying eyes. When he gradually regained consciousness, she quickly taught him Arabic and gave him a fine local name reminiscent of the past century, one people no longer used much. She dressed him like a villager from the South to make him seem like one of her relatives. She started introducing him to people as her son. For his part, he embraced his role more than he had to and adopted an emotional version of Islam, one focused on the shrines and tombs of the saints. He began to go out to protest the murder of a Shiʻi imam in the eighth century CE, the way people do. He would attend demonstrations and bare his chest, beating it like men during the annual rituals mourning the slaying of the grandson of the Prophet Muhammad more than a thousand years ago. His assimilation progressed until he raised a weapon against the American patrol that entered the neighborhood to search for him.

"Morise commented, 'Outside American security areas, people's attitudes toward Americans are hard to read. No one wants to live with a sensational horror film outside their window. I know that thousands of people love us out there, but usually bad guys infiltrate among the innocent ones. No one fights you here when you're in uniform.'

"Enki helped me to move freely through the neighborhood and to shop but could not work in the printshop. I had to jump over a high wall every day to approach the back street where the printshop was located without anyone from the neighborhood seeing me. I lived for approximately seven months as Enki without anyone catching on.

"Before the time came for the final exams after which I would be a petroleum engineer, I discovered an ancient, movable-type printing press hidden together with all its accessories and spare parts in a small cellar beneath the building. I spoke to my boss, who owned the place, and he told me the story of the press, which was the third or fourth printing press to enter the country at the beginning of the twentieth century. His great-grandfather had purchased it. The portrait in the main office showed an old man who had a stooped back and wore a red fez with a green band around it. The photographer, who had hand-colored the picture, had apparently gone overboard and made the grandfather look like an Ottoman sultan. Hundreds of little metal cubes bore protruding English letters. They were used to print pamphlets, announcements, and instructions intended for the British soldiers during the British occupation. The letters were set in a tray on which paper was pressed, and then writing appeared. That was what I understood from the odds and ends I found covered with dust and spiderwebs.

"I showed Morise one of these trays, and he was able to decipher the first words: 'Stay alive.' Then, as he watched me raise my eyebrows, he rearranged the letters to read 'I love you as I have never loved anyone before.' This was his adorable, new way of communicating. He took the letters from me and refused to give them back. He argued, 'How can I give you my tongue and my way of expressing myself?'

"In those days, I was busy writing a novel called *Computopia*. I borrowed the title from a Japanese thinker who, in the 1980s, discussed the way computers will dominate the world and how our lives will gradually turn into a virtual existence. In it, I wrote about an electronic virus that infects books of Islamic history, toying with them and turning them topsy-turvy. It attacks sentences in the programming language Visual Basic, which I was using then, and affects the life stories of heroes and merchants as well as the outcomes of the fierce battles that the Arabs waged to spread Islam. When the printshop's owner found out about the book, he worried about me. One day, though, he came to me and said he was selling the printshop and the shack behind it, including the stork's nest. He was migrating with his family to Egypt. Smiling at me, he explained that I could print copies of the novel in the printshop and distribute them myself.

"I was preparing for the book's launch party when I fled from my house in my normal form, leaving behind my books, my clothes, and the remaining copies of my novel that hadn't been distributed yet. I only had the presence of mind to take a palm-frond bag filled with the letters from the classic printing press. Two hours earlier, three women had stormed my house and seen Enki in her true form. They were not at all surprised to find I had been impersonating her but were slightly alarmed. They explained how for several days they had suspected that I wasn't female, ever since one of them—from her balcony—saw me reading by a small window. She had been surprised to see a woman read in this neighborhood, arousing her doubts. News spread to one of the former pimps, and he volunteered to break into my house. Female tact prevailed, though, and these women tipped me off about the man's plan. I doubted they were really trying to do me a favor and guessed that their generosity was motivated by curiosity, which occasionally kills the people it infects and makes life seem a daring adventure to them. I'm sure I didn't forget to thank them for saving my life.

"What helped me at that point was the need for a new translator at the checkpoint where Morise worked. This was months after Aliya's murder and the kidnapping of translators who had only been employed there for a few weeks. Most of them were young students. I was appointed immediately to a part-time position, although I spent all my time with the Americans because I had no other refuge now that the printshop was closed and I had graduated from the College of Engineering.

"I encountered Shaheen in the dean's office. He was there for the same reason I was. We both wanted to pursue an MS in petroleum and gas engineering. His face telegraphed me an eloquent message. The gist of it was that the only remaining seat in the program was reserved for him or one of his friends. His face alone convinced me to abandon this idea and devote my efforts to finding work with one of the oil companies. There was nothing easy about that either. I would have to move back to Basra, which was dominated by Sadr's militias. That same month, I found the courage to contact my father and discovered that I could still weep when I heard his voice. Before he handed the receiver to my mother, who was suffering from back and disc pain, I tried to adopt a more masculine form of weeping to make my sorrow seem more appropriate.

"'Basra's not for you. I don't want to find you tossed in a dump heap.' He repeated his sentence evoking the same nightmare. I knew I would not be found dead in the dump heap; I would be living there.

"I was returning from a routine patrol with the unit, and Morise was sick in bed, tens of kilometers away. I hadn't been able to see him for a week. I decided to remind him of me by doing something special he would enjoy. I created another female character like Enki and named her Enkida, which was the feminine form of Enkido, because I believed that Enkido had a homosexual relationship with Gilgamesh, as the ancient Babylonian epic says. My Enkida was a woman. I 'veiled' myself with cosmetics and set off for the heart of Baghdad—specifically the bookshop district. It may have been the largest market for the sale and purchase of books anywhere in the Middle East. It was redolent of the fragrance of paper, the breath of authors, philosophers, and the incense that rose from the words of Naguib Mahfouz, Virginia Woolf, and William Faulkner. This was how I imagined the atmosphere books create in the physical space they occupy. While I was looking around and enjoying the sensual feel of their covers and titles, I found myself in a narrow alley, inside a small bookstore. Squatting like someone defecating, I reached for a book entitled *Computopia*. When I turned it over and saw my photo on the back, I panicked. I sensed I was in even greater danger when the clerk approached to tell me about this new novel.

Forgetting that I wasn't Mortada then and that the salesman wouldn't recognize me, I replaced the book very quickly, adjusted my abaya over my head the way girls do in Baghdad, and fled as if carried away by the wind. It was scary to see my words in a book. My name, printed on the cover, was naked for passersby to see, and my book-shopping venture gave me indigestion for days."

Twenty-two

A week after I was discharged from the hospital, I noticed a small hard lump by my waist. They told me it would gradually dissolve. The tumor they had found at the top of my right kidney would require another round of imaging and continued monitoring of its growth. The physicians' diagnoses and the chaotic mess of papers and exam reports strewn across my bed confirmed what the doctor said when she described my vicious affliction as "happy news": accidental discovery of this kidney tumor before it wreaked havoc on my body beat discovering it too late. "The news is positive, because finding a fish in your belly today is far better than trying to hunt a whale years later." The nurse's words continued to buzz in my head like a bee trapped inside it—a bee screaming, "Namaste, namaste, namaste!" I fled from its chant as I tossed and turned repeatedly in my bed. He wanted to be nice, using what he thought was my language, of which he seemed to have mastered words of greeting. I replied to him as he cared for me, "Namaste, namaste." Then I remembered it wasn't my language and told him, "I honestly don't understand what you're saying." He flashed me a broad smile with his compassionate face and said, "Young man, you needn't be ashamed of your people and your language."

At this point, one of the priests stationed with me explained. "This young man speaks Arabic. He's not lying when he says he doesn't know Hindi. He would not be embarrassed if he were an Indian, Turk, Persian, or even from outer space."

I was writhing with pain, and the nurse administered a tranquilizer. I soon felt sedated and sensed I was floating on clouds of delight. I tossed a towel at the chatty priest to stop him from skewing the conversation toward the dangerous topic of implicit bias. The towel fell over his face, and he looked like a statue covered with a curtain prior to its unveiling.

After I threw the towel at him, the priest remained hidden beneath it, and I liked the way he looked with the towel covering his face like a veil. I would wake and doze off, rolling over in bed to hear him babbling beneath the towel. The scene might have been frightening, but it wasn't. From beneath his veil, he related the story of how Morise had helped the three men flee from their homeland, where homosexuals like them were being murdered. But Morise had done it covertly, because the priest, who wasn't a priest then, hadn't been able to come out as homosexual—not even to his mother or his sisters. Morise had sent him a letter after he heard his story broadcast while Morise was visiting South Africa as a tourist, reading, and writing. The priest, before he became a priest, was in Congo. He was fleeing with two friends from their families and from vicious gangs that had killed their companions. Morise had written him every week, enclosing a sum of money and a complete plan for their escape from Congo and flight to Seattle. Words gushed from the priest beneath the towel as he related another episode of the glorious saga of Morise.

I thought about the three monks, who collaborated openly with the three wise monkeys after the operation. I hadn't discussed Morise with them. I hadn't told them I had heard them whisper together and that I now felt certain they knew the whole story. My head was filled with fear. I was afraid to broach the topic with them in case I received a response that I didn't want to hear and that I still wasn't able to imagine. I didn't want one of them to tell me Morise had died. Likewise, I did not want anyone to tell me that everyone knew this— just not me. Except for the exciting part about the priests' relationship with Morise, I hadn't asked them anything. Instead, I wanted to complete the story myself. Because I knew the priests knew, but they didn't know I knew, my only recourse seemed to be silence, which might force them to start a conversation in which they recalled Morise's qualities for me.

On my way to meet Erick and the priests, I turned into a narrow side alley, where a rat, evidently startled by the faltering footsteps of my body, which was staggering from fatigue and my memories, almost collided with the tip of my shoe, although I managed to avoid it. The alley was dank, dirty, and fouled by the urine of homeless people. I grumbled aloud to myself about the stink and the filth. Then I heard the rat call back at me from the distance. "If you don't like this smell, go back to your homeland, idiot!"

I stopped, searching for the rat so I could finish narrating my story to it instead of to the tip of my nose, but the rodent vanished, leaving a plume of anger rising from the burrow into which it had disappeared.

Then it was time for me to meet the priests and Erick, even though there were thousands of possible items that could serve as a funnel into which I could pour the remainder of my story. Feeling anxious and bored, I searched for some special confidant. Cups, shoes, ashtrays, and angry rats no longer tempted me.

The smell of vanilla drew me out of my reverie, and I expressed an unfamiliar craving for an ice cream treat even as one of them suggested we join the spiraling queue that twisted back upon itself in front of an ice cream shop.

I took my place at the end of the line, behind them, to the right of the members of a soccer team eager to get to their green field. To my left, just inches away, was the front window of the ice cream shop, and on the other side, three women were eating ice cream and chatting. Because of the sunlight's glare on the glass, I couldn't see their faces clearly. What I could see was a small gold dinosaur inlaid with turquoise. The size of a finger joint, it seemed to be telling me, "Here I am. Finish your story with me."

Before I could begin, the light dimmed, and I made out the face of the woman who wore the little dinosaur brooch on her shoulder. I had seen this lady frequently in the 1990s in newspapers and on TV screens. Saddam Hussein had called her "the Mistress of Evil." I had heard a lot of songs and curses about her. My father, wrapped in his scarf, placing the radio near his pillow, would counter these because he considered her an experienced politician and a woman who was the equivalent of a thousand men—until the death toll of sick Iraqi children rose as a result of the American prohibitions on the importation of medicine. Then his attitude toward her changed completely. Once he saw pictures of charred children after Americans shelled their shelter in Baghdad when searching for the president, my father became furious if I mentioned her name, which had a musical ring in Arabic and appealed to a child like me: Madeleine Albright!

"That's Madeleine Albright," I whispered to one of the priests.

"Is she a novelist?"

"Yes," I replied nonchalantly.

"There's Madeleine Albright, Erick," I whispered to him while he gazed at the face of a handsome young man crossing the street with his little dog.

"I'm happy you've started talking again. Is she an actress?"

"You don't know who she is?"

"Ask her if she has a dog you can draw." He placed his hand over his mouth to suppress the kind of laughter that villains spew out in cartoons.

I felt a strong urge to meet the former American secretary of state now that mere inches separated my face from hers, which was on the other side of the window of the ice cream shop. I remembered my father. I wanted to call him. I wanted to take a selfie with her. But then I felt I really didn't want to do any of that—I even apologized to her brooch, asking the creature it depicted to leave me and my affairs alone. "Dinosaur, not so fast—I don't think you're a dinosaur. At any rate, you're some type of animal. Listen: I don't want to tell you the rest of my story."

"I washed off my ass for you." We were near the bar the priests liked when a man in his late fifties left it, wearing a black short-sleeve T-shirt bearing this phrase. The man's butt, which announced its readiness, reminded me of a letter a young man once threw at my face before he fled. So I decided to tell my tale to the man's butt, thinking it might be interested.

"Yes, Ms. Butt Cheeks, I was dressed like a soldier in the US Army, when a young man threw that message at my face. It landed on the bridge of my nose, injuring me, because the paper was folded around a rock. He may have adopted this procedure to force me to pay attention to its message. At the time, I was preoccupied by a bundle of papers that I was supposed to translate as quickly as possible and deliver to Morise and his fellow soldiers. Morise noticed the thin line of blood trickling from the top of my nose. I told him that a young man had thrown this rock-weighted paper at me and fled. I opened the letter for him, read it, and translated it. I read and translated it twice more, trying to interest the other soldiers in its message. There was something about the way the letter was written—an emotional touch and a linguistic attempt to influence the heart of anyone who read it. It stated that corpses were piled beneath the bridge and that their number doubled daily. It said the stink asphyxiated passersby. The faces of these beautiful victims were highly valued by flies. That last phrase, which I considered a powerful poetic expression, stopped me in my tracks. The letter continued: 'There are piles and heaps of young fellows whose gaping mouths say nothing, not only because they are the mouths of dead youth but because words are useless!' That's how the letter ended.

"This may have been the most eloquent letter I ever received. It made my face bleed and humiliated me. Surrounded by Americans, I had thought I was safe, especially because I was with Morise, whose heart possessed its own eyes, lips, and ears. Even so, he didn't take this warning very seriously. When I tried, in Morise's presence, to pressure the commanding officer to heed the message, I realized they thought everything I said was beyond their purview. As Morise put it, 'We're a regular army, not a militia that can chase killers like that.' Bringing the matter to the attention of the Iraqi Police would have been nothing less than idiotic. They were more cowardly than chickens surrounded by foxes. I had another excuse that I used to dull my keen concern about the matter. Its gist was that people had been dying here daily and hourly since the arrival of the American forces. Their bodies were thrown into the air by bombs that supposedly resisted the occupation. Or, they were kidnapped, and their heads were tortured with electric drills—not to mention random shots fired or people who died from shots that missed their intended victim. What was extraordinary, then, about the victims beneath the bridge? Fine, ignoble intellect, you're right, logically speaking, and let's not forget precautionary safety measures, the security situation, and the care necessary to stay alive—oh! Are we really living beings?

"As images of young people whose faces were swarming with flies never quit me, a long time passed before I went to see the mound of corpses beyond the bridge and below it. All that time, I relied on a logical excuse to dull my anger: the young man who wrote the letter provided only sketchy details, which weren't precise enough to locate the place.

"Morise stayed as close to me as my shadow during those days—to the point that his comrades said I was a man with two shadows, one provided by the sun and another that originated in Seattle. The Seattle shadow was with me even when its master wasn't. It branched out from my body instead of slipping from under it like an ordinary shadow. He would tell me about incidents in his life and would use me at times as a pocket recorder for his memories and observations on life—including his inaudible curses, the bicycle on which he traversed the small neighborhood of West Seattle, his vertically striped pajamas that he kept for his mother's sake because they made him 'look taller,' the gym of boxers without broken noses to which he belonged, his philosophy courses at the University of Washington, and the pair of light athletic shoes he longed for.

"One day when I was reading and translating for him a sermon Mahiya had delivered to her followers, we heard a racket in the street and a voice that sounded familiar to me. It was the same young fellow who had thrown the letter at me. Once again, he hadn't found anyone who would listen to him. I went out to him and asked him to wait for me at the gate at seven p.m. That was the first and last time we met. At the appointed hour, I found him waiting for me, sitting on the sidewalk, his hand on his cheek, watching the headlights of the cars. He watched them and wouldn't allow them to escape from his gaze, even after I appeared and greeted him. He smiled and told me he suffered from a persistent whisper that made him count the headlights of vehicles. I told him, 'Then you need to start the prayer ritual again from the beginning,' and we both laughed with an echoing chortle that helped the young man's chest relax and caused him to speak clearly, without any hesitation. My joke referred to the whispering, demonic spirit that attacks people when they pray, causing them to lose track of the number of prostrations and forcing them to repeat the prayer ritual all over again, from the beginning, to remain true to religious rules.

"This may have provided the youth some hint about my religious background and my previous beliefs and reassured him that I knew a lot—so there was no need for him to test my identity. That is something Iraqis frequently do when they meet a stranger, even though a person's identity can be established by not much more than his name and accent. These suffice to establish someone's sect—Sunni or Shi'i— and geographical origin. All the same, during the past thirty years, names had been adopted less systematically, and people had shifted between geographical regions and dialects. For this reason, catastrophic murders of many people had occurred when they failed to prove their identities to the slayer, who was searching for a certain victim profile to settle a score.

"The youth felt it was time to stop kidding around, because we were heading to a tragic spectacle, and remained silent once we hailed a taxi. Then he drew me by my hand as we slipped beneath a large bridge. We made our way through a garbage dump full of sheepskins and mounds of discarded rice, bread, and melon peels. He finally gestured with his hand toward the north and turned his face away, as if he wanted me to see for myself. Then my eye caught sight of dozens of corpses cast down there randomly as if they had been tossed—like wheat spilling from a large sack—from the bridge overhead and landed atop each other. They had formed piles and mounds and intertwined with each other. They were all young, none older than thirty.

"I moved farther away from him and closer to the corpses until the smell struck me like a punch in the nose. Then I returned quickly to the youth. He placed his hand on my back and pushed me up the hill, toward the street. Before I said anything, he hailed a taxi to take us back to the army post. Then we sat down on the same sidewalk where I had found him. He held out a sheaf of papers that were stuck together with the sweat of his trembling body, as if to console me for the sight I had just witnessed. The papers were copies of hospital reports for more than fifty young men who had been brought to the hospital on a single night. They all suffered from poisoning and intestinal blockages that had required surgical intervention. They were a group of homosexuals whom militias had kidnapped and tortured. Their buttocks had been sealed with adhesives before they were left to wander the streets in acute pain.

"Like me, Morise felt indignant when I told him, and his expression grew sad. After this, he took personal responsibility for collecting whatever information the international media provided about the torture of homosexuals and the sealing of their buttocks with adhesives before their noses were cut off and their arteries severed. Most of these procedures were perpetrated by members of al-Sadr's Jaysh al-Mahdi militia. This was the sectarian movement to which Mahiya adhered. It was a militia that believed it was necessary to establish a puritanical society and prepare for the appearance of one of the Prophet Muhammad's grandsons. A penitent person who had committed the most hideous and atrocious sins could find consolation for himself in this movement. He felt empowered to retaliate against the haughty scorn of conventionally religious men. Here was a door God opened for his rebellious worshipper, because he loves him. God loves his simplicity, his spontaneity, and even his ignorance. God will cleanse his soot-black heart and make it sparkling clean—cleaner than the hearts of generations of pious men who have grown up in traditionally pious homes. To stumble upon God after you have sinned and lost your way is superior to finding yourself on the straight path from the beginning—for that man and anyone else. Al-Sadr's Jaysh al-Mahdi militia was filled with people who had criminal records and who believed that God wished to use their might, audacity, daring, ignorance, simplicity, and obscenity to do good. What set these people apart was that they had stumbled upon God in a way that meant he provided them the power to dominate others. They did not want to lose the dominance they had enjoyed as a mafia. So they hit upon an idea that would make them advocates of exemplary virtues and a dominant mafia too. They felt relaxed and extraordinarily happy. Who wouldn't if you sensed that God and Satan were both on your side?

"Clinging to traditional religious teachings became risible. The authentic moral standards and values were those dictated by the youthful leader, who suddenly acquired mass popularity. Many an individual sided with him, because deposed president Saddam Hussein had killed his fathers and two of his brothers. To my way of thinking, penitence is an innocuous spiritual boost. For those guys, penitence resembled the fleece a wolf proudly treasures after slaying and skinning a goat.

"'Blocking the buttocks was their punishment for sex work. The hand that steals is cut off, and on Judgment Day, an eye that has gazed at a woman's thighs will be strung up by its lashes. According to their philosophy of punishment for homosexuals, the butt is guilty, not the penis. No one punishes the penis. It is the sacred phallus after which the shapes of minarets and mosque towers are modeled.' That's what I rattle off when I'm with Morise, pretending to be irate. Both of us pretend to be angry. What makes this even more bitter and painful is that we are pretending. Our bodies prevaricate so that our minds can take a break from thinking about the matter. We didn't feel angry so much as conscious that we were drugged by our affection for each other. An ancient maxim says that your own toothache hurts more than the death of a friend's father, but you are forced to pretend you feel bad when you're with him. I don't think I'm happy, even in Seattle, when I see happy homosexuals walk down the streets and paint gay pride flags, because I truly don't feel happy. I don't understand how I can be happy when people are still having their buttocks blocked and their feces trapped inside their colons.

"It was the right time to hear my father's voice. When I hear my father, my spirit usually feels relieved of its burdens, even when our conversation is frank and candid. The connection was bad, but I was able to hear his voice and his labored breathing. He asked me how I was doing and did not forget to advise me to work in Baghdad and to stay away from Basra. I felt he was hiding what he knew about the increase in the killing, torture, and staging of corpses of homosexuals. Everything he said to me stemmed from that reality, which he camouflaged very well, even though I felt a strong desire to return to Basra and work there as a petroleum engineer. After five years of study, that was my specialty. But he avoided referring to that. Before he handed the receiver to my mother, so she could shed her share of tears as she greeted me, he asked, 'Have you heard what happened to your friend Mahiya? The Iraqi army killed her, by mistake.'

"That explanation sounded somewhat hard to believe. It seems that when Mahiya had tired of serving as a male politician, she'd been returning, at times, to her trans status as a woman. Apparently, no one knew that politician was Mahiya. Because the army had been combatting members of al-Qaeda in the North, al-Qaeda members had been disguising themselves in women's clothing when they wished to flee and move through areas under military control. Usually the army succeeded in discovering that the woman wearing a niqab veil was a man and a member of al-Qaeda, perhaps by their overly shrill voice and gestures. When they doubted the person's identity, they searched her, paying special attention to her genitals. In this manner, they seized some individuals fleeing from al-Qaeda and ISIS. I had been able to get away with moving through Baghdad as a woman because no one suspected al-Qaeda fighters to be on the streets.

"Mahiya, who had tired of playing the role of a male politician, had returned to the way she presented herself when she was my friend. She had begun to wear women's clothes and to act like a woman, perhaps because her political projects had failed. On one of her excursions to Baghdad to visit a sacred mausoleum, the American and Iraqi soldiers manning a joint checkpoint grew suspicious of her. They didn't know that this female penitent was sympathetic toward them. They easily discovered her male organ and killed her on the spot. She was in the wrong place, dressed in the wrong clothes, at the wrong time."

During this period, I slept in the same bed with Morise every night. Nothing separated us but the tranquility that slept between us. This calm was the complete peace of an ultimate mutual attraction that may connect two bodies. We did not need to use his English or my Arabic. It wasn't necessary for me to ask him to repeat his words two or three times before I understood what he was saying—even though he normally refined his English and spoke slowly for my sake, giving each consonant its full force before clipping it short. Our bedroom chats surpassed mere words—words lead to misunderstandings; they always lie. We seemed to have agreed to this, reading without interrupting each other as our feet deliberately rubbed together to keep us from forgetting that our bodies lay side by side. He was reading one of Annemarie Schimmel's books about Sufism: *My Soul Is a Woman*, and I was perusing the same book, but in Arabic. I had purchased mine from a used-book store, whereas Morise had brought his copy with him and carried it around with his ammunition and military training booklets. He was farther along in the book than I was. While I observed his movements and reactions as he read, I wondered whether the spiritual energy released by this book would calm his rowdy vitality. It came as no surprise when he quickly returned to his normal behavior as hasty expletives leaped from his lips when the other soldiers summoned or contacted him, even though he was engrossed in discovering the spiritual "states" of Sufis wandering through the divine essence.

"We are God's brides." He liked this Sufi phrase and kept expanding on it and playing with it as he explained his thinking to me. Some Sufis did flirt with beardless youths, likening them to women. There are tons of Sufi poems that hallow boys and depict them the way a man depicts an enchanting girl. Some male Sufis have even viewed their enlightened Sufi body as feminine since God dwells in it the way a male inhabits a female and penetrates her body. Everything centers on two poles, one negative and one positive. The sky is masculine and impregnates the feminine earth. Thus, although Morise did not embrace this polar way of thinking, he did like the emotional side of Sufism and its approach to love.

When opponents of Sufism want to go to extremes in criticizing it, they describe Sufis as deviant homosexuals. This is customary. The ultimate Iraqi curse is to call your foe a homosexual. In this vein, Iraqi television used to air interviews with terrorists who had set off bombs that had ended hundreds of lives. The presenter conducting the interview would often ask the terrorist about his homosexuality. Then the criminal was expected to confess to the viewing public that he had had a homosexual liaison with his superior or with an emir who belonged to al-Qaeda—or later to ISIS. This suggested that their massacres and philosophy of maximum brutality were not sufficient indictments against them; they also had to be branded as homosexuals. The assumption was that a man who has tarnished his honor by performing a disgraceful act contrary to nature will view killing people as a walk in the park. Many of these terrorism suspects were subjected to extreme forms of torture, which might even alter their facial appearance, before they delivered confessions designed to exorcise feelings of hatred and a need for revenge. Such avowals offered relatives of these terrorists' victims some false comfort and reinforced the state's assertions of its own manliness and virility, demonstrated in capturing terrorists. These forced confessions provided no understanding of the true motives for the atrocious crimes the terrorists had committed. What counted was for the terrorist to confess he was queer. His being a homosexual had corrupted his sectarian upbringing, not vice versa. He wasn't a member of a large organization that played with him as if he were a puppet—in fact, one of thousands of marionettes whose strings became entangled, thus concealing the major partisan drives that controlled them. In order to preserve the unity of Iraq, to unite Sunnis and Shiʻis, the television presenters hosting those programs avoided attributing any responsibility for terrorist killings to sectarian disputes. It was naturally far easier to single out the killer as a homosexual. That was much safer than declaring him a partisan Islamist, since such an approach would damage fraternal feeling among Iraqis and the spirit of cooperation between two denominations that had struggled against each other for hundreds of years.

I would explain these interviews to Morise and translate them. We would laugh for a time, only to fall silent suddenly in mutual embarrassment once we remembered the victims' severed heads.

The image of Morise reading beside me overwhelmed me when I was leaving a grocery store in downtown Seattle. A young man in his thirties bumped into my cart. He apologized, saying, "Sorry. But believe me when I say I admire terrorists." I smiled at him and walked away. Then what he had said registered in my mind—a mind that leaves English sentences at its doorstep and translates them into Arabic.

"Did you say 'terrorist'?" I returned to the young man after knitting my eyebrows and adopting a stern expression. I realized that the fellow was none too bright and probably under the influence of drugs.

"I'm sorry, but believe me: I respect you even if you are a terrorist or a Muslim. You didn't give me a chance to complete my thought. I just wanted a cigarette."

I pulled enough dollars from my pocket for him to purchase a pack of cigarettes and replied, "Aha! I almost misunderstood you. Forgive me. You're a very nice young man. We terrorists are people of extreme integrity and innocence. We rarely encounter anyone who will speak to us, pay attention to us, or pick us out of a crowd like this. Even though I resemble them, we all look alike, as you know." I took a deep breath.

"Bro, I don't want to pat myself on the back, but I know a lot. I may not look educated, but I know a lot, bro." He said that as he accepted the money, smiling calmly and cheerfully.

"Yes, I agree totally with you. That's my last dollar to encourage you to be even nicer to terrorists in the future—even though you are nice to them already. Don't get me wrong."

The youth disappeared as Morise's toes continued to mess with mine. A flock of seagulls soared in from the west, descending like an arrow over the alleyways of the downtown. I heard them—these *nawaris*—squawk, "*Irhabi, Irhabi!* Terrorist, terrorist!"

Twenty-three

"'People devote more effort to correcting the errors of the past than they do to improving the future. In Seattle, Basra, Baghdad, and other places, you can see the past's skiff tugging on the wrist of every pedestrian or passenger. This is the invisible skiff we drag with us over dry land. The fact that no one acknowledges its existence makes it very powerful. The skiff that accompanies me bumps a lot when I drag it through the city's streets. It delays me at every turn. Memory's film clips, which encircle this skiff, make it capsize and wobble, capsize and wobble.'

"Morise wrote these poetic lines, which I translated into Arabic. They are still fresh, tender, and easy to digest. Morise knew only too well what they mean and realized that his skiff had rammed into mine one day, merging with it in a way that made it hard to separate them. Not even the strongest carpenter in the world could free my skiff from his. He may have realized that immigrants are burdened by their memories, which—like braids or plaits—can take time to unravel. I informed him that I had been admitted into a master's program in petroleum engineering in Texas. He was ecstatic and poked his elbow into my belly like a pro wrestler. This was an unpremeditated leap for me, but real. I would be in Texas. We would live together there while I studied for my MS. Then I might obtain a position in the southern oil fields, where we would create our new little family.

"I waited to hear about my student fellowship while Morise returned to Seattle. As I waited, I launched my career in drilling wells, spending half a month in the desert and the other half at home. This routine didn't last long, because the half month I spent in the city frightened my parents, who wanted me to spend all my time in the desert—so they would not need to fear their son's falling victim to one of the 'honor' gangs that were on the prowl, looking for victims.

"During those years, I wrote a novel called *Miknasat al-Janna* (*Heaven's Broom*), which was about a Black Iraqi family living in a house filled with cats and the tombs of pious saints. Even so, people didn't visit them or seek their blessing. The father of the family died as a martyr in the final days of the war, and no one heard his wife's lamentations because they were drowned out by the pervasive sounds of revelry and jubilation that marked the end of the war. I went to Beirut for the book signing and found Morise waiting for me there. For the first time in my life, I entered a gay bar with him. He introduced me as his 'boyfriend,' which was a delightful term I was hearing applied to me for the first time. He told me he would move to Texas to be with me. Once I finished my studies, we would return to Seattle. We would work there, buy a house on the north side of the city, and live there 'happily ever after'—like the refrain that ends old tales.

"As usual, these festivities were put on hold because after I had obtained my American visa and the grants agency had rented housing for me and registered me to study, I received a call from a number I didn't recognize while I was in an elevator in Iraq's Ministry of Oil. The speaker's voice was very familiar, although I hadn't heard it for a dozen months. Before greeting me or saying hello, he declared, 'Mortada, you're rejected. I'm going in your place. We Iraqis, we pious Iraqis, we want a man—not a sodomite—to represent us in the West.' I turned off my phone, did an about-face, and took the stairs. I raced up them breathlessly and asked everyone for the office of the director of student grants until I found someone who would answer me. I opened the door without knocking and confronted him. He seemed to be preparing for a meeting. About ten other men, dressed in suits, were in the room. I shouted, 'Have I really been rejected? After I left you, minutes ago, I received a strange call from Shaheen! Doesn't that American firm know his gang has killed people, including Americans? Has the world sunk to this level?'

"I was shouting as loudly as I could. But I was tired. I noticed that they were afraid to look at me because of the sparks flying from my eyes, which were as wide open as the jaws of a predatory animal. My outburst made no difference.

"I didn't tell Morise what had happened for fear it would disturb his queasy digestion. I decided not to tell him till he returned to Iraq on his next tour. Four years had passed since my appointment as an engineer in the National Petroleum Company. I drilled oil wells incrementally, like a manual laborer working alone with giant screwdrivers, chemical clays, and heavy equipment, until I became an old hand. I did all this while Morise watched via the emails or video calls we exchanged almost every day. Then another opportunity presented itself, and I was accepted to a training program in Tokyo. I was able to hold on to this new opportunity by staying calm. I did not believe in relying on prayers and supplications. All I believed in was creating an escape plan, any plan!

"I admit that I lost confidence in my supervisor when I saw him toss a sacred bit of clay from the tomb of the Prophet's grandson into an oil well, claiming this would fix the field problem we were encountering, a problem that had forced us to expend a lot of materials. I set about plugging the gaps by taking practical measures, ignoring all the counsels of that extremely pious supervisor, whose religiosity didn't prevent him from spewing stinging curses, extending even to mothers and aunts. After I finished the project, I submitted a critical memo about him for his review and approval—in other words a memo criticizing him that he was to certify and pass on. It frightened him, and his fear of my memo, which disparaged his superstitious turn of mind, quickly led to a truce, according to which he would not oppose my opportunities for further study. So I went to Tokyo. Morise came to visit me during that two-month training session in the tranquil city of Chiba, located on Tokyo Bay. We spent three nights on the shore, among boulders that provided an almost total escape from the world's obscenities. These boulders appeared to have been created just for us. The only downside of those moments was my confession to Morise that I would not be going to Texas that year.

"He said nothing for more than two hours. He expressed his subsequent rage not with silence but by packing his bags and disappearing. He quit Chiba and left me a piece of paper with a note:

We're finished! You don't want to apply for refugee status. It doesn't seem you'll be able to have an opportunity to study abroad. So we're finished. I'll be in Seattle after we complete our next deployment. I'm going to resign from the army and return to my apartment. I'll buy a home and build a little turtle tank in the backyard. I bought a Kurdish turtle from a shepherd near the Chaldean monastery in northern Iraq. He first said the turtle was male, but when he put it on my hand, it made a sound, and he said it was female. Isn't it neat how they determine the gender of a turtle just by the sound it makes! Do I seem disinterested to you? You know I'm not like that. But I'm tired. I've been thinking too much. I feel I need some additional cells to deal with the pains of reflection when I'm not with you. When I'm not with you, life is hard. Nothing seems to matter. The only European here is the translator. I may see you in Seattle. I may never see you again. These two feelings unite and also struggle with each other. I don't know which of them will win and become true . . . Mortada, you don't seem to share my enthusiasm for living together in Seattle. I know that you are trying to discover what you're most enthusiastic about, but compared to my goal, it seems trivial. I need to leave now and conclude this letter. I'll see you in Seattle or I won't. I'll see you somewhere.

"Incredulous that he would do this, I returned to Tokyo. I still don't believe it, not even now, not even after he punctuated his fury with a note two months after he left Chiba. It said, 'Come to Seattle. How you do that is up to you. Your next assignment in life is to arrive in Seattle. You'll find me waiting for you here.'

"While I was in Chiba, a second massacre of homosexuals occurred in Basra and Baghdad. The young man who had informed me about the bodies beneath the bridge sent me a message telling me they had gouged out his eyes and bound him with metal cable. Consequently, he discovered, as he put it, 'The world is fine when we can't see it.'

"Since I was physically cut off from the secret world of homosexuals in Basra and Baghdad, those catastrophes motivated me to meet some of them on virtual platforms. They were a terrified community that confronted one terror after another, because many recruits in the militias dealt with their own homosexuality by preying on and torturing other homosexuals. The members of this secret society were so rattled and terrified that they took out their rage on each other, and their meetings were no longer healthy or safe.

"For his part, Morise was pressuring me with amazing determination to present my documents to the office of the United Nations in northern Iraq. I refused with a determination that matched his. At the same time, I was telling him about some members of the secret society who had succeeded in escaping from their homeland. All these circumstances and my dilatory replies made Morise furious and anxious. He informed me that he had started doing stupid stuff in the military camp and was annoying his comrades a lot. The reason for my refusal to submit asylum-request papers to the United Nations was that I didn't want to use my homosexuality as an excuse to emigrate. I did not want my sexual preferences to grant me the privilege to write freely and publish my novels. The whole subject caused me excruciating intellectual pain. Morise responded, 'What are we going to do if those monsters won't leave us any other option?'

"Things continued this way until I hailed a taxi during my first day in my hometown of Basra. I was thinking of getting a room in a hotel and attempting to contact my family again—my father, mother, and brothers. The moment I set foot inside the taxi, a man, who had been hiding in the front seat, showed himself and pointed his weapon at my head. I was wearing a gold ring that was a gift from Morise. He seized my hand and squeezed it as I begged him not to take that ring.

"'Anything but that! It's my wedding ring! Take this money, this suitcase, this laptop.' I used the word 'wedding' even though I knew I hadn't married yet. I don't know why I said that.

"'I want to break your hand, not remove your ring. We'll ram it up your butt, and you can keep it there in the grave.' The man quickly broke his promise and tossed the ring out the window. I lost it forever. I felt that this was the end and that these kidnappers knew everything—in fact, that they were very good at carrying out their mission. For a reason I couldn't discern, they drove me around the city. Everything seemed carefully organized. They knew my every move and had planned for a long time to harvest my corpse. As he laughed, one of them offered me a choice: 'Do you want to die like all the others, or would you prefer to announce your repentance?'

"'Like the others?' He was referring to the last group of homosexuals they had murdered. Hundreds had been exterminated by having their heads smashed with a large concrete block.

"'Oh, fine. Thank you. If that's how it is, let me tell you something important, something your mother should have told you in the brothel where you were first defecated. I'm a sodomite, a deviant, and a novelist, and I will die that way. But just a moment! Why should I suppose you'll understand me?'

"He let me complete that sentence and then slapped my mouth with his other hand. His skinny body looked smaller now. He seemed oblivious to whether anyone in the street, outside the car, saw him brandish his revolver at my face. For my part, I was certain I would die and never see Morise again. I asked Morise secretly, 'Are you still angry at me?'

"We reached a large warehouse on the outskirts of the city. They bound me tightly to the leg of an ornate old wooden bed and placed a large concrete block on my foot to keep me from moving. The only fetter they found to use was a twisted cord of nylon strands that cut into my wrist and bared the flesh greedily.

"The shaykh arrived, sporting a sleek turban that resembled an eraser at the end of a lead pencil. It was so hot and the pain in my leg so intense that I started to see him as a pencil that was writing and erasing. He made a pretense of being compassionate by bringing in a bowl of soup every six hours and taking me to the bathroom whenever it was time to pray. This wasn't a bathroom in the normal sense. It was a bent-over palm tree they had draped with a cloth to provide enough privacy for men not to need to cover their privates completely there.

"Without interrogating or questioning me, they kept me for an entire week. These men may have learned that technique in the former president's cells, where—by their own account—they had been lifers. An incarcerated person was provided time to spill his confessions without ever being forced to. He confessed because he was bored and needed to relieve himself of his pain—because his torturer did not ask him to explain anything. Instead, he set about beating and kicking the prisoner, regardless of what he said.

"I shouted at Turban–Pencil Head, 'I want out of this barnyard. Open the door for me, and I'll leave the country and never go fuck your mothers!'

"He was praying a few meters away from me when he heard my insult. He raised his voice as he recited the prayer rituals. This showed I had angered him with my impolite words while he was addressing his Lord.

"'You're assholes. The whole country is going up in flames. Why are you pursuing people like me?'

"'All evils are evil. What's the point of letting you fiddle-faddle around on the grounds that what you do isn't important and that there are issues more important than you? You're all cut from the same cloth. All evils are interrelated.'

"The shaykh said this while he dusted off his sleeves, after praying for a long time on the filthy floor.

"'Fine. Kill me, then. Tell your Lord, "You committed an existential error by creating men who love men. Those defective goods are on their way back to you. The customer is returning them to you. Mend them at once! This being you created isn't right. He's damaged goods. He's not fully a man." Tell *him* that. Your Lord will naturally compensate you with a more virile man than me, someone who will help you wait for your Imam to return from Occultation.'

"'You seem educated.'

"'Educated enough to spit up your mother's cunt without feeling that God will transform me into a monkey.'

"'Don't you know that what you're doing is against nature? Tell me, secularist, wouldn't it be better for the lot of you to go extinct since you can't beget and perpetuate life? Isn't this a clear enough message that you're all on the wrong path? Not even nature can help you.'

"'Oh! Do you feel I prevent you from multiplying?'

"'Yes. You prevent humanity from multiplying.'

"'Go procreate with your four wives. You don't further human procreation by killing a human being. You're dumb!' When I said that, I mustered all the force I had to push the block away and kick the shaykh in the eyes.

"He staggered and landed on his back. Once he regained his balance, as he continued rubbing his eyes, he screamed, 'Come! Get him away from me! I don't want to see this filthy slimeball again.'

"The same young man who had kidnapped me appeared with the driver, and they set to work pummeling my eyes. Then the cabbie had a brilliant idea, as his victorious expression showed. He got a glass bottle and broke it on the doorstep, leaving it with teeth but no neck. I knew the goal was to make me set my butt on it—that was something inmates in Saddam's prisons were often asked to do.

"I accepted the bottle deftly and graciously and started to let down my trousers. My wounded fingers, blue from bruises, made that hard, but I finally succeeded in opening the belt and looked at my captors—only to find they had turned their faces away from me and were tut-tutting.

"'Should I do this now while you watch?'

"'God damn you!'

"Apparently my half-naked butt disgusted them.

"A flush of victory surged through my veins. I don't know how or why, but they renounced that idea, which, had it been carried out, would have permanently disfigured me.

"They led me to the car and sat me in the front seat beside the driver. Someone else, presumably a new recruit, sat in the back. He brandished the revolver over his head without looking at me. The automobile slowed down when it entered a residential neighborhood. I sensed that the door of this aged vehicle might not be locked. I learned it wasn't when I threw my full weight against it and the young man fired at me. The vehicle ran over my foot when I twisted and turned beneath it. I rose quickly and raced toward members of a family who had come out with their aged father for a breath of fresh air at the doorway. I barreled toward them, asking for help. When I was almost there, the youth fired again and missed me. That shot, though, caused the family to rush inside and lock me out.

"I headed next to a massive man dressed entirely in Bedouin attire. He had started collecting the chairs in front of his house, apparently after shooting the breeze with friends there. That man did exactly the same thing. He left me quickly and locked the door behind him, even though I entreated him not to, shouting, 'I'm your guest!' That meant 'I seek your mercy and your protection.' According to Arab customary law, a man must not deny his guest protection from those pursuing him. But this didn't work. The militias had so terrified people that they transgressed their noble customs and were afraid to observe them in moments of alarm. The man ignored me, and I raced off without any clear goal. The car followed me, and their plan may have been to fell me with a shot to the head. But I sped up a little and kept low. Since people didn't offer to shelter me, I took narrow passages till I succeeded in evading the car.

"I was going lame, and it hurt terribly to touch the pavement with that foot. My ankle became increasingly swollen. I still have issues with this ankle. Even now, I walk normally at times, only to fall suddenly, especially when I step down.

"I headed to the bank of the Shatt al-Arab to seek the shade of the red metal bridge. It was the first time I had experienced the world down there. It attracted homeless people who felt they were descending to a nether realm, climbing down to a world that was superior to the filthy bridge. I looked at my ankle, which the militia car's tires had run over. It had started to turn red, and the increasing pain was affecting my entire leg. Truth be told, I hadn't felt it till then. When I walk today, I forget I am living with a crushed ankle. It had been crushed, though, in its own special way. My ankle remembers and then forgets about this injury, as it sees fit. I usually walk naturally and then suddenly fall at times, when my foot remembers I should. Neither doctors' bandages nor splints on the joint have helped me cure my ankle's own memory.

"That day ended, but I had to wait for nightfall before going to a shop to buy clothes. Clad in my new garments, I walked upright among people. I tried to call Morise. I sent off dozens of emails that night. He was still angry with me. Perhaps his fury would last so long, he would forget me. That thought preoccupied me for a whole month. I couldn't handle the idea that Morise had abandoned me.

"Then I received his standard reply: 'Come to Seattle.'

"'How?'

"He didn't reply.

"The militia's office began sending out letters and papers with polite requests to appear before the commander of the militia in its office. They started summoning men who seemed to be homosexual. They counseled them gently and very politely and then freed them, only to drag them in once more—unless these youth had totally surrendered to the militia—and bind their eyes with wires or poke metal kebab skewers in their flanks. They would run electric drills up their nostrils to search for telltale signs of homosexuality and drive out the genes that sprang from Satan's testicle.

"I assumed that Morise and I were finished and sent him one more email in his own style: 'You can board the train and depart. Don't wait here. I'm a deserted station.' I felt my message was poetic but naive. Wishing to be more in control of my ego, body, and words, I wanted to send him a second message, but kidnapping, again, prevented that. I was in hiding—drawing and writing beneath the bridge. I enjoyed my time in the world under the bridge. It resembled a paradise. I would study the circles, triangles, and rectangles that someone had drawn on the walls—presumably an artist during Saddam's reign when the artistic directors of state television in Baghdad forbade drawing these geometrical figures. Then this unknown artist had decided to take revenge in his own way, because—for draftsmen—all of existence consists of circles and other geometrical forms: pears, grapes, the hips of men and women, even horses. Beneath the bridge existed a primal world of raw and primary art materials, and its flies, circles, and squares kept me alive.

"They stumbled on me when I was training my nose to accept the nasty smells and the pollution of the river water and then drew me gently by my wrist back to their world, which was crowded with people but devoid of circles and squares. Two veiled men placed me in a small pickup truck. It was sunset, and the red horizon was studded with storks and palm fronds. They took a corpse out of the truck and deposited it on a nearby dump heap. They loaded me into the vehicle without a word, perhaps because I offered no resistance and was obedient—as if preoccupied with some idea in my imagination or oblivious to what would happen. For this reason, I felt this was going to be the tranquil end of a docile hen, and that phrase shone in my head like the title of a book.

"In the militia's office, they informed me that this was merely a summons. They treated me respectfully and nicknamed me 'Tomato.' In their lexicon, this was a polite nickname. It indicated that the individual had many talents and could undertake many assignments— just as tomatoes are useful in many ways in the kitchen. When they explained this to me, I added, 'A tomato can also spit.' That may have been the start of the violence and what sparked their intense hatred for me.

"I spent two weeks in the militia's lockup. During that time, I was forced to yield and announce my repentance for my body and my ideas. In order to convince them that I was sincere, I drew portraits of the militia's commanders on the walls. The flies I added to the faces they understood as merely artistic touches or a special characteristic of my style. To assuage their doubts, I showed them an art magazine I had in my briefcase with reproductions of Andy Warhol's portraits.

"At the moment of my release, I was a very docile hen and didn't turn into another animal until the assistant commander of the militia tore my passport into little bits that he threw in the air like feathers. I remained calm, but any hopeful feelings I might have harbored died when I learned I would remain imprisoned in Iraq for at least a year, because a judge banned me from traveling. He believed I had torn up my passport—a charge punishable by the law."

Twenty-four

"Is there more to the story?" I felt the tip of my nose ask me.

"Yes.

"In the middle of 2016, I sent my documents and my four published novels together with some translated short stories to the Cultural Affairs section of the US Embassy in Baghdad to try my luck getting accepted to the International Writing Program, the IWP. All I know is that I had never been so lucky before. I suffer from social lethargy and am lazy about building relationships. Not even once had I felt any enthusiasm about applying for grants and awards. I hoped, though, during this period that the idea that 'literature involves an openness to rejection' would glimmer and flourish in my mind. I was happy when this phrase sprouted inside me early on. I felt that I had been training myself to expect rejections from the start and hadn't been seduced by the hyperoptimistic fantasy of nonstop success. Remaining open to rejection is a stance that is superior to optimism. Why would a toothless person fear tooth decay?

"Subsequently, I received a call from an employee at the embassy. He told me, 'We've been looking for you!' I sensed his relief when he explained I was a perfect fit for their program—especially since the embassy had been searching for an Iraqi applicant for a long time. I didn't fully grasp what he was saying and replied, 'Never mind. It's just an attempt. I'm sorry if my stories didn't qualify. I can help you find someone else.' He replied, 'Mr. Mortada, I'm contacting *you* to inform *you* that *you* have been accepted into this program. Will you be able to depart in the next few months? You must be free of obligations and ready to travel.'

"I began to treat my new passport like a glass vial that contained the elixir of life. I handled it delicately, tenderly, and fearfully, checking that it was safe and that its pages were clean, preventing it from becoming too cold or hot, and keeping it away from rodents. This was my last escape hatch, my salvation that I had postponed far too long. I told my father I was traveling for business and would return in two weeks. I didn't tell him about the program—not because I intended to quit Iraq permanently but because my father didn't know I was a writer with several published novels. For him, I was still that child whose explosive notebooks he feared officials would open and find bursting with heretical stories and drawings. Explaining the entire situation to my father might have taken more character than I had developed.

"I didn't tell anyone I was fleeing, that I was leaving the land I loved and wrote about, a country where I had shed my blood. I was keen to buy all the socks, pens, and razor blades I could—everything a writer afraid to address his homosexuality would need when other writers encouraged him and directed him to escape with his life. From Doha to London, I repressed the possibility that the American authorities might deny me entry because I was Iraqi. When I reached Chicago, the customs officer asked me whether I had any seeds in my bag. I had expected other questions and a private session in a little room, the way it happens in films.

"At O'Hare Airport, I was too scared to restrain my shadow, which I watched flow away beneath the tall windows. After the agent stamped my passport, I found a man calling my name and told myself Morise had sent someone to greet me. But I was soon disabused of that daydream. This man led me by my hand toward the cafeteria and suggested that I spend some time at his home before my flight to Iowa. He introduced himself as one of my readers. That alerted me to the fact that I was a writer and had readers I might meet somewhere in the world. Even so, my mind rejected the idea that I was a novelist. I didn't want to believe it, not even when readers surprised me with their hospitality or their revulsion.

"'I've read all your novels, and my wife keeps asking her girlfriends in the Iraqi diaspora to read your books.' I just smiled and succeeded in changing the subject without upsetting him. I was able to persuade him to wait with me at the airport.

"I spent a number of weeks in a guesthouse on the campus of the University of Iowa as one of approximately thirty-four writers from various countries. I began writing a novel I called *The Scientismist*. It is about a person who believes in science in such a radical way that he almost worships it but is then afflicted with hypertrophy of his memory. He becomes fixated on the loss of his twin brother after they have wandered aimlessly in the desert, handling war materiel during a fierce desert war. When I read the first draft of the work, I realized that I had composed this nonhomosexual work about myself and that this draft concealed—beneath multiple veils and caps—something I didn't care to show other people. Morise, who kept trying to bring this latent element to light, repeated a Sufi phrase frequently when it was appropriate and when it wasn't: 'Don't be afraid to reveal your inner truth. All blessings will pour down like rain once you strip back your veil.' He didn't feel at all inhibited and quickly transitioned to a noisy rap song that didn't match the spiritual moment when I confronted him and said, 'How about you? Why don't you come out and reveal your true identity, Mr. Philosopher?' Writing provided me what prayer does religious people. When I used to pray and now when I write, everything seems welcoming and innocuous. Only words grant me such a high degree of concentration and isolation from the world. During those days, what shone most brightly in my mind was part of a letter from Morise: 'You remind me of a carpenter's son, raised in his father's workshop, who believes the only thing he can do in this world is carpentry.'

"He was referring to writing. Each of us felt there was a great resemblance between making a chair from wood and writing a novel. We agreed that the scraps left over from carpentry help nourish the spirit.

"I tried to call Morise but failed to reach him. I guessed he was keeping track of me carefully, because he was the one who had urged me to apply for those programs. I did not doubt for a moment that he was following news of who was accepted each year and waiting for me to arrive.

"'I was looking for you. Then I saw you in the distance among dozens of students and recognized you,' the writing program's coordinator told me, after she found me wandering around the campus of the University of Iowa. 'Americans don't walk like you,' she added. 'Your body speaks a different language.' It is true that my body in those days wasn't conscious of the language emanating from it. Isn't it tedious for a person to watch not only the words that spring from his tongue but all the other signals his body gives off without his even being aware of it? My whole existence was engaged in liberation and a lasting—not a momentary—escape from the abyss. I was looking for an attorney to assist me. I abstained from buying anything that wasn't an absolute necessity and was miserly with myself. I skipped lunch and dinner to make sure I had enough money to hire an attorney to help me claim refugee status.

"When the program's coordinator asked how I was doing, I replied, 'I write and burp.'

"She replied, 'That's great! Isn't that the most a writer can hope for?'

"'I go for walks alone. Writing is good for walking.'

"'I thought walking was good for writing.'

"'If you like.'

"'There's an Iraqi who lives here—Dr. Saadi Simawe. He taught at the university in Baghdad for more than a quarter century. Do you know him? He lives in a long-term care facility. It would be great if you decided to visit him. I'm sure he'd love that. He hasn't met any Iraqis here for years. I can go with you to the facility if you want.'

"I knew that Saadi Simawe had translated a collection of Iraqi poems to English and that his brother was a well-known poet. In fact, the entire family was well known for its work in culture and the arts. I was keen to meet him and planned to tell him about my idea of staying in America. I didn't know anyone here, not since Morise stopped communicating with me. Simawe would let me voice my questions and concerns. He was my only remaining hope at that time. I prepared to meet him and collected naughty sex jokes, because the program coordinator told me Saadi loved ribald humor. I added to these a bouquet of old songs from the countryside, because I had a hunch that in the 1970s, this man had been a Communist partisan. That group loved folk songs and ballads about heroism and struggle.

"Two days later, the meeting was scheduled, and I learned that Simawe had agreed to it. I waited, in the reception room of the long-term care facility, for an Arab who had taught English. An orderly entered, pushing the wheelchair of a slight, stooped man with an aged, expressionless face. I greeted him and held out my hand, only to learn he couldn't move his. The nurse suggested I sit with him in his room, to which he took us. Simawe couldn't even speak and used his index finger to respond yes or no. All the same, his advanced age could not hide his welcome for me or his graciousness. He smiled broadly when I began playing music of the Iraqi countryside. Then I transitioned to contemporary music of Egypt and Lebanon. I felt he liked this, although they were addressed to the senses and taste of a man who could not defend himself. I abandoned my resolve to ask his assistance in my request for asylum and mocked my luck once I left his room, after saying goodbye, because the man I had sought, I had sought far too late.

"The nurse thanked me for the visit, which had cheered Simawe, and added, 'I heard you talk to him and tell him stories. He enjoyed that, and I'm grateful you did. But I want to tell you that Simawe only listens to jazz.'

"I tried to find another opportunity that would save me and keep me from having to return to Iraq. I started asking everyone I met, addressing even strangers, including a young university student who watched repeatedly when I stretched out on the ground, lying on the grass. Apparently, he felt shy about approaching me but finally found the courage to invite me to supper. When he realized that I was preoccupied and not ready for surprise romantic dates, he expressed his sexual desire frankly and said we could go straight to his dorm room. He became so intense that I didn't know how to respond. Then he allowed himself to say, 'I want to play with your brown, immigrant prick. I want an immigrant to climb on my back and hug me for hours while emptying his body's contents into mine.' That was when I realized I was an immigrant. I'm still grateful to him for quickly putting me into the picture and condensing the weeks it would otherwise have taken me to grow used to the word 'immigrant.'

"On YouTube, I found someone named Michael Failla, an American who was devoting the remainder of his life to helping people in difficult circumstances, especially those whom other people—for some unknown reason—find offensive to nature and existence. Victims of such prejudice can't say, 'This is who I am,' not even softly—without risking their lives. Michael had helped dozens of people and fought to provide them with a safe environment.

"The world still overflows with the goodness of humanity and with souls who open the windows of their spirit to fill their interior peace with distant vistas, because compassionate hearts are a power greater than hissing fire and slam-bang rockets.

"From his network, I met other people, and from them I met still more individuals who love to help others. Each circle expanded to include others, until, on my laptop, I had assembled an entire community of acquaintances. Eventually, these cyberfriends included Erick and the other monkeys, who had known Morise for as long as I had, without my realizing it.

"I came to Seattle and spent four hours with a compassionate attorney who smoothed the way for me. My hearing with the judiciary lasted four hours, during which I said only one sentence, which she pulled apart, opening and expanding it. That sentence was 'I'm in Seattle—where are you?'"

When I turned toward the priests and Erick, they merely nodded their heads and adjusted their legs, which were crossed. The longest sentence uttered that day was "Oh! You'll be fine. Most men who draw dogs survive cancer." That was their attempt to downplay the matter. When they noticed that I myself didn't care, they acted concerned and urged me to look after my health. Truth be told, I did not feel resolute in the face of the future terrors of my illness, perhaps because my shock on learning about Morise's death had embalmed my heart and turned it into a centuries-old, dried-up mummy oblivious to earthquakes or hurricanes.

The next day, the three monkeys escorted me to a doctor's appointment. There was a complete scan of the tumor on my right kidney. I asked Erick to stay with me and help the physician explain everything about my body in detail. I asked him not to use the charade of referring to good and bad news this time. As a matter of fact, I wasn't concerned about what might happen. My gland responsible for sensing disaster and monitoring my life's slow and dwindling progress was on the blink.

"Tell it like it is, Erick. I won't blame you for anything." The problem was that he sat beside the physician, who—it became clear to me—was his longtime friend. This doctor started to employ that tired stratagem, even laughing when Erick encouraged him to use it, and told me the tumor had stopped growing, and that this was excellent. The previous sample that had been tested had shown no multiplication of cells. Surgery was needed to eradicate it, and "most people" who underwent such operations survived them.

Erick helped me don my jacket and led me back to where the two other monkeys were waiting. We sat in the car, looking at each other. A minute of silence passed, as if we were in mourning. Erick started the engine and our discussion. "Everything is fine. What has happened is exactly what Morise requested. I don't need to tell you that he died in Iraq, four years before you arrived here, because I have deduced that you know that now. He did not disappear and didn't reject your presence here. He distributed around Seattle friends who would support, care for, and appreciate you."

The hair on the back of my hand stood up—from happiness, not from fright. To be more precise, it wasn't any ordinary happiness that made a person smile. Instead, it was a happiness that passed between the legs like a ball thrown toward a person by kids playing

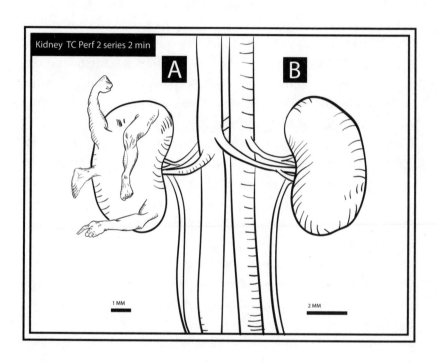

in the street—a fleeting, slight insult to a person's dignity. I felt this way because finally I had found someone who shared my memory of Morise. Morise was real, then, not a fantasy. He had not been an imaginary character I created for myself and toyed with in my head. He wasn't someone an author of magical realism concocted in the bath. I wasn't raving, then! What was engraved in my memory was real, not some PTSD hallucination.

He paused to listen to my heavy breathing. Then he continued. "At first, I did not want to tell you we knew Morise. Originally, I did not mean to conceal from you the news that he was slain on a night raid with four comrades in the East of Iraq. Morise was a very closeted homosexual. That was his personal preference, which we all respected. He feared the stigma of dishonor, which still lingers even here, in this country. You may have noticed that yourself. People don't come right out and say what they think or believe about homosexuality. They don't reveal their sharp feelings, which influence their positions and frame their relationship with us. This makes the matter abnormal and forces all of us to struggle to improve people's perceptions and to free ourselves from the last remaining twinges of shame. I also feared you would become extremely depressed if I told you about Morise when you first arrived, because I know that many newcomers need a special strength of character and psychological preparedness to confront the difficulties of starting afresh and overcoming the typical obstacles. Your mind needed to be clear and resilient for you to work diligently and achieve successes. That's why I encouraged you to forget Morise. I won't hide from you that I once conceived a complex plan to inform you gradually. I don't know whether it has succeeded or not! There is something else, something I must say. Morise himself asked us to swear not to tell you if he died, which he thought possible: 'If I die in Iraq, don't tell him at first. I want him to search for me!' I truly didn't know you were that deeply in love. He stated emphatically, 'If I happen to die in Iraq, I want you to consider Mortada just as close a friend as me.

He will substitute for me. Open the paths of this city for him. Let him embark on his new life, which will be a peaceful, happy one. Don't tell him I'm dead.' Morise wanted you to discover him in his own way. Morise loved such games."

Silence reigned again and blended with the calm of the street, over which boughs extended and intertwined from both sides. A homeless man stood on a wooden bench while beside him dozed a dog, the same breed as Heraclitus. The vagrant stripped naked, caressed by a breeze that sent the leaves near him into the air. "He's Seattle's version of Adam—fallen from the heavens to search for employment at Microsoft," Liao quipped to break the stony silence. I watched the homeless man's wrinkled body as he loped down the hill. His scrotum rocked to the beat of some earworm song that made his entire body dance. He spread his limbs out like the Vitruvian Man and peed as if urinating for the first time in his life.

About the Author and Illustrator

Iraqi novelist, filmmaker, journalist, and visual artist Mortada Gzar was born in Kuwait in 1982, grew up in Basra, Iraq, and now lives in Seattle, Washington. He earned a degree in petroleum engineering from the University of Baghdad and was later a member of the International Writing Program at the University of Iowa. Gzar is the author of four novels, a children's book, and a short-story collection; he has illustrated two books for children. English translations of his work have appeared in *Words Without Borders*, *World Literature Today*, and

Iraq + 100: The First Anthology of Science Fiction to Have Emerged from Iraq, and his journalism and political cartoons are featured in Arabic newspapers. Gzar's animated films have been featured in international film festivals, his film *Language* was awarded a grant by the Doha Film Institute, and he created the Seattle Arab Film Festival hosted by the Northwest Film Forum.

About the Translator

William Maynard Hutchins has translated many works of Arabic literature into English, including *Return of the Spirit* by Tawfiq al-Hakim, *The Cairo Trilogy* by Nobel laureate Naguib Mahfouz, and *The Fetishists* by Ibrahim al-Koni. His translation of *New Waw* by al-Koni won the ALTA National Prose Translation Award for 2015. A three-time National Endowment for the Arts fellow, Hutchins's translations from Arabic have appeared in *The Brooklyn Rail, Banipal: Magazine of Modern Arab Literature,* and *Words Without Borders,* as well as elsewhere. He holds degrees from Yale University and the University of

Chicago and has taught subjects ranging from English and Arabic to philosophy and religious studies at the Gerard Institute in Sidon, Lebanon; the University of Ghana; the American University in Cairo; and Appalachian State University in Boone, North Carolina.